IN PURSUIT OF PARADISE

Senegalese Women, Muridism and Migration

Eva Evers Rosander

Nordiska Afrikainstitutet
The Nordic Africa Institute

Original Title: Nyckeln till Paradiset; Senegalesiska kvinnors livsvägar
Swedish Original © 2011 Eva Evers Rosander and Carlssons Bokförlag in collaboration with the Nordic Africa Institute
English Translation © 2015 Eva Evers Rosander and the Nordic Africa Institute
Translation from Swedish: Alexandra Kent and Graham Long
Layout and production: Byrå 4, Uppsala
Print on demand: Lightning Source UK Ltd
Cover: Reverse-glass painting of Mame Diarra by Gadjigo with permission from Fowler Museum, UCLA, Los Angeles
This translation has been made possible thanks to generous financial support from the Vilhelm Ekman University Foundation in Uppsala, and the Åke Wiberg Foundation in Stockholm.
The photos in the book have been taken by the author unless otherwise stated
ISBN 978-91-7106-776-0
The Nordic Africa Institute
P. O. Box 1703
751 47 Uppsala
WWW.NAI.UU.SE

CONTENTS

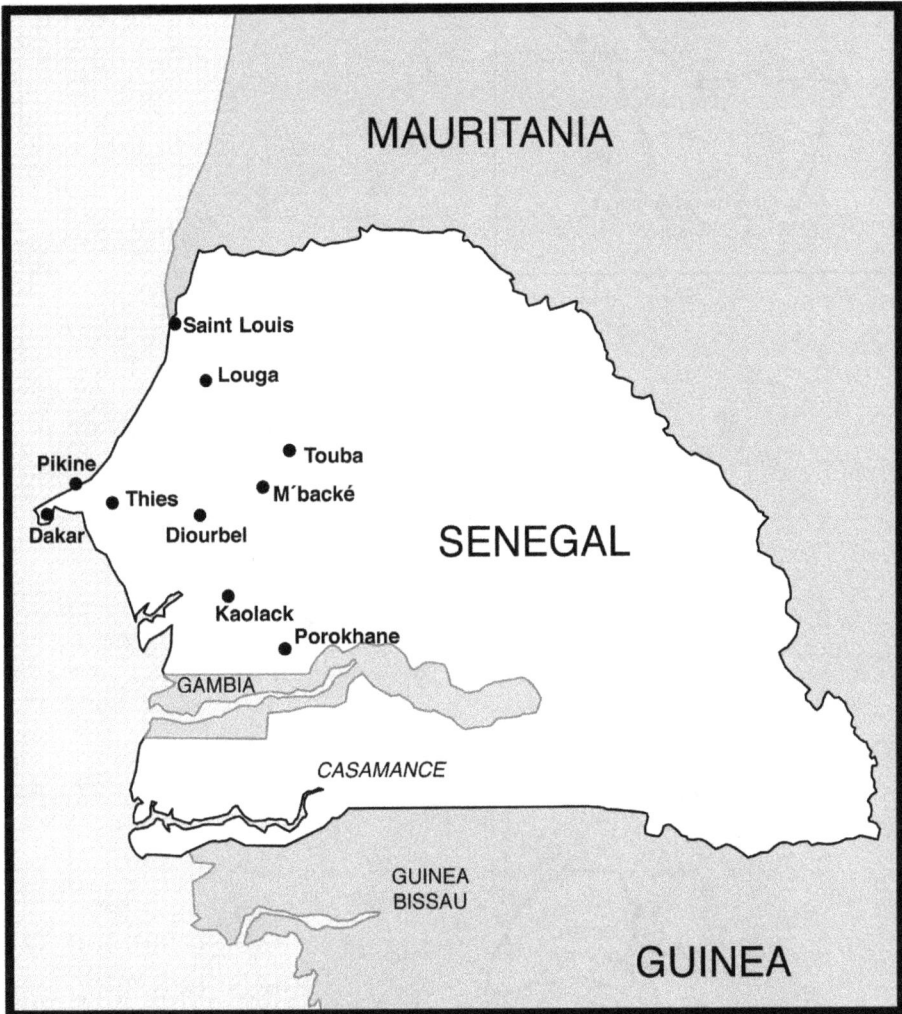

MAURITANIA

● Saint Louis

● Louga

● Touba

Pikine
● Touba
● Thies   ● M´backé
Dakar   ● Diourbel

SENEGAL

● Kaolack
● Porokhane

GAMBIA

CASAMANCE

GUINEA
BISSAU

GUINEA

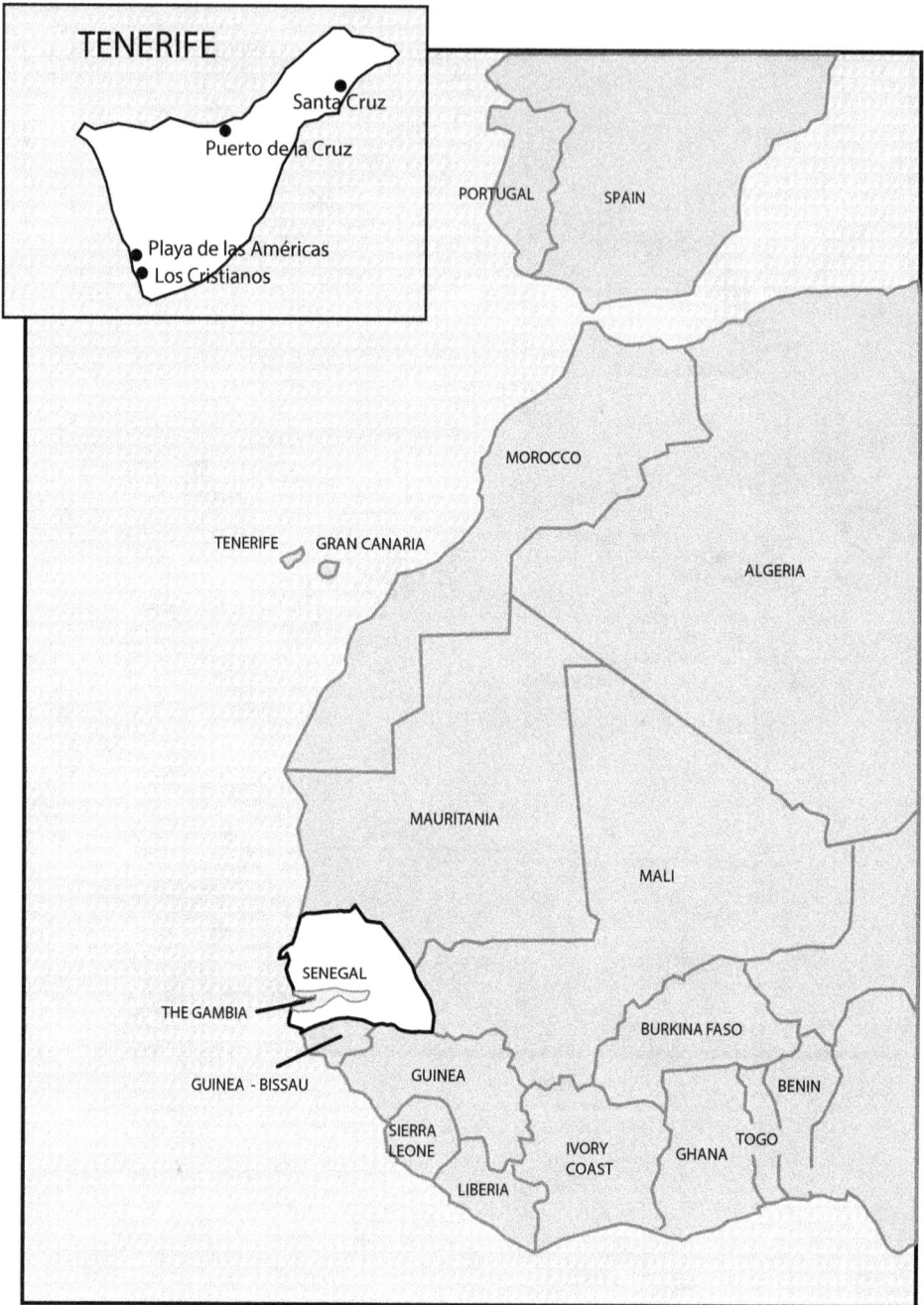

TENERIFE

Santa Cruz

Puerto de la Cruz

Playa de las Américas
Los Cristianos

PORTUGAL

SPAIN

MOROCCO

TENERIFE GRAN CANARIA

ALGERIA

MAURITANIA

MALI

SENEGAL

THE GAMBIA

BURKINA FASO

GUINEA - BISSAU

GUINEA

BENIN

SIERRA
LEONE

IVORY
COAST

GHANA

TOGO

LIBERIA

THE PURPOSE OF THIS BOOK

THE SENEGALESE WOMEN I got to know first in Senegal and later in Tenerife in the 1990s puzzled me. They seemed to be both powerful and subdued, autonomous and dependent. Their relationship to men appeared to me to be particularly ambiguous and difficult to understand. My intention with this book is to explore how issues such as religion, marriage, children, economy and involvement in women's associations are played out in their lives. I met some of these women in the town of Mbacké in Senegal and others in the tourist area of Playa de las Américas in Tenerife. Some were married, others, single. Most were involved in some form of petty trade in Tenerife. Some were also wholesalers, or working in hotels and making rasta plaits for tourists.

Almost all the women I encountered were Murids – Muslims who were members of a–Senegalese Sufi order known as the *Mouridiyya (Muridism)*. They were devout followers of *shaykh* Amadou Bamba (who died in 1927)[1], also known as *serigne* Touba, who founded the order in the late 1800s. Both men and women worship him in order to ensure a better life on earth and a place in Paradise. Many Murids also worship his mother, *mame*[2] Diarra Bousso (who died around 1850). The women I spoke with conceived of Paradise as a house with a door. The house was Amadou Bamba but the door was his mother, mame Diarra Bousso. And if there is no door, they explained to me, then there is no way into the house … [3]

In this Sufi order Amadou Bamba occupies a central position as intermediary between his disciples and God. Also his mother is believed to possess great fonts of generosity and benevolence, which she can use to the benefit of her followers.

---

1. Amadou Bamba was awarded the title of *shaykh* (the title for a Muslim leader) by his followers and *serigne* (seriñ) Touba. I shall refer to him by his first and second names only.

2. *Mame* is a title of respect used for both men and women to denote seniority. Since it will be used frequently in this book it will not be italicised.

3. See page 177..

What, then, does one have to do to open the door to Paradise, *ajaana*? Which women may enter and which ones will instead burn in Hell, *safara*? The moral rules applying to women differ from those for men because it is a woman's behaviour as wife and mother that is of primary significance for her afterlife. There are no such explicit rules governing men's behaviour.

In rural Senegal both men and women can acquire merits (*tiyaba*) for Paradise by growing crops for the highest Murid leader, the *khalifa général*[4], or for some other religious leader who owns cultivable land. Others may instead make monetary donations to the Murid leaders who are close members of the founder's family. This practice is particularly common among those living and working overseas. Such gifts, called *addiyya*, are considered to be both for the marabouts and for God Himself. Migrants are often able to make greater financial contributions, both to their families and to the religious leaders, than they could have if they had remained at home. In other words, they hope for benefits in the longer term. Mame Diarra's claimed magical powers and generosity in helping people promptly have given her an unusually prominent role in this Sufi order. I was intrigued by the fact that she held such high status in a strongly male-dominated religious movement and this inspired me to study the order more closely. For although the myth of the strong , independent West African woman is nothing more than a myth that is to some extent maintained by the women's own manipulations of patriarchal ideals and norms, the mame Diarra Bousso cult and the annual pilgrimage to her tomb is unique. I see it as an autonomous expression of women's religiosity.

Maybe I overplay the importance of these features because of my otherwise critical attitude to the male chauvinism of Muridism and Senegalese society in general. Several Senegalese feminists have suggested that I have been seduced by conservative Sufi romanticism and now see mame Diarra Bousso as the solution to women's problems. My critics point out that she does not exactly enhance gender equality. On the contrary, they argue, the wife-and-mother image she stands for, with submission and patience as its most prominent characteristics, represents a step backwards. This viewpoint is justified and I agree with many in Senegal who hope for reforms that might improve the position of women, particularly in relation to family law, which to some extent reflects conservative, religious values. The mame Diarra Bousso cult is certainly not helpful in this regard but within today's Sufism in Senegal it offers Murid women support and consolation.

Religious conditions are different for Senegalese women working in Tenerife compared with at home. Religious associations become less significant as

---

4. After the death of the founder in 1927, his oldest son took over as the leader of Muridism. He was then succeeded by his younger brother and so on until the death of the youngest son, when the oldest grandson took over the leadership in 2007. Since 2010, the next grandson in line has been the khalifa général. His name is Maty Leye Mbacké.

there is little time for meeting up and no opportunity to perform agricultural work for the Murid leaders. The most important thing for them here is to earn money, which is why they came to Tenerife in the first place. This makes it possible for men and women in the diaspora to make generous donations to the Murid establishment and it means that women gain importance for the marabouts. The motivation for giving to the visiting Murid leaders is to show that one's devotion remains untainted by secular or atheist influences from the West. Murid marabouts make regular visits to their devotees so as to maintain their trust. Muridism and Senegalese identity are closely interwoven among migrants overseas and this fuels a strong religious engagement - the belief in Paradise and the fear of Hell follow them wherever they go, as do the personalities of shaykh Amadou Bamba and mame Diarra Bousso. Above all, it would seem that fear of the eternal fires of Hell is what keeps this cult alive among today's Murids.

Amparo asks about the purpose of this book

"Okay, so tell me what this book is *really* about," said my Spanish friend Amparo, leaning back in her sofa. Amparo had accompanied me on short visits to both Senegal and Tenerife and she was interested in what I was writing. Looking me straight in the eyes, she asked, "So what's the *purpose* of it?"

Despite the Spanish summer heat at Amparo's home in Valladolid in north-western Spain I felt a chill run through me.

"Purpose?" I pondered. But I'd already explained to her. Hadn't I made myself clear?

Feeling my self-confidence ebb, I took a deep breath and decided to reiterate exactly what the book was about. I realised I would need to be more precise this time but I didn't want to start making firm statements or lock myself into preconceived notions. I began tentatively, "The book is about Senegalese women's 'keys' to Paradise. It's about the life paths they choose in order to ensure that they have a better life after this one. Their concern about Paradise is related to their fear of Hell and they believe that these are the only two options."

"That is one of my themes. The other is about the strategies women use to reconcile their daily struggle for a livelihood with religious ethics and social norms. Their lives are framed firstly by *religion/morality*, secondly by *marriage/motherhood* and thirdly by *economy/work*."

"Just a minute," said my critical friend from her place on the sofa. "What kind of religious ethics are you talking about? And what norms are you referring to?"

"I've told you that the women I'm writing about are Muslims who belong to the Murid order. Well, according to Murid ideals, women are always subordinate to men. They should be obedient, patient, industrious, tolerant and, above all, loyal to their spouse no matter what. This view of womanhood is in keeping with prevalent gender norms in Senegalese society. People say that a woman's morality will affect her children's success in later life while a man's behaviour is of no consequence for his children's futures. It follows that when a woman's children fail in life, blame is ascribed to the mother for having failed to uphold moral standards. This gives men a hold over women and they are not shy to use it. In Muridism it is said that a husband holds his wife's access to Paradise in his hands. Everything depends upon whether or not he considers her to have behaved as a good wife. Men are women's moral overlords, just as the marabouts are the moral authorities over men. The marabout's prayers open the way to God. Without this mediation between God and the faithful it is difficult for a follower to obtain the help he wants from God."

"That's dreadful," said Amparo. "It sounds just like the Catholic Church in Spain under Franco or even during the Inquisition. I suppose the priests used to play a similar role in the Church to the one you describe for the marabouts".

"Yes, it may seem so. And you'll probably be even more upset when you hear about the great role model for Murid women, mame Diarra Bousso. You can see her on the cover of my book in a painting by an artist from Dakar called Gadjigo. She's depicted holding up a part of the raffia fence from the house that her husband lives in. It's an illustration from one of many legends about this female saint. She died in the mid-1800s when she was still young but the stories about her live on. Every Murid knows this particular legend because it's a popular example of how mame Diarra Bousso enacted unconditional obedience to a man and thus embodied a central ideal of Murid womanhood. Would you like to hear the story?"

Amparo nodded hesitantly.

"Legend has it that Diarra's husband one day asked her to hold up a raffia fence that had blown down while he went off to find a rope to tie it up with. But it began to rain and the wind picked up and the husband forgot that he'd left his wife outside, holding up the fence. So she stood there the whole night long while her husband slept comfortably inside, oblivious to his wife. The next morning as he was leaving the house he noticed her still standing there and asked 'What are you doing?' To which she responded 'My master said that I should stand here so I am obeying'[5].

"Many other stories about this woman highlight the qualities believed to be

5. See also page 46..

important in a wife. The most important of these are obedience, patience and loyalty to her husband and master – the man who is the head of her household and who single-handedly decides over it. The wife should maintain high moral standards, feel shame and avoid anything that might be inappropriate for a virtuous woman."

"Well, it can't get much worse than that," said Amparo. "I feel really sorry for these women."

I continued, ignoring her comment. "It's by appealing to mame Diarra that these women hope for a good life on earth and an eternal life in Paradise. Like mame Diarra, a good wife is supposed to remain at home, where she should accommodate her husband in every way. However, the survival of the whole family nowadays often depends upon her ability to take initiative and find work outside the home. Unemployment among men is high and agriculture yields little because of droughts, soil degradation, the shortage of cultivable land and lack of modern technology. Men can usually only contribute to the basic household needs, such as with rice and millet, while everything else depends on the woman's income. This is why women are so keen to migrate. Elsewhere, they can escape the interminable struggle to find ways to generate an income without breaching the norms governing female decency. So I ask myself how ideals and reality relate to one another for these women, in Senegal and in Spain."

"Good question," said my friend. "It sounds insane! So even though the women are enterprising and well able to earn a living, their men close doors on them and society allows them few opportunities to work outside the home yet keep their reputations intact. Is that so for the women who migrate elsewhere to work too?"

"Yes," I replied. "It is a constant problem for all these women, especially the married ones who've followed their husbands overseas but also for ones who've left their husbands behind in Senegal or elsewhere. I want to describe this in detail because it's important for those of us from the countries that are hosting these people, such as Spain, to understand their situation. Female migrants face problems not only with acceptance from Spaniards in Tenerife because of their skin colour and origins. They also face discrimination by their male compatriots. But even though men may try to forbid their women from working outside the home there are ways to get around norms and in this book I aim to explore the strategies they use."

Amparo looked dubious. "Will you? So how have you been able to find out about them? Isn't it just a question of what you believe?"

"Of course it's a matter of interpretation. I don't purport to be able to deliver some kind of final truth. But I've tried my best to understand the reality these women have to deal with by first conducting studies in Senegal and then comparing my findings with their situation in Tenerife. Interwoven with this is my own reality as a western woman, through which everything I experience is filtered. But I can also check my experiences against those described by other people in the literature. Fortunately, several studies of Senegalese women have recently been published that deal with their situation both within marriage and outside of it, mainly in relation to trading and migration and these have been a great help.

"So, I want to show how Muridism is practiced by Senegalese women both in Senegal and in Spain. I want to detail the way that Murid ideals influence their lives while also considering the role that their earnings play for female autonomy. I'm thinking particularly of men's and women's ideas about the various forms of marriage."

"You mean polygamy and monogamy?" my friend asked, pricking up her ears.

"Yes, of course. Polygamy is a constant topic of conversation and a great concern for these women, regardless of whether they live in Senegal or in Tenerife. They rarely want to live in polygamous relationships. If their husband decides to take another wife, most say they'd want to save their earnings to buy their own place to live if they can afford it. Then they can either divorce and move out or remain married and receive their husband as a visitor in their new home. Divorce is on the increase these days but the social pressures on a single woman are heavy and they often end up remarrying as a second, third or fourth wife just to avoid harassment by other men. So although a woman may not wish to share her husband with other women – both for emotional and economic reasons – she may end up doing so in a new marriage simply for protection and to keep a good reputation."

"What a life of contradictions those women live!" Amparo sighed. She had divorced her husband thirty years earlier. "So different from ours."

"I don't know," I say. "The differences maybe aren't as great as they may seem, even though we don't allow polygamy. It depends on your point of view. Sufism is grounded in the idea that you can't attain the greatest reward – complete union with God and a life in Paradise – without struggling and suffering along the way. Many of the things that strike me as abusive towards women, they themselves see as trials. They say that these trials give them merits in God's eyes and they will be credited with these at the end of this life."

"I recognise those ideas," says Amparo irritably. "That's the kind of religion that's been used as the opium of the masses, or the lower classes, throughout the history of Christianity. Thank goodness we've left it behind us. Sufism and Christian mysticism are one thing but the kind of oppression of women that you're talking about is something quite different. Let's call a spade a spade. How can you keep studying this sect without becoming enraged by the male elite that you call marabouts?"

I stopped in my tracks with my effort to explain my book project. Then I took a tissue and wiped away the sweat that was starting to trickle down my face. I was trying to think of a way to respond to Amparo's objections.

"Tell me first," I began. "Do you understand what I'm trying to achieve by writing about these women?"

"Yes and no," she said. She seemed imperturbably composed. "I understand what you want to write about, but where are *you* in all this? Are you for or against the reality these women live with and their way of adapting to their religion and social norms? How involved are you? And what do you want the readers to get out of your book?"

To answer these questions I knew I needed to be perfectly clear about my motives.

"Many people in Senegal have asked me whether I want to become a Murid. From my informants' point of view it would be logical if I converted to Islam and became a disciple of some Murid marabout because of my strong interest in this Sufi order. But I don't want to.

"I think the view of women in Senegalese society as it is reflected in law, religion, tradition and daily life is worthy of criticism. In this regard, I can't say that Muridism is worse than other Sufi orders. But even if some young Murid men applaud the female virtues found in the stories of mame Diarra Bousso, she and her pilgrimage festival nevertheless have elements of a different, somewhat independent female cult and this is unusual in Islam. The qualities of the mother are given equal or even greater importance than her son's mystical, miraculous powers. With my feminist background and my interest in the mystical tradition within Islam - Sufism - I'm intrigued by this feature of Muridism and by the importance mame Diarra holds for Murid women as a source of boundless goodness, generosity and support.

"So let me recap. I want to describe the complexities of these women's lives, both in Senegal and outside the country. It's a challenge to dissect out the interconnected factors that affect their lives but I aim to present a nuanced picture in a readily accessible form. My text is a distillation of copious field notes, tape recordings, memories and comparisons with what others have written. I believe it's important to understand the people themselves before taking a stance on questions concerning such complex issues as religion, gender and economy in today's fast-changing global context. That is my vision – it's not easy but it is important."

At last Amparo seemed content. She smiled and we got up and readied ourselves for a walk in the dusk that was gathering over the city.

SUFISM AND WOMEN

N THE SUMMER OF 2000 I visited Tenerife to study religion and trading among Senegalese female Murid migrants. One day I met a woman who was carrying her hair-dressing equipment along the beach, looking for tourists who might want their hair styled in rasta plaits. She held a large cardboard screen on which she had pinned different coloured plaits and there were some photographs of various styles. At the top of the board stood the word "BRAIDS". She told me that she called her screen mame Diarra because she thought this might help her get clients. Mame Diarra Bousso was known to give you anything you asked for! So each day, she said, she would take her screen confidently under one arm and say, "Come on, mame Diarra, let's go!" This gave her the courage and energy to face another tough day of looking for business.

She brought to mind a Senegalese man I had met briefly several years earlier along a roadside near Playa de las Américas in Tenerife selling fake watches. He was delighted when I told him that I knew about Muridism, the Sufi order he belonged to in Senegal, and said I had been to the city of Touba, where the founder was buried. When I asked whether he had been to Porokhane, where the founder's mother mame Diarra Bousso was said to have her tomb, he lit up. Yes he had and he told me that mame Diarra was the very embodiment of goodness and generosity. He said he loved her as much as he loved her son, shaykh Amadou Bamba. In fact, he said, they are really just two sides of the same person. And although I was a complete stranger to him, he then insisted on giving me one of his fake Rolex watches, saying "In the name of mame Diarra" as he did so.

When I first became interested in Senegal, women and Sufism, Muridism was completely new to me. I soon became intrigued by the religious mysticism that formed part of daily life among the Senegalese. Earlier I had come across Sufism in the works of the classical Persian Sufi poet Rumi, of the Arabic Sufi poet Ibn 'Arabi and Christian mysticism in the poetry of St. John of the Cross and Sta. Teresa of Avila.

These had been literary encounters of both aesthetic and emotional dignity. Now, when I experienced this popular version of Sufism among Murids in Senegal and among immigrants in Spain I was impressed by the fervent religiosity that was so unquestioningly integrated into their everyday lives. The only word I could find to capture the piety they manifested was "spirituality".

Sufism appealed to me because of its lack of rigid institutionalisation and because of the believers' aspiration for reaching a boundless religious experience. This seemed to create a space for female religiosity that was lacking in more formal Islam. Sufism also enabled different ways of approaching the Divine. It was just as acceptable to worship a higher Being with child-like joy and enthusiasm as through asceticism and in isolation. So when I came across this orientation of Islam during my field studies, these were among the factors that piqued my interest.

Margaret Smith describes Sufism with the following words: "The goal of the Sufi's quest was union with the Divine and the Sufi seeker after God, having renounced this world and its attraction, being purged of Self and its desires, inflamed with a passion of love to God, journeyed ever onward, looking towards his final purpose, through the life of illumination, with its ecstasies and raptures, and the higher life of contemplation, until at last he achieved the heavenly gnosis and attained the Vision of God, in which the lover might become one with the beloved, and abide in him forever"[1].

Although Sufis aspire to reach and unite with God directly, in popular practice this union is achieved through mediators such as holy or learned men known as marabouts or with the help of saints. Before encountering the Murid tradition that is the subject of this book, I had already noted how, as soon as men begin to streamline and institutionalise a religious cult, women are relegated to the back seat, both in Islam and Christianity. In the mame Diarra Bousso cult, by contrast, a female figure featured as fulfilling the Murids' expectations of a major Sufi saint. It therefore seemed important to explore the meaning she held for her followers.

The historian Louis Brenner explains that Sufism is concerned not only with creating a mystical bond with God but also with salvation through prayer and with the esoteric (mystical, undisclosed) dimensions of life[2]. Sufism evolved in the Arabic-speaking world during the latter half of the 8th century along with the parallel development of Islamic social, political and legal institutions. West African Sufism is characterised by the recitation of prayers, which are first read by the leader (the imam or marabout) and then repeated by the disciple countless times. This takes place to the accompaniment of

---

1. Smith 2000: 1.
2. See Brenner 1994.

drumming and dance-like performances. In West Africa there is also a strong belief in Sufi saints and their ability to perform miracles for their followers. The disciples seek the holy power (Arabic *baraka*, Wolof *barke*) which the marabouts are said to transmit to their followers from God in order to help them in this world and into Paradise.

As mentioned, a characteristic of Islam in West Africa is the close relationship between the disciple, *talibé*, and his teacher or master[3]. This bond is particularly strong in Muridism and it is based on the *talibé*'s obedience and subordination to the marabout. Other concepts that are important in Sufism in general are: the concealed inner truth (Arabic *haqiqa*), the holy struggle (Arabic *jihad*), contemplation (Arabic *mushahanda*) and the recitation of God's name (Arabic *dhikr*). Of these, most Murid women are only familiar with the concept of *dhikr*.

For women Muridism is a whole way of life. While Murid men tend to treat the esoteric and the practical as two distinct realms, women are adept at interweaving the two. The enormous amount of food that women prepare for the big Murid pilgrim feasts and for numerous other occasions of religious celebrations and meetings is just one example of women's conviction that working for God and the marabouts will give them merits *(tiyaba)* from God.

I noted above that Margaret Smith had claimed gender equality was the rule in true Sufism. In contemporary Islamic mysticism, however, and among some of the Sufi men of the classical period (800–1100), the attitude to women in daily life was and still is ambivalent. Anne-Marie Schimmel has described how some Sufi men have derided certain women as old witches. Sufi women have always had to use diplomacy skills in order to avoid displeasing male Sufis[4]. While men often speak negatively about older women who show a strong will of their own, motherhood has always been extolled within Sufism. The mothers of famous male Sufis have often been glorified as selfless and bounteous, as in the case of mame Diarra Bousso.

The very first Sufi saint noted in the texts was in fact a woman, namely Rabi'a of Basra (aka Rabi'a al-Adawiyya). The praise lavished on her has contributed greatly to the shaping of the image of the generous, ideal woman, who is worshipped because she is so different from "ordinary" women – or so the male interpretation would have it[5]. Rabi'a's biographer Farid ad-Din Attar describes her as a person who transcended gender division in her love of God. Ad-Din Attar is known to have expressed his opinion of female saints thus: "When a woman follows the path of God like a man, she cannot be called a woman." Rabi'a was one of the first to teach the doctrine of disinterested love

3. The Muslim leaders have been known by the French as marabouts ever since the colonial era (ca. 1815–1960).
4. See Schimmel 1975.
5. See ibid.

of God, a new concept to many of her follow-Sufis, who served God largely in hope of eternal reward and fear of eternal punishment[6]. Since Rabi'a's time this "pure" love model has been said to be the essential element in the saint's relation to God. Rabi'a was also probably the first to teach that Paradise was to be conceived of as a spiritual state in the presence of God, not a place filled with individual pleasure.[7] Rabi'a al-Adawiyya was undoubtedly the greatest of the women mystics of Islam and she made the greatest contribution of any woman to the development of Sufism.

Rabi'a's stress on unconditional love of God is recalled in the mame Diarra Bousso cult. Rabi'a claimed that Sufism should be concerned with cultivating love as a true feeling rather than with calculations about divine rewards. Similarly, the Murid legends about mame Diarra emphasise her unconditional love of her adepts and God. Murid stories about mame Diarra often contain descriptions of love using the common Sufi metaphor of an endless sea and she often features helping people through the gates of Paradise.

It would seem that even in early Sufism (from the 8th century) women were permitted to attend meetings at which male Sufi preachers were delivering sermons[8]. This is not always the case nowadays. Murid women who attend meetings more often than not remain in a corner of the room and are asked not to join in the prayers and singing so as not to disturb the men.

Many Sufi women who lived during the 9th and 10th centuries are mentioned in the Arabic and Persian literature as prominent Muslim mystics. Others were acknowledged for their knowledge and were admired for their pious lifestyle. The stories about mame Diarra's family (in the middle of the 19th century) describe how she used to study the Koran and other religious literature at home under the tutelage of her learned mother. In later Sufi legends too we find women who are admired for their religious knowledge.

I have already mentioned that I was struck by how people in Senegal integrated religious mysticism into their everyday lives. In books about Sufism I had read about the ecstatic worship of holy people, the spontaneous expressions of joy and the absolute confidence in God and His representatives, such as shaykh Amadou Bamba and his mother mame Diarra Bousso. However, none of the Murid women I met called themselves Sufis or knew much about Sufism as a religious path. They simply saw themselves as Murids, in contrast to members of other orders.

There are, of course, Senegalese people of all ages and from all social groups who are quite unconcerned with religion *per se*. They experience the Islamic prohibition on eating pork or drinking alcohol and on fasting dur-

---

6. Smith 2000: 94.

7. Ibid. 2000:70.

8. Schimmel 1975: 427.

ing the month of Ramadan more as features of cultural or national identity. These people could be described as passive Muslims, who live in a country steeped in Islamic tradition and simply see it as natural. They participate in major Islamic festivals a couple of times a year, eating good food and giving presents to the children just as many Christians do at Christmas or Easter time. It is only when they travel abroad to non-Muslim countries that they note the differences between their own and more or less secular society. This is when they begin to regard themselves as Senegalese and as having a religious identity that is distinct from that of the host society. This tends to lead to an intensification of religious activity, particularly among men.

Orthodox Islam has an influence both in Senegal and among migrants elsewhere. Returning Senegalese students from the religious universities in Cairo and Yeddah are spreading Islamist ideas at home, which become readily intermingled with mystical beliefs and practices. In Senegal today the *Shi'a* Muslims form a growing minority, consisting mainly of the younger generation[9]. The country's population of fourteen million includes almost 95 percent Muslims and around five percent Christians. Many of the latter live in Casamance, south of Gambia, and along the coast south of Dakar in the areas dominated by the *Serer* (an ethnic group with its own language).

Most Senegalese Muslims belong to a Sufi order of which the two most numerous ones are Tijaniyya and Muridiyya. The members engage themselves in both practical and mystical religious activities such as pilgrimages to holy sites and tombs and to renowned religious leaders' houses. The regular meetings of members are vital for the survival of the Sufi orders. The *talibés* involve themselves in different religious associations, each of which exists in the name and honour of a specific Sufi marabout or the supreme leader of Muridism, the *khalifa général*. The evening call to prayer can be heard from the minarets while the sound of religious songs and recitations of God's name from the gatherings at the Sufi associations echo through the streets of Senegalese cities, towns and villages late into the night or until dawn. Young men can be seen everywhere reading prayer books that they have bought from sellers along the roadside. Women pray at home while the men file off to the mosques to perform their prayers. On Friday afternoons the mosques are so packed that many men go down on their knees to pray in the streets close to the mosque as the imam's voice blasts out from the loudspeakers.

Religion is not simply a private, individual affair in Senegal. The state is also involved in a way that westerners often find surprising, particularly given that Senegal is supposedly a secular state and has a non-confessional school system modeled upon that of the French. In accordance with the Senegalese Constitution religious political parties are forbidden. However, the relation-

---

9. See Leichtman 2009.

ship between religion and secular politics in Senegal differs notably from that in France. The coexistence of religion and secularism both seduces and irritates foreign visitors who are trying to understand this special situation. Senegal could perhaps be described as a religiously defined secular state. This description may frighten some and seem erroneous to others but it contains the important idea of popular government under God. Some might wish to see the patriarchal system, which is legitimised by religion, challenged by reference to secularism but instead we find patriarchy deeply rooted even in secular contexts. These factors notwithstanding, Senegal enjoys a certain harmony between the state and religious authorities and this is rare in Africa. How is this so?

In the 19th century, French colonial powers broke apart the small kingdoms that formerly made up today's Senegal. Muslim leaders soon took over power locally and they began to play a double role. On the one hand, they worked to liberate themselves and their people from the colonial yoke while, on the other, serving French interests by engaging in mutually beneficial relations in the groundnut export business. This symbiosis between the state and religious powers persisted even after independence in 1960 and after the groundnut trade more or less died out. The relationships between secularism and Sufism in Senegal therefore evolved from conditions that were specific to the country.

The term *laïcité*, secularism, was coined in France in 1905. It was originally an anti-clerical concept that was meant to express the freedom of the state from religion. The French revolution, which had struggled to break the power of the Catholic Church, was the driving force behind the separation of church and state and atheism was now celebrated. However, the situation in Senegal is quite different. Here, the state tries to help those who want to participate in religious rituals. Abdou Diouf, the country's second president after independence from France, interpreted secularism thus:

> *Laïcité* (Secularism) in itself is a manifestation of respect for others. It acts in this way if it is well understood and properly practiced.
> Such laïcité cannot be anti-religious, nor can it become a state religion if it is a true laïcité.
> I would say further that such a laic state cannot ignore religious institutions.
> From the fact that citizens embrace religion flows the obligation for the state to facilitate the practice of that religion, as it does for all other vital activities of citizens.
> Respect for religion does not only mean tolerance, it does not mean only to allow or to ignore, but to respect the beliefs and practices of the other.
> Laïcité is the consequence of this respect for the other, and the condition of our harmony.[10]

---

10. Abdou Diouf quoted in Stepan 2007: 9.

State representatives are present at religious ceremonies led by the most influential leaders and the state sponsors poor pilgrims to go to Mecca. For the great pilgrimages to Touba for the Murids and to Tiwauen for the Tijans, the government often invests in infrastructural improvements, such as repair of the roads. At the Murid pilgrimage, the *Grand Magal* in Touba in 2007 there were eleven ministers in attendance. This represented half of the entire government!

Some information about Touba

Touba lies 198 km east of the capital Dakar, in the Diourbel region. The city is Senegal's second largest urban centre with approximately 700,000 inhabitants and it is the headquarters of Muridism, a Sufi order that originates from nearby Mbacké, which is situated 8 km from Touba. The city's buildings spread out around the centrally located mosque, which is one of the largest in Africa. While population growth in the rest of Senegal is around 5% per year, in Touba it is around 15%. Many Murids dream about Touba becoming the capital of the country. The town is known as the "holy city" but administratively it remains a rural municipality. It falls under the authority of the highest Murid leader, *the khalifa général*.

Because it is a religious centre, Touba is partially exempt from the power of Senegal's local and national administration. In practice, this means that the Mbacké Mbacké family is responsible for many of the town's services. However, rapid population growth has made it almost impossible for the family to control the situation. The city's only hospital was built using private donations made by Murid followers, particularly remittances from migrants. It was built under the direction of *the khalifa général*. There are only fifteen medical clinics in the whole of Touba and these can only deal with a fraction of the population's health problems. Lack of water and sewage systems and inadequate road planning have led to grave problems such as repeated flooding, cholera epidemics and yellow fever outbreaks.

The great mosque is surrounded by quarters that have been inherited by shaykh Amadou Bamba's grandchildren. The buildings closest to the mosque are owned by his sons, behind these are buildings owned by his daughters. A lane leads visitors into the female marabouts' properties.

The courtyards belonging to the houses are big enough to receive visitors who have joined the annual pilgrimage. Each of the grandchildren owns not only houses and huts but also a mosque each, a water cistern and an open area in which to gather for discussions. In Wolof this area is known as a pentch and it is very important for the social interactions between the descendants of the founder and their disciples. The further a house is from the main mosque, the more distant the relationship of the owner to Amadou Bamba. It is an extraordinary form of urban development in which the size and position of a house immediately reflects the owner's relationship to the founder.

Source: Agence Nationale de la Statistique et de la Demographie, Senegal, publication Estimation de la Population du Sénégal de 2005 à 2015, Direction de la Prévision et de la Statistique, January 2008.

Reference: Guèye, Cheikh 2002. Touba. La Capitale des Mourides. Paris, Dakar: ENDA-Karthala-IRD.

A FEMALE
MARABOUT IN TOUBA

Three ladies go to Touba

I T WAS A RATHER cramped taxi which left Dakar for Touba one hot November day. The driver shared the front seat with two male passengers. In the back seat we three ladies sat crowded together, all of us a bit on the bulky side, dressed in large and somewhat stiff frocks, so new, in fact, that they rustled when creased as we manoeuvred to give ourselves more room on the seat. The woman next to me was holding her baby son, and he, a few months old, was in fact the real motive for our trip. He was to be blessed by the youngest of Amadou Bamba's daughters, sokhna Maimouna Khadim Mbacké Mbacké (1924–1999). *Sokhna* was her honorary title, given to all female marabouts and other distinguished women. In the following I do not use her title in my text. The child's mother had grown up at Maimouna's house. She had been left there when only a couple of years old, and had served Maimouna together with a host of other girls, a combination of 'daughter' and maid. At fifteen she had married the man Maimouna had chosen for her. Together with this woman and a friend of hers who was a Murid and a follower of Maimouna as well, I was making the trip in order to acquaint myself with Touba and meet the famous female marabout. 'Follower' is the term I use here to specify those people who, just like the women in the car, claim a special relationship to a religious leader without having sworn an oath of loyalty and obedience to him or her. The disciple, *talibé*, has established his formal loyalty by swearing such an oath, known as *djebelu*.

A tense mood prevailed in the car. It was, after all, not an everyday event for the women travelling to Touba in the company of a *toubab*, a white European and a non-Muslim as I was. Moreover, we would be visiting the big mosque alone, unescorted by the men. It was true that there were three of us paying the visit, but you never knew what might happen.

The anxiety my travelling companions felt infected me too, and I requested instructions on the proper behaviour required of me. Touba was not just another place on the map but a holy site, the centre of Muridism, where special rules prevailed. I knew that I had to cover my head so that no hair was visible. Provocative clothes were out of the question and trousers were not accepted for women. The ladies accompanying me approved of my dress, a *grand boubou*, long and wide as it was, just like theirs. In Touba smoking as well as alcoholic drinks were forbidden. Hotels and restaurants did not exist at all. The purpose of going to Touba was to visit the mosque with its famous mausoleum, and to see one's marabout, in his home or its vicinity. The marabouts who had their houses in Touba were descendants of the founder of Muridism. They received visitors at home or in their courtyard during their annual celebrations. On these occasions the marabouts' wives organised the preparing of food and camping facilities for as many visitors as possible with the help of disciples and *daira* members.

We drove towards the centre and after a while the car stopped to drop off the male passengers, who wished to go to one of the big market places in Touba. Trade and commerce flourished there all year round; goods were inexpensive as no duty rules were applied. As a matter of fact, Touba was a duty-free zone, administered chiefly by the highest leader of Muridism.

I took a good look at this remarkable place as we slowly made our way along roads mostly in a poor state of repair. The sandy surface was bumpy and uneven after the rainy season. Horse-driven carts dominated the scene, and we were surrounded on all sides by swarms of people going about their business on foot. I found the air torrid and unpleasant. The buildings appeared just as shabby as in many other places. Was this really the Touba praised and spoken about by the Murids?

Next, the mosque was silhouetted against the horizon and I gazed in amazement. It offered an impressive sight with its 87-metre high minaret reaching up into the sky. I remember how a woman in Dakar had once told me that the Touba mosque penetrated right into Paradise, and I could now appreciate what she was getting at. The mosque had been built in commemoration of Amadou Bamba, and inaugurated in 1963. Even though his father's relatives were from Mbacké, he settled down later on in life in Touba, some eight kilometres from Mbacké. Thus Touba became the centre of Muridism, a fact confirmed by the construction of the mosque.

The Murids claim that whoever dies in Touba will enter Paradise. Naturally enough, a large migration takes place to this urban centre, a result of both the spiritual element and the promising trading climate. The favourable price of goods at Touba encourages settling down there and trading with other parts of the country. Countless immigrants have invested money in land on the outskirts of Touba, and have built or intend building houses there. All Murids strive towards being buried there in time. In brief, Muridism has created a huge expansion in Touba, which if the present rate of investment continues could easily become the country's largest urban settlement.

My companions in the taxi were deeply touched by the sight of the mosque. The driver also seemed affected, and suddenly became chatty and helpful. Like the others, he was a Murid, and wanted me to have an opportunity of admiring the building from every angle. We drove round it twice. Then it was time for me to visit the mosque. I removed my shoes, and, my eyes fixed on the ground before me, I drew my shawl down over my forehead as a sign of respect a decent woman was expected to show. At the entrance stood a Bai Fall disciple dressed in a colourful patchwork robe, his feet bare and his hair in dreadlocks. These outward characteristics of the adherents to the Bai Fall pleased me. I knew Bai Fall was a sub-section of Muridism, which originated with shaykh Ibra Fall, the most prominent disciple of Amadou Bamba. The young man stretched his gourd bowl towards me begging for money and reading a prayer, but I had already offered a few coins to others, mostly small boys.

Very soon I heard a fascinating song, strange to my ears, coming from a group of men. Seated on the floor to the left of the big doorway, they recited or rather chanted Amadou Bamba's religious songs, which he had composed based on texts from the Koran. They are known as *khassaïds*, and are normally sung by male members of a Murid association. The men at the entrance were members of such an association, chanting these songs in perfect time and in unison, all of which plunged me into an unreal and almost trance-like state. The other women proceeded further into the mosque in order to pray, while I stayed close to the chanting men for a long period of time now that this was my first visit to the Touba mosque. Later on I became accustomed to the constant singing of the *khassaïds* at all the Murid places I visited and even could become weary of it, particularly when it disturbed my sleep at night. On the whole, however, the songs infused in me a feeling of insulation from life around me, and a sense of peace was kindled within me.

Calm in mind, I headed for the north-eastern corner of the vast mosque, where Amadou Bamba's mausoleum was situated behind a sturdy grating, erected to keep pilgrims at a discreet distance. I kneeled down, surrounded by other visitors, in front of the golden gate. The tomb was decked with embroidered velvet cloth. The atmosphere was tense, to say the least. The people around me appeared to be in raptures merely at *being there*, at *serigne* Touba's tomb (this is another name for Amadou Bamba). Weeping women, their tears streaming down their cheeks, as well as men, pressed against the grating to get as near the tomb as possible. I was pushed forward by their warm bodies closer to the grating door. A desire to appropriate Amadou Bamba's *barke* appeared to have taken hold of everybody. Serigne Touba himself had said that Paradise cannot be attained without a spiritual guide. His followers gathered at his tomb were confiding to him this hope, together with expectations of a better life on earth. I felt touched by the intensive nature of their religiosity. In some odd way it was contagious, invading me with a physical and spiritual sensation of communion and shared excitement at being close to something I couldn't define.

A while later we left the mosque for Maimouna. All three of us were happy that the visit to the mosque had ended without any questions arising concerning my own religious affiliation. We felt fortified and relieved at the same time – I believe – each in one's own way. For myself I reflected, mostly in jest, over the fact that mame Diarra must have been keeping a protective eye on me as I was paying a visit to her son's splendid mosque. When I smilingly suggested this to the women, they showed a serious mien and underlined the fact that this was indeed the case – you are never deserted by mame Diarra Bousso. The religious metaphors I was employing in my efforts to explore Muridism were pure reality for the people around me, and as such quite simple and evident.

Together with Maimouna

Maimouna's house and courtyard were full of women and children. The male visitors were waiting in an adjacent room. One woman had brought a live hen for Maimouna. A middle-aged man evidently intended delivering a sack of millet, which he had dumped at the entrance. A few women were carrying baskets of soaps and bottles of perfume. I thanked my lucky stars that I had a currency note equivalent to two euros in my bag. We sat down on the floor in the anteroom in front of a door which was closed. Very soon one of Maimouna's trusted assistants came along, a young boy belonging to her inner circle of disciples. He beckoned to us, opened the door and admitted us before the others in the room. I realised that it was my identity as a *toubab* which deserved this priority. I could imagine the reproachful looks behind me as we went in. I felt uncomfortable as a white woman visiting Touba's religious élite while the followers, true believers in the female marabout's powers and in sincere need of her aid, were constrained to sit and wait together with their gifts. That feeling remained with me during the meeting with the elderly lady, who must have been only two years old when her father died in 1927.

Maimouna was dressed in white from top to toe. She sat on a low sofa together with her spokesperson, a young male disciple, just behind her. She whispered into his ear what she wished to have stated to us visitors, and this he communicated in a loud voice in *Wolof.* The baby started to cry as it was handed to the female marabout, who spat into the palm of her right hand and smeared the baby over its entire body, reading a prayer in a scarcely audible voice. The purpose was to transfer by means of the saliva her inherent holy power. The mother was beside herself with happiness and pride. Somebody in the group explained to Maimouna that I was a European wishing to learn more about Muridism. She promised to pray for me, and I delivered my small note to the man at her side.

Maimouna straightaway suggested I remain at her home for the rest of the day. I could sit close to the wall while she was receiving her visitors, and then spend the evening together with her. There was a language barrier, however. My travelling companion with the baby acted as interpreter, but was unable to remain there. We talked the matter over and asked if we could return another time.

Later, I asked myself why I hadn't stayed there at Maimouna's house, irrespective of the language problem. It would of course have been a perfect opportunity to become acquainted with a person who occupied a central position among the Murid élite. Deep down, however, it probably had to do with the fact that I felt ill at ease with the system as such. I quite simply did not believe that this woman could transmit her blessing to me, or that she had anything else to offer merely by being Amadou Bamba's daughter.

Like a feudal lord Maimouna had inherited her position and now earned her living similarly. I asked my fellow-travellers what it was that made Maimouna so special in their eyes and those of many other Murids. The question seemed to be rather unnecessary. "Well, because she is serigne Touba's daughter", was the answer, implying that she was in possession of *barke* and capable of transferring it to others from a source which never dried up. Yes, for sure, I said, but what was it she did for her followers in a purely concrete fashion? The women declared that Maimouna had sufficient power and influence to help her adherents whenever they needed it. They might, for example, be suffering from problems related to health, marriage, fertility or finances. "She is a rich woman, a sure sign that God is with her and she does share with others."

Before we left Maimouna's house she performed the act called *ñaan* – she blessed us. We received the blessing kneeling in front of her, our arms stretched out and hands cup-shaped. I followed the others: lifting our hands to our faces and allowing the palms and fingertips to stroke our bodies, from forehead to stomach, by which the holy force was infused. Then we thanked her from our position on the floor and left. That was the last time I saw her. A few years later she passed away.

As proof of Maimouna's generosity and essential goodness the women named her annual celebration of *Leylatoul Khadri*, the night God is purported to have sent the Koran down from heaven to the Prophet Mohammed. The exuberant festival originally took place in the village called Darou Wahab, but had been held at Touba for the past few decades. On that occasion she used to invite the people to generous portions of food, cooked under her supervision by her disciples. The female marabout financed the purchase of poultry, oxen, sheep and camels, oil, rice, millet grain, tea and sugar, using the money yielded by the harvests from the fields in her village. She had herself founded the festival with permission from the highest Murid leader, her half-brother.

All gatherings arranged by marabouts are defined in religious terms within Muridism. The biggest festival of them all has already been referred to – the Touba *magal* in remembrance of Amadou Bamba. Maimouna had also, along with many other female marabouts, inherited arable pasture land. The custom goes back to that period in time when Senegal was divided into small kingdoms and the daughters of royal families were able to inherit land on both the paternal and maternal side. When the kingdoms disappeared as colonial power took over, giving way to the religious leaders' control of the countryside, many daughters of royal descent were married off to marabouts and took with them the arable land they had inherited.

Christine Jean's doctoral thesis on female marabouts at Touba underlines the fact that Maimouna lived her life entirely in accordance with the Murid view of religion and finance.[1] She devoted a lot of time to studying the Koran and teaching Arabic. Maimouna had grown up aware of her father's, Amadou Bamba's, doctrine that work and prayer were equal in importance before God. A pious life took into account hard work leading to prosperity, something which was to be shared with others. Generosity and an industrious spirit were core concepts within Muridism.

During the years that Amadou Bamba lived, 'work' implied agricultural work and the cultivation of groundnuts and millet in particular. The area around Mbacké and Touba in the province of Diourbel formed part of the zone known as the 'groundnut belt'. Groundnuts were the chief crop for the market. It was the peasant population in this region who constituted the basic element in Muridism. They belonged to the *Wolof* ethnic group but also to the *Halpulaar*. From being landless illiterate people they gained access through the marabouts to fields they could cultivate. As a means of compensation for the land they acquired, they devoted one day a week – often a Wednesday – to growing millet and groundnuts for their religious leaders.

Maimouna had lived through the groundnut boom in the region around Touba. She had access to arable land in the neighbourhood of her village Darou Wahab, and it was there she opened a number of *daaras*, a type of boarding school with instruction in the Koran for young boys in the village.

---

1. See Jean, 1995.

The boys' duties included ploughing the fields bordering the huts where they slept. These youngsters were handed over to the *daaras* while still very small, but were not put to the agricultural tasks until they were older, most often at the age of between ten and twelve.

Maimouna's source of income was chiefly agriculture, although trade and commerce were important too, in addition to the financial donations from religious associations in her name and in her honour. The money was handed over by the respective presidents at the annual village festival or on monthly visits to her. She also received presents and money when her followers went to see her at the afternoon receptions.

During the second half of the twentieth century groundnut exports dropped sharply. Trading in other products assumed a more important role for everybody in the Diourbel region, not least for the female marabouts. Agricultural work on marabout land was carried out as part of a religiously defined activity and it still is. Did trade in clothes, textiles, materials, shoes and cosmetics have the same religious significance; or, to put it in a better way, could trade and commerce be related to Muridism in the same quite obvious way?

The answer is manifestly affirmative. Trading became for Maimouna and other women in a similar position one more activity among others in the religious sphere. She had her female disciples sew clothes in her dressmaker's workshop. They were sold in Touba at a profit which fell to her. Customers interpreted as a sign of good fortune the purchase of clothes manufactured at Maimouna's prestigious workshop. Moreover, it was common to think that there might be elements of *barke* in the garment, to favour the new owner. The female marabouts regarded it as quite natural to make trips together to Gambia to purchase inexpensive material at the market places for sale among friends and acquaintances in Dakar. From a secular, Western viewpoint, this activity may not be what we would term 'religious practice'. As far as Maimouna and her customers were concerned, however, everything these female marabouts did, or what they worked with in order to earn money, was religiously legitimate, as long as the actors were descendants of Amadou Bamba. The prevailing idea was that they would share their prosperity in different ways with their adherents.

Maimouna had not only founded a village and ran an agricultural business and traded in a similar way to the male marabouts. She also had *talibés*, disciples, who helped her in her various commitments. You became a disciple by swearing an oath of loyalty, a *djebelu*, to your religious leader. In Maimouna's case, she had sworn the oath of allegiance to her first husband. This is the mark of the true Murid woman, serigne Touba has said, and it is not until this ritual has been performed that a married woman can enter Paradise.

Maimouna's husband died, however, and she remarried without moving to the new husband's home or swearing the oath to him. This she did instead to the highest Murid leader, the *khalifa général*. Many of her own followers swore their oaths to her and thus became her disciples. The majority of them were girls. This happened in spite of the fact that a number of Murids claim that no female marabouts may have disciples.

In point of fact a lot of Maimouna's followers and disciples left their daughters with her from as early an age as two or three. Parents had given their daughters Maimouna's name as a sign of their veneration for her. In all there might be more than a hundred 'Maimounas' at her household. Roughly speaking, there were two categories of girls living with her. The first comprised children whose parents were distant relatives of the Mbacké Mbacké family with some form of marabout connection. The second comprised girls from common families where the often poor parents' purpose was to deliver their daughters to Maimouna as a gift and a proof of their trust in her, their spiritual leader.

This was also an established way of getting their daughters provided for while small, and later favourably married off by Maimouna's agency. The first category of girls were allowed to go to the Koran school, and they performed fewer household chores than the second, who were little more than serving maids as soon as they were old enough to work for Maimouna.

The woman I travelled to Touba with had belonged to the 'maid' bracket. She had nothing but good words to say about growing up with Maimouna, who she addressed as 'Mother'. Maimouna had acquired a much older husband for her. He had been well off, and she had enjoyed a good life together with him until he died. When the children had grown up she had remarried a butcher who already had two wives. She did this because she found it difficult living as a respectable woman without a man in the town she came from. The second husband had no son with his other wives, and as fortune would have it, she turned out to be his favourite, giving birth to a strapping little baby boy. The woman felt that Maimouna, with her *barke*, had been instrumental in some way. It was evident for the happy mother that the female marabout was in possession of this very special power.

Barke manifests itself as a primary factor in the Murid belief system. It is the access to *barke* which regulates people's relationship to the religious leaders in terms of subordination and its opposite. Like royal personages the Murid marabouts inherit their portion of *barke* and it is distributed unevenly, in accordance with the predominant ideology, and depending on gender; female marabouts inherit less *barke* than male marabouts. Murids who are not related to the Mbacké Mbacké family cannot expect any inherited *barke*. A sign of affiliation to this eminent group of close surviving relatives of Amadou Bamba is that they add an extra 'Mbacké' to their name to mark their exceptional status. Murid leaders normally declare that female marabouts are *unable* to possess *barke*, and should they by chance do so, they cannot transfer it to other people. In actual fact a great number of exceptions are reported, as noted, Maimouna being one of them. Examples are brought to mind of women who are the daughters of marabouts and the family is without male issue.[2]

Apart from inheritance, a marabout's personality and charisma play a decisive role. For a female marabout to attain a place of importance in the Murid establishment, she must have some form of allurement. Her father's and her brothers' attitudes towards her are also of great importance. If she gains a reputation for having *barke* confirmed by her wealth and the miracles she is said to have performed, she will soon be popular among the Murids. The number of disciples a marabout has points to his or her success, both socially and financially, as well as with respect to religion. One thing is sure: disciples must remain convinced that the marabout they put their trust in really has something to offer them in spiritual and material matters. A marabout who cannot provide sufficient – or none at all – of what has been requested is considered to have no *barke*. He will have fewer followers and disciples in the long run, and thereby less power. The most important aspect is of course the belief that the marabout can help the individual disciple to enter Paradise. Maimouna had not herself created the ample network in which she was active. As a member of the Mbacké Mbacké family, she was one of the Murids capable of functioning in a well-organised and totally integrated manner, both within the religious order and outside it. Murid leaders are to be found in positions of power in the transport industry, the building branch and the trade and commerce sector. They maintain important contacts with members of the government, not least by marrying into certain families to men occupying influential political positions.

The biggest market place in Dakar, Sandaga by name, is dominated by Murids whose families originally come from the area around Mbacké and Touba. Generally speaking, it might be said that the Murids' activities constitute a fascinating fusion of subordination and seniority in a decidedly strict, religious hierarchy. Added to this we find a large degree of fellowship and sense of responsibility among Murid disciples. Moral issues are important and a tough social control is exercised. Within the wide framework of religion Muridism represents a Senegalese variant of modern life bound by tradition and in line with the aspirations people have of leading a better life both spiritually and materially.

Touba representing the heart of Muridism and Maimouna as a model for its female leadership are interesting objects of study in themselves. I should now,

---

2. See Coulon, 1988 and Coulon, C. and O. Reveyrand, 1990.

however, like to focus attention on women other than those belonging to the immediate Mbacké Mbacké family. This means moving away from Touba. I have chosen to make a stop in the nearby town of Mbacké, a place also deeply marked by Muridism but less than Touba. Here, too, live surviving relatives of the Amadou Bamba family, although not in a direct line of descent.

It is not only among members of the religious associations but in Senegalese society as a whole that the associations appear to act as a platform for women's activities. The women's association forms the legitimate basis of everything that is done in support of the family's good and one's own. I made a thorough study of the various types of associations and alliances which existed in the city and the countryside before making for Mbacké. It proved to be a rewarding initiative.

MBACKÉ:
THE FIELD EXPANDS

ARRIVED AT MBACKÉ in the afternoon heat in a cloud of dust and sand stirred up by the city jeep which I had travelled with. The perspiration ran in streams down my arms and between my shoulder blades, sticking shirt to waistband.

We stopped outside a Lebanese shop. I crawled out of the vehicle, my legs stiff. The first thing I noticed was the large number of carts travelling along the street, loaded with passengers and goods, and drawn by emaciated horses. The horses presented a pitiable scene. Several of them suffered from large weals where their flanks had been whipped, their clearly visible ribs and blood-soaked skin witness to hunger and ill-treatment.

I was shown into my living quarters around the corner from the ironmonger's. I would be living there on a number of occasions. It wasn't until my fourth visit that I rented a house of my own. This first time all I could think of was water as I entered the house: cold water to douse myself with and to drink. After buying thirty litres from a vendor who was passing by with his water tank, I washed and changed to a loose and ample Senegalese cotton dress, and ankle-length trousers of the same material.

Then I went shopping to obtain the most essential items, plus a bottle of sparkling water in the only shop in town which sold such. This was a luxury I permitted myself on very special occasions. As a European I was almost alone in the town and roused a certain amount of attention. *"Toubab, toubab!"* children shouted when they saw me. An elderly French couple lived together with a host of cats and a dachshund in an old house nearby. The husband had sold wine and spirits in Mbacké, but the sale of these articles was put to an end by the Murid leaders in Touba in 1980. The remainder of the population was made up of the ethnic groups of *Wolof* – the majority – *Halpulaar* and *Serer*, together with an ever-decreasing sprinkling of Lebanese born in Senegal.

I later learned that many Lebanese had settled in Senegal during the first thirty years or so of the twentieth century. They enjoyed both Lebanese and Senegalese citizenship. Only a few Lebanese families remained in Mbacké, however, subsequent to the year 2000. The Chinese who had arrived in Senegal as from the 1990s ousted much of the competing Lebanese trading community. The younger generation of Lebanese found their way to France for further education and training, and tended not to return to Senegal.

I strolled past the line of tailors sitting in front of their sewing machines at the wide entrance to the ironmonger's, with their eyes on the street outside and all that was happening out there. Women balancing loads on their heads wobbled past, shouting to each other from across the street. Bunches of young boys stood around, and thin, long-legged dogs sniffed among the piles of rubbish littering the corners of the market place. The market place stretched further along the road opposite the ironmonger's where a number of multi-storey buildings, their pastel coloured paint peeling, came into view.

In 1992 none of the roads and streets in Mbacké was surfaced, and sewage was disposed of straight into the sandy street, where pedestrians and horse and cart passed. I recall how the dirty sand scorched my heels as it seeped into my shoes. They were without a back strap as it was easier to remove them that way and shake off the sand before entering a house.

The heat was oppressive in Mbacké even during the 'chilly' months of January and February. My first visit took place in September when the intense heat following the rain period increased the humidity. The early morning, around six or seven o'clock, was the only time of the day I could move around with a certain degree of comfort. I used to stroll out from the centre of the town and follow the road to the hotel situated on the outskirts and then return. After that it became too hot to walk any longer stretches.

Now, however, it behoved me as a recent arrival to get in touch as fast as possible with the persons I wanted to look up. Therefore, in spite of the sweltering heat of the late afternoon, I went in search of my future assistant, a woman who would be helping me to find people to interview in the local language, chiefly *Wolof*. Most of the women in Mbacké knew no French since either they had not gone to school at all or had been to school for a very few years. All education was imparted in French at school, but at home only the local language was used.

A neighbour had given me instructions of the streets to take, and I followed them assiduously to avoid getting lost. All the greyish-yellow sandy roads looked alike, and on first glimpse the low-strung houses behind the fences of sheet-metal or raffia lining the roads didn't seem to vary greatly. It was not long before I found myself surrounded by a swarm of children. Two of them belonged to my assistant's household. One of the children, a little boy, led me to his mother, whose name was Penda. I'd found her! The boy was her youngest son.

The last time I visited Mbacké, in 2005, more cars could be seen in the streets than before. The number of surfaced roads in the central parts of the town had increased, and horse-drawn carts were fewer in number. There was still a shortage of restaurants, cafés and hotels in the inner city. Whatever entertainment existed was stamped with the seal of secrecy owing to the vicinity of Touba, where anything associated with sinful activity was prohibited. This included tobacco, beer, wine and spirits. Smoking and alcohol were allowed in Mbacké, but the open sale of these items was not permitted. The many bars and brothels said to exist in Mbacké were surreptitiously frequented by visitors from Touba, where representatives for the Murids kept a close eye on matters. The flag of morality was held high, at least superficially. Women's arms and legs had to be fully covered in Touba, and men were not allowed even to light a cigarette. None of these rules and regulations applied to Mbacké, which in any case did not occupy the same high status as Muridism's holy capital. I was apparently the wrong person to judge what went on in certain places after nightfall since, on a par with most other women, I seldom left the house after sunset. Mbacké's reputation had, however, long been established negatively in the chastest of circles.

When I arrived Penda was sitting on a mat in the courtyard chatting with a group of women who were sifting millet. She was a *griotte*, and like most *griottes*, she specialised in singing and dancing. She used to be invited, on the occasion of their celebrations and festivals, to sing the praises of certain families with whom she had a number of mutual obligations and commitments. The *griottes* form a sub-division of the *ñeeños*, a minority group traditionally divided into handicraft guilds or 'castes', occupying a low status in contrast to those who represented the opposite end of the scale, the *geer*, who are the majority. This means that the latter are not from birth divided into inherited handicaft trades but are so to speak 'independent'.

Penda was a highly appreciated graduate from a school of social studies, trained and educated in Dakar and employed by the social welfare office in Mbacké. I discovered in time that her marriage was monogamous, a circumstance which probably caused envy among a number of other women. Penda would continually do overtime, earning extra money. I was convinced this was, at least in part, in order to be able to spoil her husband and his family with food and gifts so that he would not get around to acquiring a second wife. Penda also spent money on bleaching powders for face and body, apart from cosmetics and aphrodisiacs. The four children were sent to good schools. Her husband contributed to part of the daily domestic costs and retained the rest of his modest salary as a local government officer for himself. I often had the impression of seeing him sitting in the shade of the tree in the yard while his wife was constantly busy with home, children and other tasks.

In her role as *griotte* at the different festivals, as informant and interpreter for a variety of development aid and research projects, and as person in charge of matters at the social welfare office, Penda gathered a wealth of information on the local community. This woman became my mainstay during the years 1992-1995. Towards the end of 1994 and 1995 I was joined by two female sociologists working a few months together with me in Mbacké and the surrounding villages. They were both, however, from Dakar and Saint Louis, and consequently in no way as well-known or as acquainted with the town as Penda. She was the genuine insider who knew most about most matters. The problem was often what information she considered suitable for my ears and what she kept for herself.

Penda and I had a preliminary chat sitting there on the raffia mat, and then I put forward my business. I wanted her help in locating various types of female organisation – religious, social, financial – in Mbacké and its environment. Could she introduce me to a number of female networks or groups and interpret my interviews with members of these associations both in the city and in the countryside? In addition, I was keen to get to know a Murid marabout and his wives.

Penda was eager to collaborate with me, delighted at an opportunity, as implied earlier, to earn a little extra money. She immediately had a number of excellent suggestions. To start with we decided to get in touch with a woman by the name of Awa, who was the president of a religious association in Mbacké in commemoration of mame Diarra Bousso. Then the turn would come to a likable marabout in a village called Touba Belel, whose first wife Penda knew via a Swedish-Senegalese Development Aid Programme, operating in three villages around Mbacké from 1992 to 1994. The marabout was the grandchild of the founder of Muridism and Penda believed that he would be well disposed to my research project.

I hurried back to my living quarters at the back of the ironmonger's before it got dark. My visit to Penda made it feel as though the field – the research field – had begun to open up and I would be admitted to this unfamiliar reality. Simultaneously, however, it was a long and lonely evening I spent. With the lamp switched on I was invaded by insects crawling through my hair, over my neck and plunging down into my dress. The air was hot and still as I crept into bed under the mosquito net. Insects buzzed around the room and the sheets stuck to my body. Cats hopped in and out of the room through the window and scared me. The horses tied to their stables whinnied in a heartrending manner down below – or were they donkeys? All of this I had to get used to. Would I manage it?

When the house-owner's private night watchman began his round and shuffled through the courtyard, his presence gave me peace of mind. In the early hours of the morning a cool breeze swept by and I nodded off.

"BECAUSE WE LOVE HER"

Meeting the president of the Mame Diarra Bousso Association

A FEW DAYS AFTER I met Penda she called on me to take me along to see sokhna Awa, president of a Murid association or *daira* by the name of the Mame Diarra Bousso *daira* in Mbacké. Awa had received the title of *sokhna* by virtue of her role as president of a religious female association in honour of mame Diarra.

On our arrival at Awa's home in Mbacké the penultimate meeting was being held prior to the pilgrimage to Porokhane. Members were gathered in the courtyard of the president's house. Thirty or so women were seated on mats spread out over the sand, chatting. The shell of a gourd fruit stood in the middle containing money, a sort of savings bank, and it bore mame Diarra's name. The members greeted us amiably, as did Awa, and expressed their pleasure at my interest in mame Diarra. In different ways they declared their love for this mysterious person and their trust in her by uttering: "All I have in life I have received through her" and "Three there are; God, his Prophet Mohammed and mame Diarra".[1] These people were keen to persuade us that we had everything to gain by accompanying them to her tomb in Porokhane at the *magal*, the pilgrim festival, shortly to be held.

Awa put her heart and soul into her work for the association in honour and in commemoration of mame Diarra. Her devotion to Muridism's saintly maternal figure appeared to be in line with the very core of the order's essence. An approach to the Divine via personalities such as mame Diarra constitutes a self-evident part of the cult. Some regarded Awa as something of a fanatic in the manifestations of her love. She was, nevertheless, not alone in this respect but surrounded by women with the same yearning to experience a bond with mame Diarra, their source of hope for a better life. Answering my query as to

---

1. See Evers Rosander in Ask and Tjomsland (ed.) 1998.

why the women were members of just this association, the president warmly replied for all of them: "Because we love her."

Every Monday afternoon during the past year they had met at Awa's court-yard and gathered together to pay their dues, which in 1995 amounted to 40 CFA francs a week (approx. 5€ centimes), and another 200 CFA francs once a month.[2]

If you were not able to be present in person, it was acceptable to send somebody else in the family with the dues. Failure to pay on time brought a small penalty charge. This very act of paying your dues was the most impor-tant single item of activity carried out on home ground. The pilgrimage to Porokhane was of course the highlight of the year. The money saved would go to mame Diarra's representative here on earth, a descendant of hers in Porokhane. The cash-box in which the money was kept remained at the vice-president's house, situated opposite Awa's. Half of the sum was donated to a member of the Bousso family called sokhna Astou Boury, with whom the president was in contact in the course of the year. Food and transport costs accounted for the other half.

Keeping the money in the cash-box causes a certain degree of tension. Have the funds saved during the year been in safe custody, or has the president or vice-president had reason to open the box at times and borrow over the year? The notion of collecting an amount of money which is not being used seems unfamiliar and unnatural, and represents a temptation; everybody is agreed on that. At the same time, the unauthorised borrowing of money is deemed a dishonest act, even though it might be returned after its use. Furthermore, who can check that the right sum has been returned if neither the president nor the vice-president can keep proper accounts?

The older women dominate the scene at the meeting. The younger ones sit together on one side of the yard while the older ones occupy centre stage. The young male singers, when they are present chanting their Murid songs, the *khassaïds*, sit right at the back of the yard in a ring around their amplifier and loud speaker equipment. Apart from the fact that the members of the association are ranked by age, a certain hierarchical pattern marks the group as a whole, reflecting the general social structure of the community. The president and the vice-president are *geer*. They belong to what one might, with some caution, classify as an upper class, and maintain contacts with the higher strata in the local community and with Murid marabout families in Touba and Porokhane. Members from the lowest social spheres, the *griottes*, run errands for Awa when necessary. A division into 'mother and daughters' is another peculiarity of the association. Awa is often called 'mother' by

---

2. CFA francs is the currency used in six West African countries, including Senegal. 100 CFA francs was at that time the equivalent of approx. 15€ centimes.

members, who in turn see themselves as her 'daughters', first and foremost the younger members.

The day's agenda concerns preparations for the trip to Porokhane. A check on how many have paid their fee for the trip is carried out, a decision is made as to what colour in common will be chosen for the dresses to be worn on the pilgrimage of the year, and a lively discussion is had of the menu for the picnic which is traditionally enjoyed during the stop before reaching Porokhane.

The meeting over, we entered the president's house and made ourselves at home, sitting on the edge of her bed. Bedroom and living room were all one. What struck me were Awa's simple attire and her Spartan surroundings. Her neighbour the vice president, who lived on the other side of the road, had an entrepreneurial husband and a relatively prosperous household, and thus distinguished herself completely from Awa in this sense.

It was quite noticeable that Awa was accustomed to having people drop in at her home. She did not wish to spend more time than necessary, quickly giving a brief summary of the association's activities. Awa did not belong to the higher female strata of the Murid establishment, whose privileged style of living differed considerably from that of common Murids. Nonetheless, she entertained certain ambitions to climb the social ladder, and she was determined to create a career for herself within the religious field. Awa was one more woman among those who were seeking a platform in the world of female associations. This was something the Murid female élite – Maimouna, for example – did not need to do. She had access to every imaginable resource in the powerful Mbacké Mbacké family network.

It transpired that Awa was the widow of a 'lesser' Murid marabout, an expression used to signify that he had had a distant relationship with the founder of Muridism. Shortly after becoming a widow, Awa had married a younger brother of the deceased husband, in accordance with the prevailing custom, known as *levirate*. She had remained living in her old house. She went to see her new husband from time to time in Touba, where he lived together with his three other wives. He was too old and too weak to call on her as was the normal habit.

Serigne Mbacké sokhna Lo

In addition to her own association, Awa devoted time and effort to another Murid association dedicated to a well-known and important marabout. The man I am referring to is serigne Mbacké sokhna Lo, Amadou Bamba's eldest great-grandson, an elegant, stylishly dressed and charming marabout, (1934 –2005). He had added his mother's title and name, sokhna Lo, to distinguish himself from the numerous marabouts who bore the name of serigne Mbacké. He was enormously popular among people in Mbacké and the neighbouring villages. As a member of this association, which went by the name of Wilaya, Awa knew exactly where he lived in the Darou Khoudoss district of Touba. He had in fact inherited the district from his father. His charismatic personality attracted large numbers of disciples and followers, and his reputation for performing miracles was an important factor in the adherents' judgment of him.

Members of the Wilaya association visited the marabout at Darou Khoudoss once a year on the occasion of serigne Mbacké sokhna Lo's *magal*. Money was collected in the course of the year from each member. In 1995 the organisation had set the amount at 50 CFA francs a week per member, in other words 200 CFA francs a month. Awa collected not only the dues for her own association, the mame Diarra Bousso *daira*, but also those for this marabout from his members. She performed other duties for him, firmly convinced that her work constituted a sacred duty of the utmost esteem. Her argument was that she thus acquired special merits – *tiyaba* – in the eyes of God and the Murid leader's blessing. [3]

These assignments and work in the political field sometimes overlapped. Awa was part of a female network of election officers who, in her capacity of president of her association, were mobilised by serigne Mbacké sokhna Lo. It fell to her lot to make sure that members voted for the 'right' candidate on election day. Nevertheless, the marabout was not always able to steer her in the direction he wished. Good turns required services in return, and Awa was not the one to obey any religious leader blindly, despite all that was said about subordination to one's religious leader and the obligation of loyalty. So much Awa made clear to me in the conversations we had.

The male disciples were generally less inclined to question the marabouts' volition than the women. The men appeared to be more fanatical in their obedience to the Murid leaders and less given to negotiation. Since childhood they had been more or less brain-washed into doing whatever the marabouts said. The many years spent in the Koran school exposed to the imams' often rigid indoctrination, accompanied by the swish of the cane, had taught them this. The girls in their younger years were seldom treated to the same uncompromising teaching procedures. I made a note of Awa's combination of devoted religiousness and common sense, qualities which steered her through the successes and setbacks she was to experience during my time in Mbacké.

The highest Murid leader had assigned serigne Mbacké sokhna Lo responsibility for the cultivation and harvest of the large agricultural area known as Khelcom under the ownership of the *khalifa général*, and it was an undertak-

---

3. Buggenhagen 2009:203, Evers Rosander 1998:152

ing carried through with the help of his disciples and followers. Whenever he summoned them via a radio broadcast, they dropped whatever they were doing and whole-heartedly placed themselves at his disposal, performing whatever tasks without remuneration. Actions such as these were regarded as religious tasks, well rewarded in the eyes of God. The cultivated soil provided huge income for the highest leader – and possibly for serigne Mbacké sokhna Lo too – when the millet and groundnuts were sold. The marabout was seen as a sort of channel through which the holy force, desired by all, moved its way. Everybody was aware, moreover, of the enormous wealth he possessed, and this widely impressed. It was important to keep a high profile, perform services for the marabout, work for him and make financial contributions for him to share.

Awa received the marabout's summons to Khelcom a few times a year. Her messenger, the female *griotte*, informed all the association's members they were to join the task force in clearing the land and harvesting. She told me that as president of the mame Diarra association she enjoyed somewhat better living conditions and better food than her companions in Khelcom. The other women spent the night in the open sleeping on the ground without the benefit of roof or tarpaulin, and were served only cooked rice and water. According to Awa, all of them were extremely keen to have the chance to work for the marabout, for the khalifa in Touba, and for the prospect of Paradise, in spite of the fact that - or perhaps just because - they invariably returned home from Khelcom quite ill, grown thinner and exhausted.

At this stage of my field work the financial and social structure within Muridism had become clearer. The basic Murid unit was the *daira* and its members. Each religious meeting held in the name of one particular Murid marabout assembled people, who spent the night singing or listening to others sing the *khassaïds* and gathering the *addiyya*, the gift of money to be offered the Murid leader on his or her annual reception for the adherents. Above them in the Murid structure we have the disciples, serving different Murid marabouts or the *khalifa général*, to whom they have given the vow of allegiance. The disciples work free of charge wherever they are needed and called upon by their religious leaders. Among the Murid marabouts there exists a ranking depending on linear distance of kinship to Amadou Bamba, as referred to earlier. The closer the links of kinship with the founder, the more status and prestige for the Murid marabout. Those marabouts having property in the countryside get part of their income through the *dara*, the Koran schools whose pupils supply cost-free agricultural work for the marabouts. In the case of serigne Mbacké sokhna Lo, he was himself in charge of many *daras* spread throughout the country in eight different villages.

Some marabouts have opened urban Koran schools in a number of cities.

Small boys and young disciples are sent out from the schools to beg for their living and on behalf of the marabouts. They often live in conditions of abject misery, with the risk of ill-treatment if they have not collected enough from begging. These *daras* are supervised by marabouts from all types of Sufi orders. Begging of this type was prohibited by law in the autumn of 2010, but the law was rescinded later. Protests had emanated from those who wished to give alms for religious reasons and were in favour of *daras*.

Today Amadou Bamba's grandchildren represent the élite of Muridism. Awa's position, then, was somewhere above the lower levels of the Murid hierarchy, while sokhna Maimouna Mbacké Mbacké belonged to the upper echelons. They both shared a large measure of piety and a detachment from all worldly glamour. In this respect they had little in common with the marabout recently depicted. He attached a high degree of honour to being elegant and modern, and worked towards steering Muridism into international financial networks with the purpose of achieving good business results. This attitude and outlook was shared by several Mbacké Mbacké marabouts among the younger generation.

Awa in the flesh

When I paid my first visit to Awa she was about 45 years old and had six children living. Her two sons were tailors, and their workshop was located at one end of Awa's sandy courtyard. They lived together with their own families in simple tin-roofed houses built around the yard. The houses were partly joined, and Awa herself occupied two rooms. She rented one of the houses to a local policeman, and this probably gave her a certain degree of safety and respectability.

Awa travelled by bus to her customers in the neighbouring villages and sold material and the clothes her sons had sewn. Her links with the marabouts in Touba enhanced her reputation, to the benefit of her business affairs. Most of her income derived from sales of dresses and the material for the piece of cloth, called *pagne* in French, used by women around the waist under the dress. The textile trade showed better profit than selling oranges, as she had done previously. Not only was the fruit a short-term commodity but it was a heavy business dragging the oranges around. She bought her material at the market places in Touba and Dakar where they were least expensive.

Apart from trading, Awa devoted her time to the raising of sheep which she sold to be slaughtered for *Tabaski*, the great Muslim feast celebrated in recognition of Abraham's readiness to sacrifice his own son as proof of his allegiance to the will of God. Every Muslim family that can afford it, slaughters a sheep. Every year Awa would sell a number of the animals she had breeded to a healthy profit. One of her sons was working in Italy and regularly sent her a remittance, an assistance which dispelled any immediate worries she might have had for her financial position. Between the sales trips she found time for the association and its activities, and for maintaining contact with her husband and other marabouts in Touba and their wives. Domestic chores were mainly in the charge of her daughters-in-law.

Awa was like a mother for the members of her association as well as being a good business woman. Her purpose was to give as many of the members as possible the opportunity to make the trip to mame Diarra Bousso's tomb in Porokhane. Once at the tomb, they could themselves make their personal pleas for help with their respective problems. Awa was also working hard to improve her own economy and that of the association, seizing every opportunity to haul in money for their activities. One of her objectives was to make me a fully paying member, a goal she achieved. I gained the impression that I was the only one ever to pay the full annual fee during the current year. Awa was deeply and sincerely grateful.

Penda and I, each in her own way, stood for the possible channels through which Awa hoped the imagined resources could be funnelled. In my capacity of foreigner I was, seen through her eyes, a contact with the existing Development Aid Programmes. Penda represented a definite possibility of assistance when they were applying for state or municipal support in the form of loans. Awa did not, however, realise that such organisations would seldom or never stake their money on elderly city women. Instead rural women were given priority. Nor were the members of her association in a position to gather the 20,000 CFA francs required to make an application. It was far too large an expense. They had once made the effort to apply for the money but had subsequently seen no trace of either money or application. Furthermore, in order to acquire a permit to open a bank account for the possible loan, you were expected to make a contribution of your own when all the conditions had been satisfied. The loan ran for six months. The women's reluctance to part with any money without a guarantee that it would bring something in return was therefore based on experience. There was no attraction for the older women in the notion of cooperative work and collaboration. They wanted to discover means of attaining individual initial capital for their various activities.

The members of Awa's association were women of modest means, with the exception of the committee members who were somewhat better off. They all dealt in some form of trading, striving thus to improve their living conditions. Even women who enjoyed regular employment engaged in some form of commerce, but among the members of the association they were in a clear minority. Some women resorted to selling goods at the roadside in front of their houses. The goods for sale would be small bags of frozen lemonade, water, deep-fried doughnuts, a few boxes of match-sticks or the odd orange, purchased at a cheap price at one of the markets. Women who could afford to leave their homes, unhindered by the need to care for their children or by men who quite simply prevented them from going out, hired a stall at the market place in Mbacké. There they sold textiles they had bought in Touba.

There was a constant need for more money. The husbands couldn't be relied on as breadwinners. As part of the struggle for existence it was solidly believed that mame Diarra could contribute towards a better life. The pilgrimage and visit to Porokhane were therefore primarily intended to yield an immediate and abundant dividend in the form of material resources in response to the visitor's invocation. This was what the annual *magal* to Porokhane, commemorating mame Diarra, was famous for. In addition, the women wished to keep alive their contact with her, the good mother, by visiting her tomb. This way her support was surer at life's end in order to reach Paradise. Awa quoted from the Koran – "Paradise is to be found at the mothers' feet"[4], as if to convince me in case I was sceptical. These words also acted as a guiding star for the members of her association.

The Mame Diarra Bousso Association was an entirely informal creation. It was not registered anywhere and had no bank account. The board was made up of six women with posts boasting impressive titles, a legacy from the time of French colonial rule when attempts were made to organise the swarm of Senegalese associations. The Mame Diarra Bousso *daira* consisted of a president, vice-president, treasurer and a number of secretaries. There were, for example, a 'conflict' secretary, an 'organisation' secretary and a 'general secretary'. In point of fact, however, work was mainly carried out by the president and the treasurer. The latter was the only woman in the association who could read and write. None of the committee members knew anything about book-keeping. The young man who led the singing of religious songs at some of the association's meetings acted as accountant. In almost all of the situations in which money and accountability were involved, the women were dependent on this man's help.

It put huge demands on the man's honesty and left the women particularly vulnerable. The women's lack of education hampered their progress throughout life, not least in the activity they had given priority to, namely trade. This was the case both within and outside their association activities.

As far as status was concerned, the Mame Diarra Bousso Association in Mbacké led by Awa was fairly insignificant in comparison with other *dairas*. Unknown women traders handing over small gifts of money to a female marabout in Porokhane land a long way down the ranking list. For the wom-

4. Also quoted by Schimmel 1998 (1995):105.

en themselves, however, the association offered a religious, moral and socially acceptable platform, enabling them to legitimise their meetings and their trips to Porokhane. The Murid profile provided room, moreover, for other women's activities. The *daira* women had long been members of a so-called *mbotaye*, an association providing mutual support among members in the shape of financial aid, donations and lending a hand in connection with weddings, name-giving ceremonies and funerals. The president dissolved the *mbotaye*, however, when it transpired that the women preferred to invest their money in it rather than in the religious association. The donation to the female marabout in Porokhane had become embarrassingly small, a source of much concern for the president.

Mame Diarra Bousso

I decided quite early on to join Awa's association on the pilgrimage to Porokhane to visit mame Diarra Bousso's tomb. First of all, however, I needed to learn more about the event and its principal character, mame Diarra. With Penda as my interpreter, I made once more for Awa's house, this time for a lesson in Muridism. The sokhna spoke uninterruptedly for an hour on the subject of mame Diarra and the annual pilgrimage to her tomb in Porokhane. Awa then asked me if I was willing to make a financial contribution to the association in exchange for the information she had provided, which I naturally offered.

In short, Awa narrated the following, translated from the *Wolof* language to French and condensed by me into first a Swedish version:

Amadou Bamba's sons have all contributed towards making Muridism a successful Senegalese Sufi order. The eldest son succeeded his father as highest leader of Muridism. Another of the sons, serigne Bassirou, established Porokhane as a pilgrimage site. During Amadou Bamba's final years in the mid-1920s interest increased in mame Diarra Bousso and her life as a female model and ideal figure of piety.

In 1948 the first organised commemoration meeting was held, a *magal*, in Porokhane. Nowadays the annual *magal* in Porokhane has assumed political dimensions, just like the *magal* in Touba. Every year growing crowds invade Porokhane to visit the holy sites during one or two days, and donate their collected *daira's* money to the religious leaders under whose protection they find themselves.

I already knew from previous conversations with a Murid marabout in Dakar that mame Diarra's parents had not been particularly wealthy or in any other way conspicuous. This fact has led to mame Diarra being toned down as a historical figure in leading Murid quarters. Her father's name was Abdou Bousso and her mother sokhna Walo. They belonged to the *Halpulaar* ethnic group, termed *Toucolor* by the French, and they derived their origin from the Fouta region. On account of the unstable political situation of the 19th century mainly due to the presence of French colonialists and the disintegration of the various kingdoms, they moved from Fouta to Kayor in central Senegal, where the husband taught the Koran as a living.

Both parents were deeply religious. The mother educated her daughter in a thorough knowledge of the Islamic doctrine. Mame Diarra was married to mame Mor Anta Sali and became one of the several wives in his polygamous marriage. After having lived for a time in Mbacké the family moved to Porokhane. Mame Diarra had three children, the youngest of whom, and whose exact date of birth is unknown (between 1855 and 1865), became in time the founder of Muridism.

Mame Diarra became ill on the long, exhausting march to Porokhane. She never recovered, and consequently was unable to accompany the family when it started its return to Mbacké-Touba. Few detailed biographical data remain of mame Diarra Bousso. The little we know refers to her birth around 1840 and death in Porokhane some 25 years later. Awa said that at that time Amadou Bamba was about five. He lived in Mbacké with his father's wives, and his brothers and sisters from all the families. He later settled down in Touba and lived there as a religious leader until his death in 1927, with the exception of the periods of exile in Mauretania and Gabon enforced by the French colonial powers. His order had grown stronger and stronger and caused unrest in the colonial Senegalese community.

Following these brief pieces of information, Awa then proceeded to feed me with her favourite subject: the numerous legends about mame Diarra Bousso which flourish in Senegal. I already knew when I arrived in Mbacké that this female Sufi saint differs from others inasmuch as she has not bequeathed any text material of her own in the shape of poems and prayers. Nor has she been attributed any famous scholarly biographies dealing with her life, as is usual in the case of well-known Sufi saints. She only exists as a female ideal figure in the legends, poetry and songs referring to her in the oral tradition. She has attained her position among Sufi saints via the tales told of what she had performed as mother and wife in every-day life. Her reputation as a good and generous wife, mother and saviour in moments of distress, lives on in the popular legends related in Murid circles, in Senegal and the worldwide diaspora.

All the legends concerning mame Diarra speak about her diligence, generosity, endless patience and tactfulness, chiefly in relation to her husband. Mame Diarra's high degree of tolerance and adaptability in order to avoid conflict is also made special mention of in her daily life together with her co-wives, husband's family and his disciples. Her blind obedience and total sub-ordination can occasionally, however, reach exaggerated levels in the legends. What she sometimes does in order to please seems almost a madness. "That's how we Murid women are", said Awa. "We're crazy. We'll do anything we're told, merely to approach the Divine. And in order to be a mother like mame Diarra and have a son like shaykh Amadou Bamba."

Polygamy as a life style can easily lead to conflicts among the co-wives con-cerning the distribution in the home of domestic work and resources. Insecu-rity and jealousy sometimes result in quarrels and accusations of witchcraft, and consequently serious problems in the individual wife/mother-children units. On the other hand such a system can relieve the amount of work both domestically and in agriculture. In mame Diarra's day people lived together as now in large households in the countryside. Each wife had her own hut where she lived with her children. The husband had his own hut, occupying a central position in the fenced-in area, which constituted the farm itself with room for livestock. The imam's and marabout's disciples worked with the cultivation of millet and groundnuts, and were taught the Koran. They shared living quarters under simple conditions. Wives took it in turns to cook, and fetch water and wood for the entire household.

The legends Awa told me about mame Diarra gave a clear picture of the Murid ideal of the perfect wife. Mame Diarra's conduct in her marriage to mame Mor Anta Sali is an often repeated subject. One of the most well-known tales concerns the following, referred to in the introduction to this book and illustrated on the cover, here in Awa's version:

> It is said that one of the raffia fences surrounding the courtyard had once fallen down, and that her husband told her to hold it up while he fetched something to repair it with. Storm clouds covered the sky and it began to rain. The man went to look for some rope and entered the house to avoid the rain, forgetting all about mame Diarra. She stood out in the pouring rain all night holding up the fence. The episode also occurs in the song about her: "She stood out in the rain until dawn. When her husband went to pray at sunrise, he passed her and asked: 'who are you?' She answered: 'It's me, mame Diarra'. He asked her: 'But what are you doing here?' She replied: 'It was you who asked me to hold the fence up, and that's why I've stood here during the night in the rain.' "

Awa has a lot more to tell about mame Diarra as wife and house-keeper. She recalls a song about mame Diarra Bousso including the following verse: 'When it was mame Diarra's turn to cook the food, the disciples were as happy as could be.' The song alludes to mame Diarras's generosity. This is followed by a more detailed description of daily life, and then a well-known legend of which Awa is especially fond:

Each time mame Diarra put down the pail of water she had brought for cooking, the disciples rushed to drink from it and left it empty. So she fetched more water, time after time, without a complaint or asking for help. That is why the well at Porokhane has never dried up and the tale is told of mame Diarra's ocean. It is endless.

Other legends tell of mame Diarra Bousso waking up in the morning and saying her prayers, after which she would make her way through the courtyard, wishing everyone a bright 'Good Morning'. She greeted her husband, kneeling, and then his relatives and her own co-wives. Her next tasks were cooking breakfast, tidying the house, fetching water from the well and preparing the midday meal. The disciples appeared on the scene as she was serving the meal and ate their fill, hardly giving her time to finish the cooking. But they all got their portion of food, however many they were. This is why there is more food nowadays than there was then, Awa is quick to point out. Rice is not as expensive as it was then; or oil either, for that matter. You can have enough to eat nowadays. Mame Diarra's good deeds, in other words, had paid dividends. "You have to sow good seeds to have a good harvest" said Awa, quoting the words of a song about serigne Touba's mother: 'Mame Diarra, nobody knows how large is your ocean; not even the angels.'

Another famous legend involving mame Diarra and her husband mame Mor Anta Sali reflects the wife's ideal behaviour in the marriage. It concerns a woman's *soutoura*, her tact and discretion in never revealing the husband's weaknesses, even at the cost of her own happiness and well-being. The tale tells the story of mame Diarra's pearl necklace, which she had received from her mother. Her husband found himself without money to pay for the daily purchase of milk, and mame Diarra bought it in secret. The important thing was to prevent the word getting around that the man was without means and might thus suffer dishonour. Every day, therefore, she paid the milkman – a nomad – with one of the pearls until the necklace was quite bare. Not even when her mother reproached her for spoiling the necklace would she own up to the sacrifice and good deed. Finally it was the milkman who reported to the mother what had happened and for what purpose, and then her mother purchased the pearls back for mame Diarra.

The men sing their khassaïds while the women sit and listen

Awa's long account revealed the fact that there existed a treasure of song material on the subject of Bamba's mother. These songs are often chanted by a group of women led by a female conductor. They always sing in *Wolof*, but never using texts drawn from the Koran. They often sing about mame Diarra

Bousso in a softer voice so as not to lose self-control, as they put it, and in the thrill of the moment behave in an unconventional way. In Mbacké I began to understand the significance of religious song in the Murid culture. All the *dairas* had male singers who would strike up their songs at the meetings in the afternoon, evening or into the night in the various districts. The sacred songs, the *khassaïds*, were sung in Arabic and only by men, and were considered by the Murids themselves as expressing the innermost yearning for community with God. Chanting the religious songs and listening to them brings one to the very core of Muridism, for both men and women.

I thought I could see how women are marginalised in Muridism by not being considered worthy of singing the *khassaïds*. That, at any rate, was the impression which struck me. They themselves lamented more the fact that they were not allowed to take part in the meetings by dancing and by other bodily movements. A prohibition had been issued by the highest leader in Touba and applied to all female Murids everywhere. At Murid association meetings, open to both men and women, the normal arrangement is for the men to sit opposite the women, or else they each occupy a set part of the room. While the men are singing, the women listen. The men sit on the ground, their hands clutching their ears in an effort to concentrate on the lyrics, gripped by the profound feelings their song inspires.

The songs, in fact, serve as an intensified form of prayer. Awa's son explained the meaning behind the songs thus: "*Khassaïds* represent the very heart of Muridism. They draw you towards them, you are drawn to them, it's their message. They have magic qualities, too, for singing them and believing in them make your wishes come true." The leader of a *khassaïd* group of singers at Awa's place said the following in an interview:

> I'm not related to Awa but it is the association that has brought us together. My father was a *khassaïd* singer, and he himself taught me. Now it's my turn to teach other boys. I joined the association in order to make a contribution to *mame* Diarra Bousso. Her son, shaykh Amadou Bamba, never had the time to work for his mother, and so I joined. I want to collect a bit of money for *mame* Diarra Bousso. I do so by singing, and I donate it to the great marabout in the Bousso family. That's my work – doing that is working towards Paradise.

On one of the occasions I attended a meeting of the Mame Diarra Bousso Association the young men singing appeared especially inspired by the holy songs. It happened at a time when they were running a campaign to collect money for a new amplifier. Their song had a hypnotic effect on the listeners and was heard far and wide. One of the women sitting on the ground some way away from the singers started to sway back and forth, her body moving with the music, but the president did not stop her. Instead she got up and performed a very dignified dance, a far-off look on her face, without the wild jumps which otherwise characterised the women's dancing. She moved as if in a trance. Everybody knew that the *khalifa* in Touba had forbidden women dancing to the accompaniment of the *khassaïds* so as not to distract the men, but this was something out of the ordinary. People from outside looking in at Awa's courtyard stood stock still as if enchanted by the music.

The song leader takes an active part in the other more important association, the Wilaya, already referred to, where he teaches the young boys to sing *khassaïds*. He points out that the songs contain at least three different themes. They are songs of praise to God, they teach high morals, and they provide consolation and relief in the case of illness and accident. Furthermore, many of the songs of greater length record Amadou Bamba's life and the miracles he performed according to oral tradition. These miracles have given rise to a number of anonymous songs as well as works of art using motifs with which all Murids are acquainted. Awa's son stresses the importance of using the correct expression: the *khassaïds* are *sung* and not recited. The word used in *Wolof* is *wai*. He reminds me of the fact that the texts have been compiled by Amadou Bamba himself, on the basis of the Koran.

The group's young leader not only teaches but also travels around, singing together with his colleagues at different meetings held by the religious associations, at mosques, and during pilgrim festivals. He emphasizes the fact that the single purpose of Awa's association is to make the annual pilgrimage to Porokhane. He intends accompanying the women in order to express a wish at the tomb. He is adamant in his conviction that whatever is wished for at her tomb is fulfilled in the course of the following year. That, in his view, is a measure of the power – *barke* - expelled by mame Diarra in her capacity of mother of Amadou Bamba. The same applies to the son, the founder himself, but mame Diarra is of a more generous nature and renowned for fulfilling your wishes sooner.

The singer's supposition concerning mame Diarra's mystical powers was fully in line with Awa's. After Awa had become a widow following the death of her first husband, she set her sights on a life after this one, in Paradise. At least she claimed that this was her chief goal. It was in order to invest her all-female association with a particularly good reputation in a fully acceptable framework that she had invited the young men who themselves were reputed to be excellent *khassaïd* singers. She had registered them as members without requiring a membership fee. Quite the contrary – the female members occasionally gave them a few tips when they had been singing at one of the Monday meetings. The women always helped the young men with donations of various types in conjunction with weddings or other family ceremonies where a financial boost was necessary.

TOGETHER WITH MAME DIARRA
IN POROKHANE

The last meeting prior to the pilgrimage

"Madame Puit (Mrs Well!), Madame Puit, stop, don't forget me, please!" Fatimata is the name of the woman who is calling to me as she sees me hurry past her house. I am on my way to the very last meeting of the Mame Diarra Bousso Association before we leave on the pilgrimage. We are to check the financial situation for the excursion and plan the bus trip. This means that the cash-box containing the money collected has now been opened by the president and the vice-president, and the contents are to be gone through and accounted for. Through the orange-coloured clouds of dust stirred up as I stride along the path, I see Fatimata sitting at the entrance to her yard in front of a small trestle table. On the table lie a few mottled oranges and two match boxes.

The nickname 'Mrs Well' has been given me because Fatimata believes I am connected in some way to a development aid programme, and am therefore in a position to produce money and equipment for the drilling of a well in her village, 20 km north-west of Mbacké. The people in her village belong to the *Halpulaar* ethnic group. Raising cattle is their livelihood, but their supply of water is getting dangerously low and the animals are suffering severe thirst. It costs a fortune to provide the water they need, water which has to be purchased and transported to their village from a great distance by horse and cart.

Fatimata was married at nine years of age and had her first child when she was fourteen. In the course of time she was to have six children, a large number of grandchildren, and one great-grandchild. She is the first wife of a polygamous marriage. Her husband and son earn their living raising and selling cattle. They paid for Fatimata's pilgrimage to Mecca the year before by selling three of the head of cattle, and the pilgrimage earned her the title of *haja*.

Fatimata is about 50 years old. She has moved into town to look after her ailing mother. Her co-wives remain in the village and their jobs are to take charge of domestic duties, the children, and the milking of the cows. She says that looking after her aging mother constitutes a good deed, ensuring her a better chance of entering Paradise. Her husband and son, however, criticise the petty merchandise she devotes her time to at the roadside in Mbacké. Their argument is that it is beneath her dignity as the wife of a man whose business is the breeding of cattle to sell other products than butter, fresh cheese and whey. Fatimata's devotion to this petty merchandise, however, derives from her desire to get out of the house and be able to observe what is happening outside and along the road. Inside she is bored; the domestic help does the shopping and keeps the house tidy. Her mother sleeps for much of the day. If Fatimata is unable to sell her oranges, she will give them away to the children who pass by the house on their way home from school, she explains to me. She is indefatigable in her efforts to acquire means to pay for a new well and a pump for the village. "Aren't you going to the meeting with Múskeba?" I wonder. "Yes, of course, but not just yet; I'll be along..." she replies. Penda laughs and gives me a knowing look: "What did I tell you? We're far too early...!"

As a result we were the first to arrive at the meeting with the general secretary, Múskeba Diop, the Monday before the pilgrimage to Porokhane was to start. An hour later there were still not many members present other than the core troop of elderly ladies. Múskeba's big disappointment in life was the fact that her husband, having promised her gifts of jewellery and expensive clothing at the time of the marriage seven years previously, never fulfilled that promise. He had, on the other hand, recently acquired a second wife, who – according to Múskeba – he had proceeded to shower with expensive gifts. She felt bitter about this, while her sense of pride would not allow her to show her private anguish for others. Moreover, the refusal to expose the husband's imperfections or defects to one's environment formed part of a wife's duties and moral conduct. To me, a foreign *toubab*, however, it was quite acceptable for her to complain. Múskeba assumed that, as a probable western-style feminist, I would be indignant at one more example of Senegalese men who let their wives down. She was right. All I could do was fully agree with her and establish the fact that this was not the first time I'd heard of this kind of deceit on the part of a married man.

On arrival I greeted all the women I knew from earlier on in a particularly intimate fashion with two kisses on each cheek, while the rest of those present I shook hands with. This was to be the last opportunity for paying the fee for the Porokhane trip. A further sum of money was required for the trip and the cost of the food. It had been set at 500 CFA francs, with 200 CFA francs in addition to the gift of money for sokhna Astou Boury. She was the representative of the Bousso family in Porokhane for the Mame Diarra Bousso Association. The president declared that an extra charge had to be made since she feared there was not enough money in the funds. She was reluctant to expose us once more to what had happened the year before. On that occasion there had been almost nothing left in what came to be known as the 'envelope' (the gift of money for sokhna Astou transported in an envelope to Porokhane on the day of the *magal*) as food and transport costs had swallowed up practically all of the money that had been saved. In the end Astou Boury had received no more than 10,000 CFA francs (roughly 14€).

A woman said: "Sokhna Awa, you have said that we have to pay so and so much money for our trip, but you don't know how much money is in the funds since you say that you haven't yet opened the cash-box". The president admitted that she hadn't counted the money in the cash-box yet, but she thought there would not be enough. Another woman agreed with the first woman. The extra amount should not be paid until what was in the cash-box was ascertained. For myself I wondered why Awa had not counted the money. Had it been withdrawn on loan and not been reimbursed? The fact remained that it was only those women who had paid the full sum, including the latest addition, and who had this amount together with their names registered by Múskeba in her book of accounts, who were allowed to travel to Porokhane. This was Awa's decision, and firm in this knowledge we left and went our various ways after sipping the customary cup of Touba coffee, the bitter beverage which was the Murids' speciality, and which was widely appreciated by all those present. Awa explained to me that Amadou Bamba is reported to have taken plants of this bitter-tasting coffee bean home with him from Gabon, where he had been exiled from 1895 to 1902. I had already noticed that "*Café* Touba" (Touba Coffee) was an extremely popular drink among all the Murids.

Preparations for the pilgrimage

Leaving for a *ziyara* in Porokhane means making a tour of Porokhane and visiting the various holy sites there. To attend the *magal* commemorating mame Diarra is a great adventure, above all for the women who seldom move so far from home. It is, however, an enterprise which requires a good deal of organising and planning. This is the job of the president.

The custom is to stay away two days and a night. Apart from the transport, the picnic and the 'envelope', there is a moral element involved in the planning. Women are not of course expected to travel alone without some form of male escort; in any case, not for such a distance and in possession of the *daira*'s accumulated financial assets. As members of the association the group travels in a respectable fashion, with an honourable, religious purpose. The president has a good reputation for competence and piety, but she does need to have the company of some of the *khassaïd*-singing youths on the journey or one reliable male person. Transport costs are high, too, and there is never enough room for everybody on the bus. All of these matters have to be taken into consideration by the president before the trip so as to ensure that the women will be travelling in as safe and respectable manner as possible.

My own preparations for the pilgrimage to Porokhane were partly of another kind. My assistant and a few colleagues wished to make the journey as well as myself, even though they were not Murids. I therefore had to search for a spacious vehicle with a reliable driver, at a not unreasonable cost. During the Porokhane *magal*, however, transport is hard to come by and charges rocketed skyhigh. Nevertheless, a few useful contacts within the Murid-dominated transport enterprise solved this problem, and I then got down to compiling a list of the things I should be needing. A white scarf to cover my head was top of the list, followed by a water bottle, an assortment of biscuits, paper handkerchiefs, a small plastic mat to sit and sleep on, camera, pen and paper, as well as a plastic bottle sliced off at the lid. This would serve for toilet purposes as I had no intention of wading through a morass of urine at the shed, which according to all reports would accumulate during our stay. I had also followed the advice of an American anthropologist and acquired pills for an upset stomach which I took prior to our departure. I dressed in a particularly attractive *boubou* with a *pagne*, a piece of similar material swept around my waist, and left home at the given hour with butterflies in my stomach, excited at the prospect of the entire undertaking.

The departure

The members of the Mame Diarra Bousso Association who were to make the journey gathered in Awa's courtyard, most of them wearing the same blue grand *boubou*, with a *foulard*, a long scarf twisted around their heads of the same blue material. Even though each year a new *boubou* colour was chosen, common to all the members of the association, my colleagues commented on the *boubous*, pointing out that they appeared old and well-used. The year before white had been the colour opted for, and the dresses now being worn were probably from earlier years. Only committee members seemed to be wearing *boubous* made of a beautiful rich damask fabric, imported from the Netherlands and dyed in Senegal.

There were 17 women in all, which meant that two more women had been

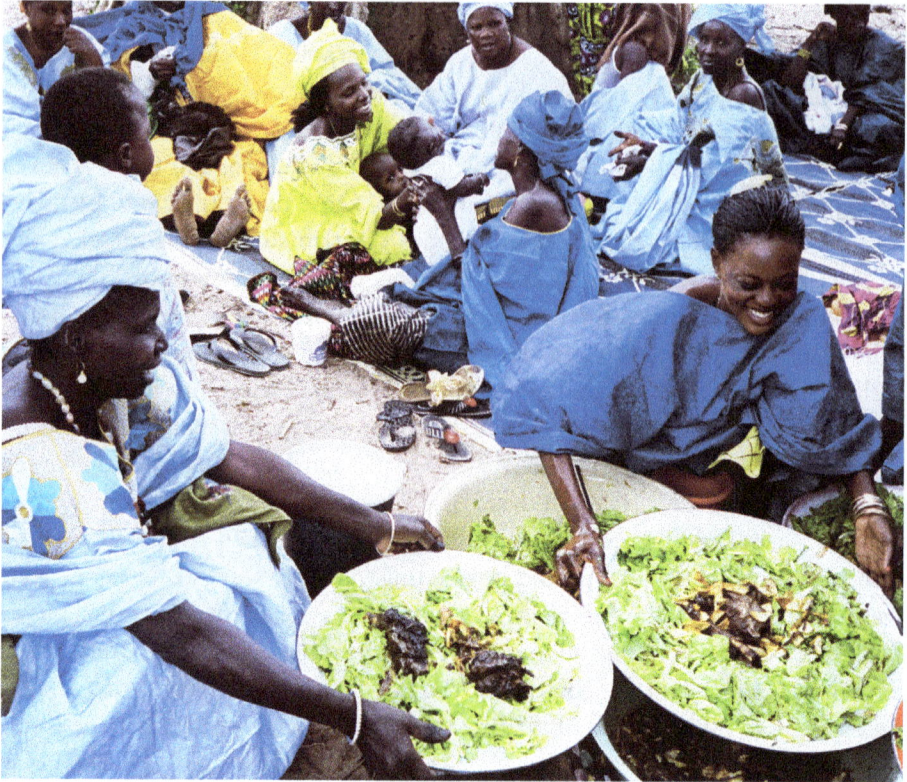

On our way to Porokhane: a short rest for a picnic before arrival. 1995.

added to the list since the last meeting. They paid their fee to Múskeba on the spot before getting on the minibus. In an effort to save money Awa had rented a small vehicle, so conditions on board were fairly cramped. In order to help out we took two people in our own vehicle so that nobody should be left behind. The policeman who lodged in a house at Awa's compound accompanied us, a circumstance which considerably calmed Awa's nerves on the eve of the journey. He sat at the front of the bus next to the driver and one of the *khassaïd* singers. The president was fully aware of her responsibility so that nobody should meet with a misfortune. This time, as well as myself, she had three other persons, not members or even Murids, to keep an eye on and care for.

The outside temperature rose and the traffic got denser the further south we drove on the big highway towards the city of Kaolack. Some three hours later we passed Kaolack, and it wasn't long before it was time for a picnic at Njoro, the customary place for a break. An artesian well supplied drinkable water and huge trees provided the shade we needed to enjoy our picnic. The stop at Njoro was one of the topics of conversation which had occupied the women before the start at club meetings. Who would purchase the food and cook it? What food should be bought and what was it to cost? Now, however, it was time to enjoy a rest, stretch our legs, and refresh our weary bodies after sitting for hours squeezed into bus and car. We had high expectations of the picnic. Many of us watched as the hampers were unloaded from the bus. I felt a sense of frustration, however, as I saw what was being presented on the big round serving dishes: large quantities of lettuce leaves, a few slices of potato, and a small number of fried legs of lamb, carved into tiny pieces. The loaves of white bread, enough for everybody, saved the day. The other women kept a straight face, but the question on everybody's tongue was what had happened. Quite simply, it turned out, the money had not stretched to cover the cost of food, after Awa had hired the bus and put away 20,000 CFA francs in an envelope for sokhna Astou in Porokhane. Awa had stood for the cost of the food herself, she told us, and had one of her own lambs slaughtered. It had been sold to provide the money needed, save a few bones which had been spared for us pilgrims. Nevertheless, I soon got over my blighted hopes imagining the large barrels of meat, rice and millet in spicy sauce which would be served us by members of the Bousso family in Porokhane during the pilgrim celebration. I had been made to understand that this was the custom both in Touba and Porokhane during the *magal*.

Each marabout and sokhna is accustomed to inviting their disciples to a meal as a means of expressing their gratitude for the financial donations the members of the religious associations make them. The food is cooked by female disciples, while the heavy dishes loaded with food are carried out to the pilgrims by sturdy male disciples. The men and women who are close to the core of the Murid establishment experience, as mentioned earlier, their task of preparing and serving the food at a *magal* as highly privileged because of its holy character. I was told that once in Porokhane our association would of course make its way to the house of our sokhna and her courtyard, where we would camp down for the following twenty-four hours. There we would receive the share of food allotted us. Astou Boury was from the start of the association's activities the member of the Bousso family to receive the donation of money. According to Awa, she was closely connected to the founder of Muridism since mame Diarra Bousso was her great-grandmother.

Before leaving Njoro all the travellers had filled their bottles with water from the well. They then moved away from the shade of the trees to a bushy area to perform the prescribed ablutions in accordance with Islam before entering holy ground, in this case Porokhane. I followed suit in like manner, which my fellow-travellers highly appreciated. None of them would have demanded such of me, but they surely would have felt hurt at the thought of me approaching mame Diarra Bousso's tomb or the mosque, without performing this ritual. I covered my hair in proper fashion with my white scarf and put my sun-glasses on. In this way I felt comfortable not having to show my white face among the vast crowds I knew would be thronging the areas for the visits to the holy places. We arrived at two p.m. and made straight for the patch of ground allotted us in Astou Boury's courtyard.

At Porokhane

Judging by my notes on the Porokhane *magal* during January 19 and 20 1995, the conclusion I must draw is that it was indeed an adventurous celebration that took place there. I remember making up my mind to try and adopt a calm and composed attitude, allowing myself to record events one hour at a time.

As we approached the area occupied by the Bousso marabouts' houses, I was struck by the number of people already sitting on the ground on their plastic mats in the open air. They were pilgrims without any *daira* connected to mame Diarra Bousso, and who therefore were without a marabout to provide them with a space in their courtyard. We forged ahead past the many pilgrims on the road with some difficulty, pushing our way along, while Awa was afraid we would lose touch with each other. The policeman's task was to keep me under close surveillance. Penda and my colleagues followed hard on the heels of the *khasssaïd* singer, who had his eye on the youngest and prettiest of the women in our group. Reaching Astou Boury's courtyard, we found the tenting equipment in place. Using all hands, we hoisted the tent to provide sufficient shade. The sandy surface of the yard was covered with tarpaulins, over which we laid matting fetched from inside the house. On top of this we placed the plastic mats we had brought with us, and made ourselves comfortable. One of my colleagues disappeared to look for her mother-in-law, whose association was established at another marabout's house. The elderly lady was supremely happy at the fact that her daughter-in-law – not a Murid but one of the *Tijaniyya* order – for once had come to Porokhane on a pilgrimage. Her son had experienced a religious conversion, and had left his Marxist persuasions to become a fully practising Murid. His mother now held the hope that her daughter-in-law would follow in the husband's footsteps.

A long wait sitting on our plastic mats lay ahead of us. As time passed the entire courtyard grew fuller and fuller of members of other Diarra Bousso associations, which also claimed Astou Boury as their patron. Two or three at a time, our members left to complete their *ziyara*, the tour by foot to the holy sites. The most important of all, besides the mosque, of course, was the visit to mame Diarra Bousso's tomb. Next came the visit to the well to take home some of the holy water, reported to possess magic powers. Afterwards, it was

At Porokhane: members of the Mame Diarra Bousso Association in Mbacké squatted down in the courtyard of the female marabout Astou Boury. 1995.

the usual rule to go and see the place where mame Diarra was purported to have lived at one stage, where she pounded the millet and hung out her washing. You were to roll over in the sandy path leading to a small wooded area in imitation of what Amadou Bamba did as a small child. Many pilgrims plucked leaves, said to have healing powers, from the trees. Others would tear off bits of their clothing and fasten them to the branches of the trees. These pieces of cloth symbolised the hopes and wishes which it was expected mame Diarra would fulfil. You were to visit the mosque the afternoon of your arrival, unless you proposed attending the Friday prayers the following day. The market place was another attraction with its many duty-free articles, but most of my fellow-travellers would not be going there until Friday morning. Prices were said to be high, however, which perhaps made the tempting offers less appealing. You might also run the risk of having to pay duty on the goods in the event of getting caught at a police check-point on the way home.

While waiting for Awa to give me the go-ahead to complete my *ziyara* in the company of the male members of our group, I suddenly felt sharp pangs of hunger. It had not escaped my attention that food was being cooked in large quantities not far from where we were sitting. The people who had been invited to the sokhna's house and the surrounding buildings belonging to some of the Bousso family's marabouts, were beginning to enjoy the generous portions of meat and sauces being served on big plates, borne by brawny male hands right in front of our eyes. Appetising smells from the plates wafted towards us as they passed by over our heads, and I was once again invaded by the same sense of frustration as earlier that same day during our picnic. Awa served us the remaining leaves of lettuce, only now they were more shrivelled than before. After some remarks from her to one of the male servants, a few bowls of white rice appeared for us. In the evening we were also able to share a dish of millet, although without meat sauce. By that time a number of our members had called at another house and asked for some more nourishing dishes as our own food situation looked a bit bleak. I chomped on my biscuits, reflecting somewhat wistfully on the fact that this was the way things go when you donate such a small gift of money as had been the case last year to the Bousso family...

Having remained seated for such a long time on my plastic mat, my legs were aching when I got up and left, together with one of the women in our company and the young male singer, to tour the holy sites in Porokhane. We started by making for the well, only to find a long queue in front of us. I felt almost squashed by the tight crowd, and beads of perspiration ran down my back. It was about six in the afternoon, and the entire area was thick with pilgrims all wanting to visit the same sites in the course of their *ziyara*. In spite of the enormous crowd people were in a happy mood and they acknowledged

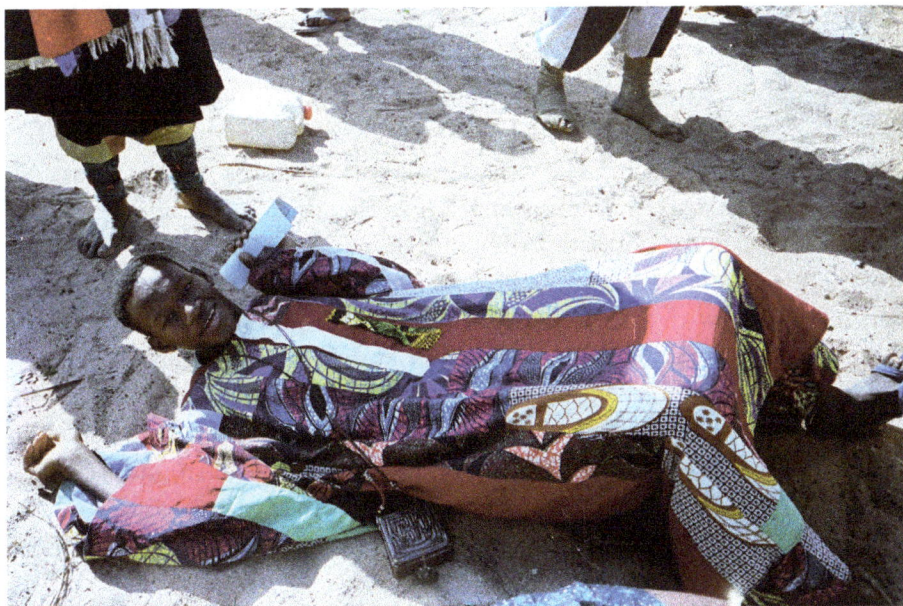

At Porokhane: a member of the sub-group of Muridism called Baye Fall rolling in the sand at the spot where shaykh Amadou Bamba is said to have played as a child. 1995.

and greeted each other in a friendly fashion while jostling in the queue. They talked about the miracles Diarra Bousso had performed, and how often they had visited her tomb with favourable consequences. The policeman's warning to heed possible thieves had put me on the alert, but as time went on I became more and more relaxed, impressed by the kind and friendly atmosphere which prevailed among these people. I made special note of the common expressions of joy in "being together with mame Diarra", as people called their visit to Porokhane.

After the well, the tour approached the spot where mame Diarra had performed her domestic duties. We followed a sandy path as far as a point where two Bai Fall disciples dressed in colourful patchwork kaftans, on each side of the path, called out to us. They were inviting the passing throng of people to pound millet with a large mortar in imitation of mame Diarra herself – in exchange for a small charge, of course, money which went to one of the marabouts. This millet ritual was central in the mame Diarra cult. During her lifetime – the mid-nineteenth century – rice had still not been introduced as a staple item in Senegal. Millet was the crop grown for daily consumption, and its preparation was a woman's task. It is said that mame Diarra was charged with this task during serigne Touba's first years of childhood in Porokhane. As a form of homage to the mother's skills and to the essential nature of agricultural work – interpreted as woman's life-giving contribution

– men and women imitated the pounding of the millet, a necessary process in the preparation of grain. The young singer in our troupe, who would never have dreamt of performing such a woman's job back home, gladly seized the mortar and applied a few hefty blows. He then rolled around in the sand just as Amadou Bamba is said to have done close to his mother's hut. All of this took place amid much laughter, together with a certain measure of solemnity in commemoration of mame Diarra. No other Sufi ritual comes anywhere near this one exalting a woman's work to almost spiritual dimensions. On a par with this tradition in memory of mame Diarra Bousso, her great-grandchild, sokhna Gad Bousso, would supervise the cooking of three tons of millet couscous which was offered to visitors at the Porokhane *magal*. The young woman from Dakar, the colleague accompanying me, broke out in surprise and exclaimed: "It's a remarkable fact that Muridism, male-centred that it is, permits such a ritual as this, which elevates the woman and her crucial importance in life to such absolute heights." We others could not but agree, and we felt reassured by what we had experienced.

We didn't pluck any leaves from the branches of the trees, for they looked already rather bare. Nor did we hang any bits of clothing there. Instead we decided to save our wishes for the visit to the tomb. The queue for the tomb, however, was if anything even longer than the one for the well. We separated into two parties – one all-male, one female. Night had fallen quite suddenly and it had turned cold. I began to tingle with excitement as we stood there waiting. The subject of the women's conversation for such a long time was now to become a reality – the visit to the tomb. What would it offer? How would it feel? And yet...as it turned out, in spite of everything, we had been waiting quite in vain. The tomb had been temporarily cordoned off because of unruly behaviour, while the culprits had been driven out using tear gas. The commotion was caused by too many people entering the precincts and throwing their garments to the guardian of the tomb. His job was to hold up one garment at a time facing the tombstone, whereby the clothes would be impregnated by the power which was thought to radiate from the stone. People got wrong garments back, however, and some lost their items of clothing in the tumult which arose. All we could do now was return to Awa and the other women, with a fresh attempt later on to visit the tomb.

The next port-of-call was at Astou Boury's house to deliver our gift of money, otherwise known as the 'envelope'. The other members of our association were seated on their plastic mats in expectation. When we arrived after the frustrated visit to the tomb, I was overwhelmed by the sincere and heartfelt feelings of friendship the women showed me. They had been worried because of our absence, and were truly glad to see us back. We made our way as a squad to the sokhna's house, to the left of the courtyard seen from our 'camping-ground'. We were admitted to an anteroom by one of the sokhna's aides, a young male disciple of the sokhna's husband, who asked us to sit on the floor and wait. I adjusted my scarf to cover half of my forehead. We were all excited at the prospect of meeting the sokhna and how she would greet us. Would she be satisfied with the 'envelope' or not? Her attitude towards us during the rest of the *magal* would constitute proof of that. This was in any case Awa's conclusion, and she was the one most concerned.

We entered the sokhna's room, heads bowed and led by the young aide. He indicated the part of the floor where we should be, and we dropped down to form a semi-circle in front of Astou, with Awa in the middle. Astou Boury sat on a bed, her head largely hidden wrapped in a shawl, and with a disciple – her spokesperson – standing just behind. All communication with the sokhna was channelled through this man, and he was the one who accepted the 'envelope' when it was offered by our president. Awa addressed the man, introduced our *daira* to Astou Boury, and begged her blessing. After this message had been whispered into Astou's ear, she greeted us via the man while we finally lifted our eyes to behold her. The personage seated on the bed, I sensed even at a distance, radiated a keen aura of authority. Beside her lay an assortment of presents she had received earlier that day. Among a variety of objects could be seen a number of bottles of perfume and a few packages of soap. I was unable, however, to make out our 'envelope' containing the donation.

A conversation ensued via the spokesperson between the sokhna and the president. Awa told her of the difficulties facing the members of her association, and that they had come to seek her help. She mentioned among other matters the lack of finances, serious illnesses in our community, and marriage problems. Astou promised to pray for all the members of the *daira*. It was clear that the president and the sokhna knew each other, and that there existed a good rapport between them. I was introduced as a person who wrote books and consequently made mame Diarra Bousso's name known in Europe. Sokhna Astou promised to pray for me too, for my assistant Penda Seck, and for my colleagues. The reception was terminated by Astou Boury's giving us her blessing. I left the sokhna's room struck by her charismatic personality – yet another compelling Murid woman! She reminded me of Maimouna in Touba. Outside her room sat a new group of women together with a few men, waiting their turn.

The night that followed rang loud with *khassaïd* singing, as well as with the noise of people streaming past us, in decreasing numbers as it got later. Most of the women beside me lay asleep. I, too, huddled up on my little mat after going around and saying good-night to people in other courtyards. At three a.m. the policeman approached us and assured me it was safe to visit the tomb after he had made a check. He considered it peaceful enough now to escort me there without risk, together with the young woman who had been with us earlier. Now that it had grown dark his endeavours to provide for our safety grew too, and he wouldn't leave us unobserved for a single minute – Awa's orders, I assumed. She thanked me for not crossing the bridge and venturing into the woods on the other side of the stream. All kinds of night entertainment were in full swing there of every possible type, including dancing, frowned upon in the present circumstances. I had noted a growing impatience in Penda Seck and the woman who had returned from seeing her mother-in-law. They belonged, of course, to another Sufi order, the *Tijaniyya*, and they felt it was time to draw the line at all these Murid and pilgrim activities. They were keen to make their way home, in other words.

My partly edited notes from the visit to mame Diarra Bousso's tomb took the following shape:

> The place was teeming with people, even though it was the middle of the night, and the closer we got to the entrance to the chamber with the tomb, the more excitable everybody seemed. The friendly mood which had captured my imagination during the daytime had vanished. People had one thing in mind – reaching the tomb. For a moment I considered turning back – eveything seemed so insecure, I became scared. An irritated police force, beggars turning aggressive. A Baie Fall rattling his gourd bowl under my nose angling for money. Lots of people (women, that is, only women, I was in a queue consisting only of women and Awa's policeman had left me), all over the place, pushing us along from behind. A guard ordered us to remove our shoes and hold on to them, and cover our heads better. He pulled my scarf – brutally, I thought – way down over my eyes, and I felt harshly treated. At the entrance itself it was almost a matter of every man for himself – crammed full, you couldn't move an inch. Suddenly I found myself shoved inside, right in front of the tombstone. Another guard stood behind the grating which protected the tomb, charging money. I hadn't been made aware of this beforehand, but I watched the others kneel down at the tomb, say their prayers, and express their wishes to mame Diarra. Then the man, a picture of boredom, got his handful of coins. The girl with me saw my confusion and produced some money. Under stress, I was unable to request anything more complicated than a simple "Give me courage!" to mame Diarra, which I repeated several times. I felt I needed it – courage! We were hustled along, and before I knew it we were outside, stumbling down the steps. We had come out into the night air and lost our bearings, picking our way through a mass of sleeping bodies, spaced over every square foot of ground available. Then we wandered around, between the buses in the parking lot, past small tables advertising religious tracts, with oranges and Touba coffee for sale. I was still in a daze, stunned by what I had been through. The pilgrims' frenzy and the guards' tough attitudes on the one hand, and on the other my meeting with the holiest of Murid sites, second only to Amadou Bamba's tomb at Touba. Tears welled

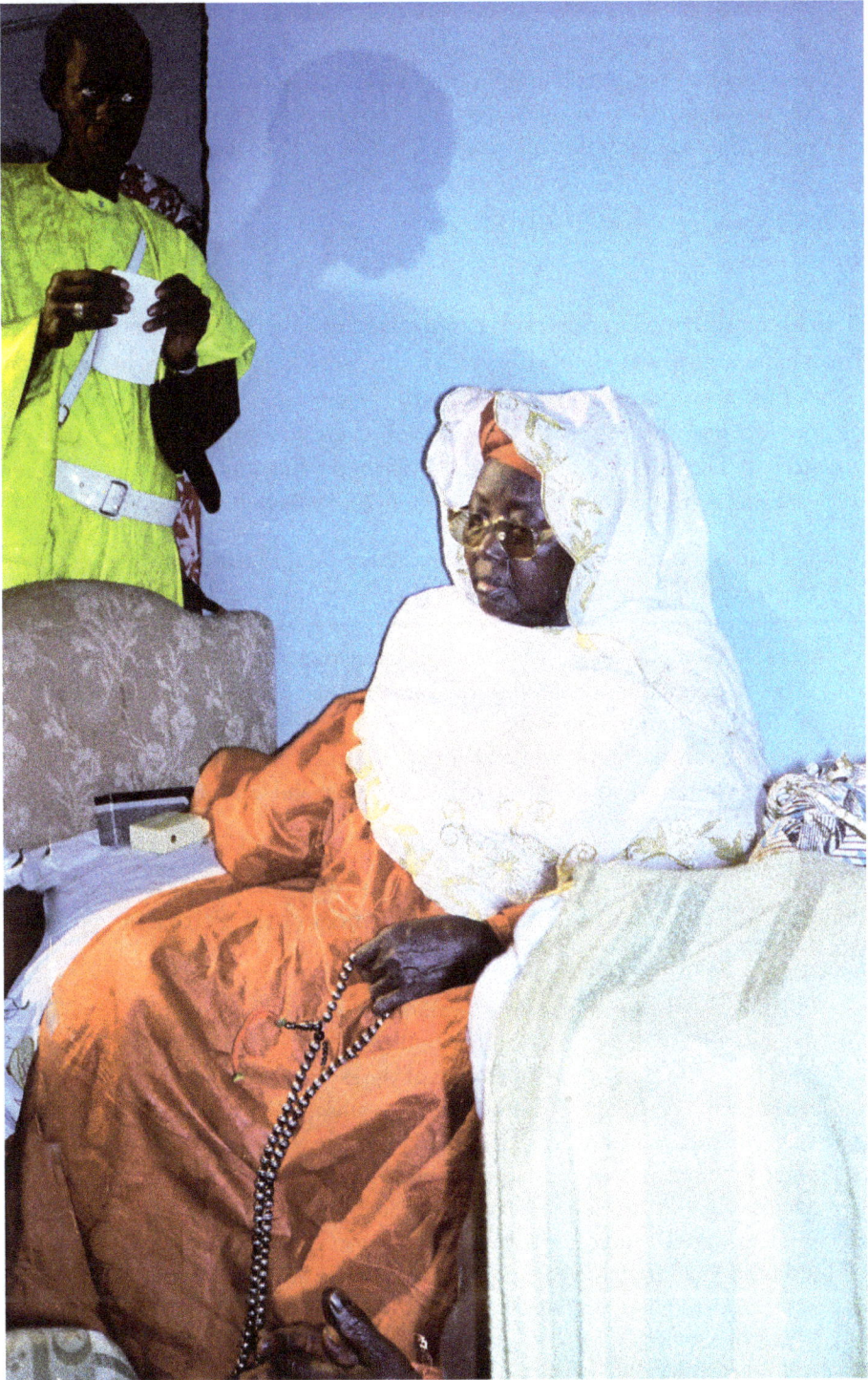

At Porokhane: the female marabout Astou Boury together with her assistant and spokesperson receiving the Mame Diarra Bousso Association in Mbacké. 1995.

in my eyes as I grabbed my young colleague by the arm. She guided me slowly but surely to our car. In the back seat sat Penda and the other woman, eager to return home. We found our policeman and asked him kindly to thank Awa for all the consideration she had shown us. The driver was sitting in the front seat, fast asleep. At four in the morning we started back to Dakar and Mbacké.

Reflections

A week or so later I received Awa's account of how the second day of the Porokhane *magal* was spent. She was immensely happy, and in her opinion Astou Boury's courtesy and attitude on the Friday was demonstration enough of how satisfied she was with the 'envelope' she had received and with our visit to her. This is how the president described what they had done together with sokhna Astou before leaving for home on Friday afternoon:

> On Friday morning we went to sokhna Astou Boury's room once more, sitting together with her and singing mame Diarra Bousso songs while she prayed for us. She then came along with us to mame Diarra's tomb. We went as a group, escorted by a policeman, who blocked the entrance for others while we were there. We stayed inside close to the tomb for half an hour, alone with sokhna Astou Boury, after which she accompanied us to the mosque for the Friday prayers. With the prayer session over, we returned to our spot in sokhna Astou Boury's courtyard, gathered our things together, and left for home.

Shortly after our trip I was walking past the home of Fatimata, the woman who had dubbed me 'Mrs Well'. Sitting there at the roadside outside her house in Mbacké, she recounted her experiences of the Porokhane *magal* in the following words:

> In Porokhane I went a first time to mame Diarra Bousso's tomb on the Thursday, and then a second time on the Friday to beg her for a number of things I need in my life. The others (members of the association) went to the market on Friday morning, because whether there's a *magal* in Porokhane, Touba or anywhere else there are always a lot of market people with their goods to make a bit of money from the visitors. For example, a lot of salesmen from Gambia selling handkerchiefs, fabrics, jewellery, shoes… a lot of stuff. What I was most interested in were the dress materials. So I went to the market to buy a *khartoum*, a special kind of cotton material I could use on the next *magal*, and I bought another material as a present for my sister-in-law, because I didn't intend buying and selling any materials to make money.
>
> When we had bought what we wanted, we all went back again to Astou Boury's room and sat and sang songs about mame Diarra Bousso and chatted about things that had to do with Porokhane. About two in the afternoon we

went to the mosque with sokhna Astou as it was Friday prayer time. It gave us an opportunity to be with her at the mosque. Luckily enough the *magal* was a Thursday-Friday event, which made it possible. After prayers we went straight back to our spot at the courtyard and gathered our things together for the trip home to Mbacké. Even if the pilgrimage is tremendously tiring, I'll always be praying to God to take me to Porokhane every year with the mame Diarra Bousso Association and to let all Muslims who want to go there.

Certain differences can be noted in Fatimata's and Awa's accounts as to what happened the final day in Porokhane. Awa, inclined towards more of a myth-creating report, offered a grander description of the visit to the tomb than Fatimata. Both summaries, however, reveal the fact that Astou Boury devoted more time to the association on the Friday. Fewer people were around to grab her attention. It was these Friday hours together with sokhna Astou - which I missed – that evidently contributed to making the association's journey to Porokhane an important experience for the pilgrims.

What, though, did my three fellow-travellers think, all of them Tijans who had never before been to Porokhane? They share the basically sceptical conception regarding Muridism, common among members of the *Tijaniyya*. They feel that Muridism is a superficial order, and that far too many marabouts have a soft spot for luxuries, at their disciples' expense. The marabouts, in these women's eyes, exploit their disciples' ignorance and lack of education in order to exert power over them through the use of magic and superstition. Disciple and marabout are too tightly bound together, the one with the other, while the blind submission this implies is a dangerous phenomenon, contradicting the doctrine of Islam, the three Tijan women thought. The Prophet Mohammed is toned down and is pushed into the background while Amadou Bamba is given a more prominent role, as if he were the leading figure. The Touba *magal* has turned into a big jamboree, in their opinion, lacking in true religious gravity. The Porokhane *magal* is a smaller affair. It was, in spite of everything, a fine experience as a result of the tour to the various places connected with mame Diarra Bousso, and also because of the friendly mood among the participants. They all agreed on this.

It was not until they saw the regrettable treatment we were afforded in Porokhane that my three fellow-travellers realised how small and insignificant Awa's Mame Diarra Association from Mbacké was. Astou Boury, under whose supervision the association came, must also be comparatively unimportant and occupy low status by the side of the other Bousso family leaders. Her house and her courtyard were small and off the main area. No group of male *khassaïd* singers dropped by. The most insulting aspect, however, as all three saw it, was being ignored when the portions of food were being served. It mattered not, they claimed, how much the president tried to embellish the situation with tales of Astou Boury's kindly care of them on the Friday. The fact remained that the way Awa and her members were treated on the Thursday gave a direct pointer to the association's low status. Criticism of a general character was also levelled at the selective manner in which the pilgrims were entertained. It contradicted the notion of a generous spirit, something which Muridism particularly prescribes.

And some thoughts...on 'being there'

Subsequently I jotted down the negative aspects of the *magal*: the thirst, the hunger, the dust, the flooded urinal floor, the teeming crowds, the hysterical queuing...And then the positive factors: the tender and motherly care shown me by members of the association, but also the kind and amiable intercourse existing among the pilgrims themselves, men and women, strangers to each other, but who saw themselves as brothers and sisters united at Porokhane to appeal for guidance and support from mame Diarra.

The president and the members of the association, including myself, spent most of the time at Porokhane on our plastic mats in Astou Boury's courtyard. *We were there*, we were at mame Diarra Bousso's, whether we were engaged on our *ziyara* tour, praying at the mosque, requesting the hearing of a prayer, greeting Astou Boury, or just being in her courtyard. The very expression 'just' is what I use to convey my own very personal idea that it was uncomfortable, a little boring and tedious 'just' to be lying on a plastic mat in a dusty courtyard in the midst of a pilgrim site . But circumstances are similar, on an even larger scale, at the big Touba *magal* in commemoration of Amadou Bamba and his departure from Senegal, exiled by the French colonial authorities. Pilgrims often stay longer there than at Porokhane, while the *ziyara* tour does not offer the same picturesque elements as we were able to enjoy, imitating mame Diarra's domestic chores in an attempt to gain access to her support and generous rewards.

Nor is the general atmosphere at Touba as friendly; crowds are much larger and the queues for the mosque, the tomb and the well are longer than at Porokhane. All the same, what people appreciate most of all is *being there*, which includes the sensation of being a participant, on the spot, as it were, during the *magal*. The vital holy force associated with *barke* penetrates the earth, merges with the sand, whirls around in the clouds of dust and radiates the air at such holy sites as I have described here. Every pilgrim wishes to appropriate for himself as much of this *barke* as he can. Whether they are aware of it or not, this holy force, invisible but for many almost palpable, makes them wish to 'just' *be there*.

This was the first aspect I discovered in assessing the members' experience of the pilgrimage. I had not previously understood the full impact of attending the *magal* at Touba or Porokhane. Not such a remarkable discovery in itself, but the interesting point for me was to see and feel how being present at a pilgrim site created almost extraterrestrial dimensions or visions of Paradise for the pilgrims. The other insight I gained concerned the market place and the women's interest in the assortment of goods on offer. They had all brought along money for purchases, either for gifts or to sell back in Mbacké and its surroundings to customers who couldn't make it to Porokhane. Both Fatimata and the other women were particularly interested in purchasing materials, head scarves and other textiles.

Here, too, the notion of the *barke* element inherent in the place itself was prevalent, linked to mame Diarra Bousso's tomb and the pilgrims' clothes. The same power or force prevailed in the goods being sold in Porokhane and gave them a special appeal to the customers. The market combined religion and money, creating an extra attraction for the women.

Finally it may be said that the Porokhane *magal*, by focussing on mame Diarra, makes the women more visible in religious life than anywhere else in the Murids' Senegal. This acted as a positive impulse for me, depressed as I was by the male dominance which characterised Muridism. The rituals performed in Porokhane during the *magal*, by both men and women, were marked by the daily activities of women, which, as inferred earlier, rose to spiritual levels.

IN TOUBA BELEL

A T PENDA'S SUGGESTION I set out for Touba Belel, a village close to the city of Touba, in order to have an opportunity to meet the marabout serigne Cheikhouna and his wife sokhna Mai Habou, the first wife of his polygamous marriage. Penda considered it was high time I got acquainted with the countryside around Mbacké and Touba. The fact that her choice fell on Cheikhouna in Touba Belel and his first wife Mai Habou was due to his good reputation as a friendly and generous person. He was popular among the villagers of Touba Belel but also among business people as well as the local administrative officials and the Development Aid Programme office staff in Mbacké.

Cheikhouna was Amadou Bamba's grandson and the son of Abdoul Ahat Mbacké, the *khalifa général* in Touba in 1988 and 1989. His father's fame as a charismatic person, renowned for his *barke*, spread far afield during his short time at the head of the Murid order, and he acquired a large number of disciples. As a consequence he became both powerful and rich. His son Cheikhouna had taken over the father's many disciples who were organised in *dairas* in memory of Abdoul Ahat. Cheikhouna had also obtained his own disciples who had inaugurated *dairas* devoted to him.

I had been informed that the marabout occupied an authoritative position in the village, emphasizing the fact that he exercised a certain degree of control over the people both spiritually and materially. Most of the villagers were poor farmers, and they were also his disciples. Their oaths of obedience to Cheikhouna placed them in a special position of dependence. Though his power was considerable, their subordination was voluntary, as they saw it, and formed part of the Murid identity. The motives and purposes were known to everybody: the desire to reach Paradise. This was their hope and expectation. They also believed that the marabout would reward them for their struggle on earth, and this belief was perhaps even more intense than their hope to enter Paradise. Their toil and drudgery working in his fields would be compensated for, as well as any other tasks they might contribute. Devotion to Cheikhouna was an investment in his magical powers to produce what they asked for.

An official at the local office of the *Ministère des Eaux et Forêts* (equivalent to the *Ministry of Natural Resources)* in Mbacké telephoned the marabout, and a visit was arranged for Penda and me together with the official. Together with two of his wives, Cheikhouna lived in Touba Belel on the property he had inherited from his father in his capacity of eldest son. He also had a house in Touba, and was there from time to time. Otherwise he remained in Touba Belel or travelling abroad, visiting disciples in Germany, Italy, France and Spain. Cheikhouna regarded his village as his 'own', in the manner of a feudal lord. He felt responsible for it, and had made a number of investments and improvements, according to all the people I spoke to in Mbacké. Many of them were his friends, who admired him for what he had achieved. Among other things he had had a mosque built and arranged for the local council to equip the village with a clinic and school. Electrification of various parts of the village was under way. He placed particular interest in acquiring another school for the village, teaching not only religion and Arabic but French too.

We arrived at Touba Belel late in the afternoon. We entered the large court-yard, boarded in by a breast-high sheet-metal fence. In the centre of the yard lay the marabout's house, surrounded by the wives' quarters and several other buildings, all covered with corrugated iron roofs. Further inside I glimpsed circular straw-roofed huts.

Penda and I stepped into the first wife's house and asked if she was at home. A tall, straight-backed woman came along and flashed a friendly smile at us. She and her husband were cousins, closely related to the founder of Muridism. She had four children together with Cheikhouna.

On a par with other female marabouts, Mai Habou had initiated a sewing workshop in Touba where some of her disciples worked. They sewed, embroidered and sold *boubous* and *pagnes* on her account. In the village Mai was eager to start the growing of vegetables when the rainy season arrived. She had been the driving force in creating a female collective body enjoying local council support and foreign aid, cultivating and selling their products at market places in the surrounding district and in Touba.

In the twilight there in Mai's house we surveyed the scene. The room was furnished with cushions and pillows lining the walls. The woman impressed me with her grand and stately bearing, simply dressed in her splendid *bou-bou* and a *foulard*, a piece of material matching the dress, ingeniously wound around her head.

Mai Habou sincerely regretted the fact that I was not able to speak the *Wolof* language. Through Penda as interpreter she wondered whether I wouldn't like to come and stay in one of the vacant houses in the courtyard and sew for her, which I interpreted as an offer to become her disciple. I thanked her but let the matter rest there, even if I did feel a sense of contentment over being accommodated within the only context suitable for her: as a disciple. I also knew that, even though it was the habit to affirm that there were very few female marabouts with *barke* and with their own disciples, this did not tally with reality. They were very much in evidence, and these women were blessed with their disciples' oaths of obedience, just as the men were. Since there were no little girls or youths visible in the house, I asked Mai Habou whether she had any of the villagers' children lodged with her. I was thinking about the boys and girls whose parents might have requested her taking charge of them to receive a religious education. Oh yes, she did, she said. The reason I could not see any just then was because they were in another building together with the older girls, who took care of the little ones at this time of the afternoon.

A very hospitable marabout

After a while we were summoned by the marabout. He was at home in his own house, accompanied by his closest disciples when we entered. Cheikhouna was as tall as his wife, and dressed in a long garment. I was aware that I should not meet his eyes as he greeted me, and that I shouldn't reach out to shake hands. He would not take my hand since I was a woman and he a man and a marabout. I still felt somewhat insecure about how I should conduct myself. He apparently observed my confusion, taking my hand and greeting me in the European style. This must have been for him an exceptional procedure, and I appreciated the gesture all the more when I saw how surprised the others in the room were over him seizing my hand.

As distinct from the other buildings, his house was equipped with electricity, a telephone, and a ceiling fan. The main room was decorated with low sofas along two of the walls and a carpet in the middle covering most of the floor. The marabout sat as we did on the floor, but at some distance from us. In a spatial perspective, therefore, he did not occupy a position superior to our own. This was apparently a gesture towards me, for in the normal way the marabout always sits in a position higher than his disciples and followers. His more intimate disciples, who served his every need, brought cold drinks, which were followed by a cup of Touba coffee, the bitter beverage, closely associated with Amadou Bamba and Muridism.[1]

---

1. For more details concerning this drink, closely associated with Muridism, see page 46 and Guye 2002:141.

Cheikhouna's cell phone and his landline were constantly ringing, and the disciples conveyed the substance of the conversations to their master. They expressed their satisfaction to me at being able to serve their marabout, repeating the fact that working for the marabout was equivalent to praying and was a great privilege for them. Their ideals of blind obedience and submission appeared to be closely connected to the notion of *yole* (sacrifice), which together with *barke* formed part of the foundation-stone of Muridism. I might perhaps add: 'seen mainly from a male Murid perspective'. In the case of the women, their moral conduct and degree of submission to the husband were, as mentioned already, linked to the religious ideology. Concepts such as *soutura*, tactfulness or discretion, and the ability to tolerate wrongs and injustices within the marriage, and *tiyaba*, religious merits gained through self-sacrificing work, were systematised in the female Murid ideal.

Initially Cheikhouna asked me to repeat a few common phrases in *Wolof*. "Serigne will say a word and you repeat", Penda said in a determined voice, and I realised that here it was a matter of doing as I was told. The marabout did not, that is, speak French. He probably felt isolated with no other knowledge of languages than *Wolof* and some Arabic and had therefore begun to study French with one of his disciples who lived in France but had chosen to spend his holidays in Touba Belel. At the present moment (1993), however, he had not made sufficient progress for us to be able to make any meaningful conversation.

The mood was a trifle tense before I made a start with my questions which Penda had promised to interpret. My conversation with Cheikhouna touched upon the same subject often repeated during my visits to Touba Belel. It was the core matter for my study: women's co-operation and participation in the religious cult and its rituals, not least the singing of the *khassaïds* by women, which it turned out Cheikhouna firmly opposed. He considered their female voices served to distract the men from praying. The marabout was, however, to begin with more interested in my background and civil status. Was I married, and if so, where was my husband? This Murid leader in Touba Belel had no idea of my purpose in visiting him other than that I wished to learn more about Muridism. For my part I did not know why he had received me in his home, but plainly he had decided to offer me a very friendly and discreet reception. He invited me back for lunch three days later and promised to provide an extra tasty meal if I came.

Before we left the room he blessed all of us with a prayer, which we received with our hands stretched forwards and the palms facing upwards. This was followed by the usual custom of stroking our hands over our faces and down to our waists. The marabout went with us out to our jeep and stood at my side of the vehicle, fondling my arm resting against the frame of the door. It was not an unpleasant sensation, but all the same I felt a certain sense of relief mixed with marvel as we drove off. Female co-operation and participation, what were they, really? A proposition had been made for me to become a dressmaker if not a disciple by the female partner of a marabout couple. The male partner may have insinuated that my role as disciple would implicate participation of a more sensual kind, although no words to this effect had been uttered. What, however, was it that he believed I was looking for in him?

During my first visit to Touba Belel I never confronted myself seriously with this question. Now, as I write these words, I think that my hosts were convinced my urge to visit them was an effort to acquire *barke* through them in their capacity of God's proxy, as well as an enquiry into more information on Muridism. This perspective most certainly left its mark on the relationship between the marabout and myself. Gradually, following many visits to Touba Belel, I found myself obliged to make it clear that I had no intention of becoming a Murid. This was why I put an end to my visits to Cheikhouna and Mai Habou. This was the price I had to pay, but their hospitality and amiability were unforgettable.

At Pikine

One of the marabout's disciples had offered to take me along to 'his' own *daira*, the association founded in honour of Cheikhouna. It operated in Pikine, a suburb in the north-west of Dakar. The young man repeatedly begged me to have him perform a number of services, whatever they might be. His spiritual leader had ordered him to obey me. The biggest favour I could do him was to offer him this chance, because the greater the submission the larger the divine reward. I found this situation quite novel and confusing. I was only capable of issuing a few commands, and unfortunately for him they could not always be carried out. There were evidently limits to the type of obedience he could show me, a European woman and non-Muslim besides. I asked, for instance, to be able to attend a meeting where the male members of his suburban *daira* were to sing *khassaïds*. It turned out to be impossible for women. They were only welcome once a week. Females were constrained to take their places in a narrow, adjacent room while the males sat in a circle in the courtyard singing with the aid of amplifier and loudspeaker, the songs penetrating the immediate neighbourhood. As in all associations of this type the procedure at the meeting consisted of the men singing their *khassaïds* and collecting money for their marabout. Certain people were invited to hold religious lectures.

All the members of the Pikine association were young men whose conception of women was decidedly conservative. The same situation prevailed in Touba among the young, well-organised male Murids, who were members of *Hisbut Tarqiyya*, an expanding association in Touba for young people.

I was surprised by how limited the Murid women's participation at the meetings was both in Pikine and in Touba. Their role was principally that of listening, and this was even the case in the so-called 'mixed' religious associations, led by a male and a female president. I noted now, as I did earlier, that the men's obedience to the marabouts was something they had taken upon themselves and which was expected to be fully rewarded by the leaders – if not now, then later, in Paradise. The women's obedience was of a double nature: they were subordinated to both men and marabouts. What choice did they have? What woman would risk her children suffering because of her bad conduct? This was the old argument continually repeated if you brought into question women's subordination in the compulsory marriage. Woman's lot was to obey and endure, if we were to labour the point of the way the young Murid men reasoned in their discussions with me.

The women and children of Touba Belel

All the women in Touba Belel took part in the social, financial and religious associations' activities. If they didn't, they would soon find themselves under a cloud of suspicion. Being absent was the same as withdrawing from the collective body in order to hide what one was up to. Both boys and girls had their respective associations, the *maas*, where they trained to be practised members. Male adults tended to be most active in the religious associations. They did not have the same need for social and financial support through the associations as the village women. The men's possibilities of moving independently outside the village and avoiding gossip were of course much greater than the women's. This enabled them, for instance, to seek financial aid if necessary from distant relatives and friends. The men were accustomed to borrowing money from each other through their male networks in a way distinct from that of the women. The same situation prevailed, as mentioned earlier, for female marabouts. They had families enjoying a wide range of contacts, and through close and distant relatives had access to a variety of resources.

The individual female villager did not have any appreciable sums of money at her disposal, but relied on either so-called 'self-aid organisations' (*mbotaye* or *aide-entre-aide*) or rotating savings credit associations, in *Wolof* called *nat*. *Mbotaye*, a name which originally referred to the burden women used to carry on their backs, nowadays corresponds to the gifts, donations and the work done which female members, in case of need, offer each other in conjunction with *rites-de-passage* feasts such as marriages, name-giving ceremonies and funerals. These rotating savings associations are also present in the village. The *nat* phenomenon has become all the more popular since the village women have started to sell more at the local market places and thus gain access to ready cash to invest in a rotating savings and credit association. A *nat* comprises a group of women who meet regularly and hand over a certain defined sum of money to the president. Lots are drawn each time they meet to see who is 'rewarded' with the total sum for her personal use. She is then struck from the list, and at the next meeting another woman is the fortunate one. This procedure continues until everybody has had the chance to gain access to the total sum of money. The condition is, of course, that all women will turn up every time they have a meeting and make their stipulated contribution.

The women in Touba Belel usually employ the money as initial capital for remunerative activities in parallel with crop-growing in the fields and care of the home and their children. The money might be spent on the purchase of a number of lambs to raise and later sell at a profit. It is sometimes used for the purchase of a stock of products which are then sold to neighbours or at the local market, or buying white cloth and dyeing it for sale, or for groundnuts to press and produce oil. The rotating savings concept is not without risk, however. If any woman moves from the village, or passes away, or for any other reason leaves the group, the sum of money will be that much smaller. Nevertheless, the advantages lie in the fact that money which the women might spend on trivial matters or loans they might feel the need to grant to their husbands remains with them, even though it is inaccessible for the moment in accordance with the rules of the rotating savings credit association.

Mai Habou was both president and treasurer in most of the associations, the traditional and informal ones as well as the new formal type under national control. These associations, such as the *Groupement de Promotion Féminine,* (equivalent to the *Cooperative for Women's Economic Development)* had appropriate participant lists and a bank account of their own. The hierarchical nature of society in these villages lends itself to a situation such as this. Committees are claimed to be elected democratically, but in point of fact it is only women from the marabout's family and possibly one of the village leader's wives who come into question. In Touba Belel the exception was the self-help organisation. Mai Habou did not belong there either economically or socially, as she was a wealthy woman of much greater status and prestige. The members made their own contributions to each other's celebrations and parties directly and reciprocally. All of these village women had a similar financial status and stood more or less on the same level of the social scale.

At the village of Touba Belel: a meeting of the women's association (mbotaye). 1994.

I brought to mind a *daira* such as the one Awa managed in commemoration of mame Diarra Bousso in the town of Mbacké and compared it with the situation concerning women's associations in Touba Belel. A *daira* with a similar purpose and ambition was unthinkable in the village. The women lacked sufficient money to be able to finance a pilgrimage to Porokhane or to achieve the degree of independence necessary. The village men would not allow their women to leave the home, let alone sanction an overnight stay somewhere else. This attitude caused a great deal of problems in the families, not least of a financial character. The women needed to travel to markets outside the village to sell their products, while at the same time the men set up obstacles, in spite of the fact that the money they apportioned to the upkeep of the home and the children's needs was insufficient. Husbands wished to have their wives under constant supervision.

During my visit to the village Mai Habou once managed to assemble the members of the *mbotaye* at Touba Belel to sing 'women's songs' together. They gathered by a field at a spot far from the spying eyes of the men, who were of the opinion that women singing was something that should not be heard. To begin with, the women remained silent, rather embarrassed. The presence of both Mai Habou and myself was new and disconcerting. In order to ease the tension somewhat, I started to sing a few verses from a couple of Swedish melodies associated with Christmas. Everybody soon appeared to be more relaxed. Following my rendering of a rather melancholy Swedish ballad, it now seemed as though it was time for the women themselves to break into song. Mai Habou was keen to seize the opportunity to perform the Murid songs, and she asked a *griotte* whose voice was widely appreciated to lead the singing. She began with a well-known song about mame Diarra Bousso, the others joining in with the refrain. I then realised what a particularly solemn moment this was, above all for the female marabout, who otherwise always had to be content with reading the words of the songs together with her husband. The singing lasted about one hour, after which the women hurried back to their work.

Originally no religious associations existed in the countryside other than *daras*, referred to earlier as a type of boarding school, teaching the Koran for the sons of Murid disciples in the village. These boys were expected to perform agricultural work in the marabout's fields. The marabout informed me that he had nine *daras* in Touba Belel alone. The purpose was to take care of the religious education of the farmers' and male disciples' sons. Parents who leave their sons in the care of the marabout demonstrate in this way their obedience and loyalty to him. As far as the village women are concerned, they leave their daughters in the care of the marabout's wives. The farmer's consignment of his own son – his prime possession, we might say – to his religious leader is considered a worthwhile sacrifice, a *yole*. Nowadays boys are also sent to *daras* in the cities. They are often the children of men who have migrated from the countryside to the urban areas. Parents have to pay a fee at the *dara*, otherwise the marabout will send the boy out on the streets to beg for his living. In Touba Belel the older boys at the *dara* are employed in the fields owned by Cheikhouna, who cultivates millet, groundnuts or manioc both for his own requirements and for sale. The boys' labour serves to increase the marabout's well-being, while in return they receive instruction in the Koran from the imam, daily not-too-generous portions of food and somewhere to sleep at the edge of the fields they work in. The imam lives in Touba Belel, and on a well-known parallel with many instructors of the Koran, maintains the habit of including corporal punishment in the teaching.

Toddlers remain at home with their mother as long as they are being breast-fed. Mai had up to 30 children aged between two and six in her care, she told me. At the age of six or seven the children were separated, the girls remaining with her and doing domestic work, while the boys left for the *dara*. Each family in the village normally delivered at least one son. The boys alternated between the Koran school and work in the fields from ten years of age, generally doing their homework in the mornings. Girls also attended Koran school to some extent, working more or less as servants in the female marabout's house. Their lives were less strenuous than the boys', however, and the religious drilling on the part of the imam less tough. His ambition to have the boys recite the Koran off by heart was decidedly higher. Around 17 to 20 years of age the boys would marry the bride obtained for them by the marabout and his wives. The boys were provided with a field to cultivate and thus became farmers or emigrated, while the girls were married off at an early age.

One day Penda and I took a walk to a few of the nine *daras* which Cheikhouna supervised in Touba Bebel. Our guide was Mai Habou. I was completely overwhelmed by what I saw, even if I had thought I was fully prepared through the objective descriptions I had read in books replete with facts about what sort of institutions the *daras* were.[2] Now, as I write in 2010, it is sixteen years since I was first confronted with this milieu, which more than anything else reminded one of a work camp for children. I know that large parts of the *dara* system are still in operation in rural areas, a robust system based on the notion of sacrificing everything – even one's own son – in order to obtain everything. The bigger the sacrifice the greater the reward. Furthermore, the object is to instruct the young generation of male Murids in the value of submission and obedience free of protest or bringing into question the procedures. This is the message Muridism wishes to convey and spread far and wide through these young boys, engraved in their bodies in sweat and tears, and in the sore eyes that comes from all their reading of the Koran. The boys are forced to endure ten years or more in fear of not learning their lessons by heart or having the strength to get through the work schedule. The years spent at the *dara* leave a mark on them for the rest of their lives; both the marabout's own sons and the farmers' children are put through the mill as one. They share life at the *dara*.

Leaving the centre of the village we approached a large fenced-in area of sand, stones and thorny bushes. Along the side were a number of huts supposedly used as sleeping accommodation. At one corner of the enclosure kitchen equipment was visible, dominated by some large kettles for the cooking of rice. A group of boys of various ages were sitting or lying down, rattling off parts of the Koran or scribbling on wooden boards. Their lives consisted of completing the work schedule out in the fields, and in this enclosure. Their strict teacher, the imam, awaited them at the Koran school. Punishment was regarded as an essential part of the upbringing, a sort of sacrifice in a dignified quest to reach God. The fact that the girls were not subjected to similar harsh treatment depended on their being considered incapable of standing up to the pain.

General opinion was that the girls were not mentally capable of meditating for long periods or tolerating solitude, hunger and thirst. I imagined that it was these elements which gave the women a more practical and realistic view

2. See O'Brien 1972, Copans 1988.

of daily life, enabling them to see to it that the community functioned in all its basic tasks: health, reproduction and nutrition...

The scanty fare offered at the *dara* consisted mostly of cooked rice. The boys' clothes looked too big for some of them, and on others they hung like patchwork quilts. Laundry was the job of Mai Habou's girls who worked for her at the yard. Three older boys, assisted at times by a fourth, were in charge of the entire *dara*. They cooked the food, supervising the group as a whole, some hundred or so in ages ranging from seven to fifteen. These were approximate figures since nobody really knew how old the boys were.

I felt really sick at heart at the *dara*. What could I do to better their lives? How would I tackle such a problem when the current thinking was that their 'sacrifice' was what gave them a reward in both this life and the next? The boy chosen by the 'guards' to be interviewed by me had an absent look about him and did not appear very willing to talk to us. As thin as a rake and ill-clad, he made a disheartening impression. The look on his face was the most depressing feature we noticed, vacant as though his presence were neither here nor there. He said he didn't know how long he had been at the *dara*, nor when he would be leaving. When the marabout came and 'liberated' him was the expression he used – that was when he would be leaving. The guard told us that permission was granted for the boys to be at home twice a year in conjunction with religious feasts. During *Tabaski*, the sheep-sacrificing festival and one of the most important celebrations of the Islamic year, they were allowed to stay at home for an entire week.

A little weeping boy of four or five years scurried past us on the path between the *dara* and some of the huts. He refused to go to the Koran school and attempted to rush home. He howled loudly as he was fished up by an adult and carried back to the school. Mai Habou told us that truant children are punished by having their hands and feet chained. This had happened to one of her sons when he was small. She remembered her own distaste for the Koran school. All the children felt that way, she said, but it was of course a necessary evil. She was quick to point out, however, that the girls, who did not have to endure the *dara*, spent a milder and more pleasant childhood than the boys. They are less brainwashed, I thought to myself, and consequently less tied to the demands of authority under the compliant surface.

How, I wondered, could these women, less influenced than the men by the demands of Muridism for total devotion, bear handing over their sons to a *dara*? Penda was now eager to inform me of what she considered were the women's true feelings on this subject. She didn't want me to draw hasty conclusions of a negative character concerning what I saw and heard, without first understanding some of the background. Penda said she knew for a fact that the mothers suffered for their children, and that there was nothing they would wish for more than that their children be spared going to the *dara*. Moreover, it was not just a matter of sheltering them from the overly tough work they were supposed to carry out. These children were without sufficient proper supervision, with dangers lurking in every corner in the shape of poisonous snakes, scorpions, risk of malaria and other illnesses. This, however, was something that must not be spoken about. Everything lay in the hands of God, and it was absolutely out of the question to make a complaint so that others heard it. Such behaviour could be interpreted as pure blasphemy and irreverence towards God's representatives, the marabouts. Penda said that in most people's eyes the years living at the *dara*, despite everything, involved activities divinely inspired, deeds of a holy character, implying an act of sacrifice on the part of the boys and their parents.

The adult males in Touba Belel, who had spent many, long strenuous years of their childhood and youth at the *dara*, devoted one day a week, normally a Wednesday, to working in the marabout's fields. The men also made themselves available on other occasions when the marabout decided he needed them in the cultivation of millet and groundnuts, or clearing woodland and bush. The driving force here, of course, are the Murid ethics, based on the notion that work is equivalent to prayer.

After we had returned to the marabout's house, a woman approached from a neighbouring village with an assignment to Penda and me. It was Fatou, who I had earlier met in Mbacké. She greeted Mai Habou in a very respectful manner. I immediately noticed that the two women enjoyed a special relationship. Meanwhile, a rather thin and untidy little girl of about eight appeared shyly in a doorway. Mai grabbed hold of her with a friendly word or two and disappeared, returning very soon with the little girl dressed in a pretty frock and a shiny smile on her face. She approached Fatou, who was evidently her biological mother. The girl, called 'Mai' after her new mother, had been left in Mai's care by Fatou when she was a three-year-old, as a token of loyalty and obedience. Both the biological mother and her daughter did their best not to show their spontaneous joy at seeing each other. I imagined that it would be out of place in the presence of Mai. They stood in silence, Fatou's arm cuddling her daughter, until the moment Penda and I left together with Fatou. The little girl remained, her arms hanging listlessly by her side, without a word or gesture of farewell.

During the many years that have passed since my last visit to Touba Belel (in 1995) the village has by all accounts expanded, and is nowadays said to be a popular migration centre. The vicinity of Touba, which has also increased in size, is a strong contributory factor in this expansion. The last I heard was that Cheikhouna was living in Touba permanently. Have any of his sons taken over the village empire after their father? They have lived abroad for a long period of time and presumably adopted another life style. How can the marabout/disciple relationship be maintained? How many *daras* exist today in Touba Belel, and how are they run? These are some of the many reflections and queries, which might give rise to new projects and deeper insights.

I was never able to influence Cheikhouna in either direction in the course of our discussions concerning the boys' suffering at the *daras*, or the women's wishes to sing *khassaïds*. He remained convinced that he was doing right in maintaining the religious ideas in Touba Belel in accordance with the prescribed formula. The Mbacké Mbacké marabouts, his closest relatives, lent him their support on this issue. The young men outside the family circles, too, campaigning for Muridism within the various religious associations shared Cheikhouna's point of view.

FATOU'S FRUSTRATIONS

I N PREVIOUS CHAPTERS I have described my encounters with three leading Murid women each within her own sphere of activity:

Maimouna, the daughter of the founder of Muridism, lived a comfortable life out of and together with the religious order residing in Touba, and in the village founded on her account by its highest leader, the *khalifa général*. She was the most prominent of the female Murid marabouts, and a large number of disciples attended her.

Awa, the president of a female Murid association in Mbacké, admittedly worked in trade and commerce, but she herself considered her real task was organising and carrying through the annual pilgrimage to Porokhane on behalf of the members of her association. That activity provided her with both status and prestige, not only among people locally. It also supplied her with useful contacts in Touba.

Mai Habou, the grandchild of the founder of Muridism and married to her cousin, a man whose father had been the highest leader for the entire order, ruled over her realm of disciples and followers among the village women in Touba Belel, and ran financial affairs in the name of religion with the aid of her followers both in the village and in Touba.

Fatou, a married Murid woman

Fatou, the principal character of this chapter, is a Murid woman, living in a small village on the outskirts of the city of Diourbel. Like almost all the villagers, Fatou is a member of a mixed *daira* run by the men, honouring the highest Murid leader. She also considers herself an active member of another association dedicated to her neighbouring marabout, serigne mame Mor Mbacké.

Fatou makes no money from the work she performs in the name of religion; on the contrary, this activity is a contributory factor in the marabouts' overall income. She clears their fields and reaps their crops, loyally offering her help to the highest Murid leader at his millet and groundnut farms in Khelcom, in the same way as Awa does. On one of my visits to Fatou's village, she explained to me that the purpose of her work was to gain sufficient qualification or merits in the eyes of the Divine (*tiyaba*) to be able to enter Paradise. In addition she very much wanted to do what she could for her marabout. Fatou represents the rank and file, and as such she and the other members of the religious associations make up the foundation stone within Muridism.

I was keen to get to know how she lived in her village, and thus become acquainted with the characteristic features of these women's religious practices; not just those of the élite, but among the disciples and followers in the countryside. As we had met before in Touba Belel, Fatou asked me to come home to her for an interview, in order that she might relate her life undisturbed. Before I give an account of the contents of this interview, I should like to briefly describe her village and the rural environment in which Fatou lives.

Fatou's village

Fatou's village is situated inside the groundnut belt, an area which extends between Louga, Diourbel and Mbacké. There is a striking degree of emigration as conditions for farming with profit are few. During the bad years – and there are quite a few of them – the villagers have emptied their stocks of food five or six months before the harvest is due. For the remaining period the villagers resort to purchasing food on credit from the headman of the village. He owns the only existing commercial centre and consequently controls a price monopoly. The inhabitants are faced with a variety of difficult problems. Among these may be mentioned the encroaching desert, shortage of water, poor soil, shortage of pasture ground for animals, animal disease, lack of know-how in agricultural technology, scarcity of natural fertiliser and artificial manure, shortage of wood for cooking and finally an under-sized labour force owing to emigration.

The young boys leave the village and make their way to the big cities, to Europe and to the United States. The young girls move into the cities to their relatives and seek employment as domestic help. The women, too, are emigrating abroad in increasing numbers. All the women are occupied with petty trade regardless of where they live. A number of them land up in some form of prostitution in the cities in an effort to make ends meet. Later they turn their attention to becoming married to a suitable husband. What remains in the village for the rest of the year are middle-aged married women, the children and elderly persons.

The middle-aged men claim their migration is a seasonal feature. At harvest time they return and work in the village. Many of them, however, if truth be known, avoid returning home for the harvest, according to the reports of women in Fatou's village. This means that all the work is left in the hands of their wives, children still at home, and elderly people. The women strongly disapprove of their husbands in the diaspora acquiring fresh wives with the money earned abroad instead of investing it at home in the village. The wives who have remained in the village see far too little of the money the men are said to be earning abroad. I am given to understand that this emigration in point of fact means nothing but an increasing amount of work, which is heavier too, for many women.

The emigrants are almost without exception Murids of the *Wolof* ethnic group. In general, they have had few years of education, apart from the Koran school. The girls usually spend less time at the Koran school, and no time, or two years at the most, at the public school, since the custom is to remain at home and be of help to their mothers or to their sokhna.

I already knew that Fatou's marriage was polygamous. Her husband was a farmer who cultivated a few acres of land and raised a number of calves. In the village the crops grown were millet, groundnuts, *niambi*, the tuber of a tropical bush similar to manioc, manioc and *bissap*. The red flowers of the *bissap* were dried and turned into a very popular drink. The other main village activity was raising cattle. Millet was generally grown for personal use while groundnuts were for sale. Fatou had fields of her own she had received from her husband, which really meant she had them on loan. Whatever she reaped she was able to sell as she wished, and the money earned she retained. In addition to her own cultivation she helped her husband in his fields and, as referred to earlier, also performed agricultural tasks for the marabouts.

Fatou's story

We agreed upon a day when I could interview Fatou. We had a long conversation in French, which she had learnt as a little girl living in the city of Thies, where she had gone to school. She had no objection to me recording our conversation, and I tried to avoid interrupting her unnecessarily. Fatou appeared to be eager to talk, and was in no hurry. I suspected there were perhaps twin purposes on her part: the desire to share her trials and tribulations with me, an outsider, and rouse my sympathy, but also the expectation of earning a little for the trouble. I understood full well both of these possible intentions, because Fatou's time was precious, and I was making use of it in a rather self-willed manner. I proved to be on the right track. At the end of the interview she laid bare her expectations of me as a European and person of resources.

I grew up in Thies. I went to school in town like most of the others and learnt to read and write French. I also learnt how to count, and we spoke French at school. My father died and my mother met another man and remarried. But my mother's new husband didn't like me very much as I wasn't his own child, and he never had any children with my mother. So there was a divorce and my mother and I moved to this village since we have relatives here. My own father is from this village and his family lives here.

I was married off when I was fourteen years old and became the third wife of a man who was my father's age and that of the village headman. He was that much older and would be very kind to me, is what they told me. He'd give me a lot of things too, when I married him. Money to buy material, for *boubous* and *pagnes*, for saucepans and bowls. That's what he said, but when we got married, nothing. Not even a wedding present. He promised me that after the next harvest he'd give me what he'd promised. All broken promises, and I ended up with nothing. Instead he put the money away and got himself a fourth wife five years later ..... she was the one who got what he had promised me – clothes, kitchen stuff .... I swallowed all of this inside of me. Even my mother thought I should leave him. But I didn't. I said it was God who had brought me this far, and that I would keep married by my own two hands. Fatou explained that by this is meant that she would work and earn her own money since her husband gave her none.

And now I don't have any financial problems as there is work for me through the development aid projects in operation here. I can provide for my household, for my children. But what I can't get over is the way he treated me. As I showed *soutoura* and hid my shame, nobody noticed anything. I went to wedding parties, name-giving celebrations, I danced and had a good laugh, but all the time I felt bitter inside me, and suffered from the deceit I had endured. There you are – that's an example of *soutoura*.

I asked Fatou to explain a little further what she meant.

Soutoura is something a woman needs to have. It's a female virtue. A man who marries a woman with soutoura is a lucky man, because he's got hold of a woman who can keep a secret, and who can hide inside her what's good and what's bad. With soutoura, you can look forward to a good future and bring children into the world who are going to get on in life.

Fatou was thirty-five years old at the time of the interview. She was *Wolof*, belonging to the large group of people who were not 'caste-graded', and who made up the vast majority in the village. There were only a few families belonging to the traditional blacksmith or professional singer 'castes'. Her literacy made Fatou a true resource in the village. She had far more knowledge about what was happening beyond the corner of her own house than the other women. Fatou came to the assistance of many of them in reading and writing their letters, and explaining how the cooperative credit association

Preparing rice for the name-giving party. Mbacké 1995.

worked. She also kept their finances in order, making a list of the amounts they had borrowed and repaid. Her position as secretary of the cooperative credit association brought her into contact with leading women in the village, such as the headman's first wife and one of the marabout's wives, as these women occupied the positions of president and vice-president respectively on the village cooperative committee.

The struggle to improve one's private economy was a constant process among the village women. It was particularly acute in a marriage involving three co-wives, each of whom endeavoured to assert her own position in relation to the others. It was a matter of outdoing each other in everything: in the cooking of meals, and in the objects they owned or acquired. This is not to mention the merciless competition that went into the beauty element, which continued until the wives had passed their fertile age and began to be classified as old. The first wife, known as *awo* in Wolof, always enjoyed a privileged position in relation to the husband, not finding it necessary to make the same effort to assert herself. In her opinion, Fatou as third wife was forced to take a back seat in most household matters. It was particularly important to create a positive profile of oneself as a generous, open-handed person at *rites-de-passage* ceremonies such as weddings, name-givings and funerals. The hostess' reputation was at stake at the name-giving ceremony where the family's resources played a central role. The mother was expected to make presents of large sums of money to the father's family on such occasions. Maximum respect for one's family and person was called for.

Fatou was upset by the huge outlay of money and goods implicated by these feasts and festivals. At the same time she was painfully aware of the fact that if she did not take part in the rituals her position among the co-wives would deteriorate still further. In the polygamous household in which she lived, the youngest wife's constant giving birth and the subsequent name-giving ceremonies were a thorn in her flesh. It annoyed her that the husband spent so much on buying meat for these ceremonies, even though tradition required this expense when the husband became a father anew. Fatou's fear was that these expenses risked making a big hole in the household's finances, affecting all of them.

During our conversation Fatou spent a considerable time pouring out her feelings for me over how desperate the situation was in her household, and how much she yearned to be able to return to Thies. She hadn't been there for the last two years because she had her job to see to and the trip cost money. Her unhappiness and discomfort with life derived in the first place from her marriage and difficulties with her husband. He was a moody and penny-pinching individual, she said, and his careless attitudes towards his wives made Fatou indignant. She told me that the man refused to accept any

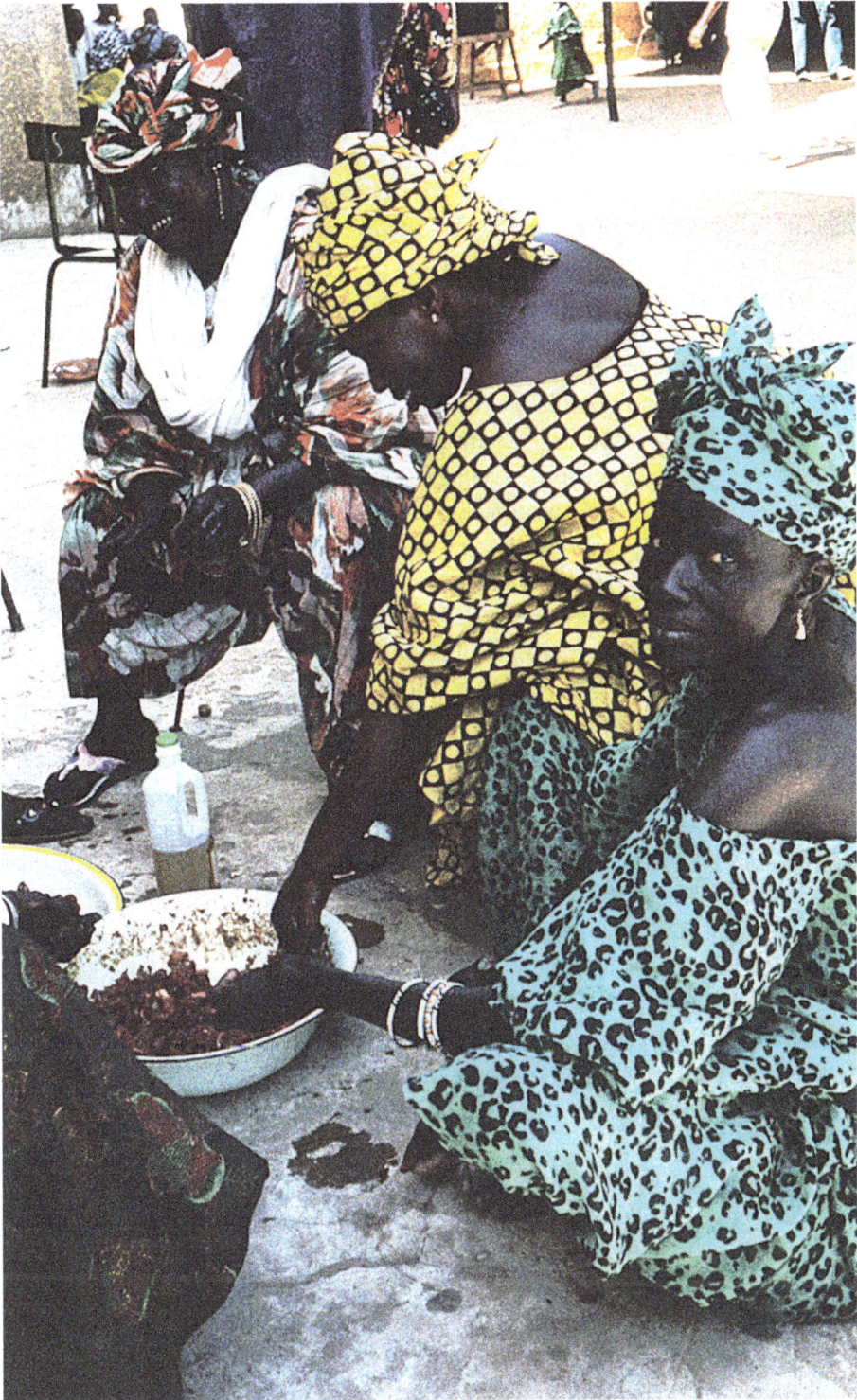

Guests on a name-giving party. Mbacké 1995.

form of contraceptive precautions while, with two boys and two girls, she was unwilling to have more children. It wasn't an easy situation, she complained. Fatou was also unhappy with the fact that the husband was having one child after another with the latest wife, whose health was jeopardized by the repeated pregnancies. Moreover, her many children gave the fourth wife a position of privilege in the household. I asked Fatou how many children the husband had in all. At the time of the interview the number of children born of the four wives came to twenty-two.

In second place after the husband, it was her co-wives who created most problems, she thought. By way of insinuation I was led to believe that she feared they could hurt her and her children through sorcery. It was practically impossible to defend oneself against this threat, she implied, since they lived almost shoulder to shoulder sharing kitchen duties and much else. I understood this to mean that she was referring to the risk of being poisoned by one of the co-wives. It was common knowledge that the fear of evil forces was always present in polygamous marriages. Fatou felt that she differed from the other members of the household and was therefore particularly exposed. Furthermore, she possessed more modern and more defiant ideas about health and cleanliness, and was often critical of the other women's standards of hygiene. She had of course gone to school in Thies and learnt about various diseases and how to combat them. This sort of knowledge made no impression on her fellow wives, who tended to regard her as putting on airs. Nor was the situation made easier when Fatou complained of the howling children in the fourth wife's hut. They disturbed Fatou's sleep at night, but the mother was offended.

More than anything else Fatou badly missed having a person she could take into her confidence in the large compound. Her mother had previously been her support and comfort in life, but she was now old and blind and seldom spoke. Fatou had an elder sister living in the village and she was a faithful ally, coming to Fatou's defence whenever the situation demanded. Fatou was much younger than her sister and had great respect for her. Nevertheless, she mostly felt ashamed at bothering the sister with her troubles. Feeling as she did that her environment had little trust in her, she would suffer from nervous periods of tension resulting in stomach pains and headaches.

The wives had followed the traditional pattern in polygamous households for cooking duties. The women and children ate their meals together out in the yard from a huge dish after a portion had been carried in to the husband, who more often than not had his meal alone inside his house. If he had guests visiting or male relatives, they would share the meal. Each wife with her children had living quarters of her own, which were not much more than a sheet-metal shanty of the simplest construction.

The women purchased the food required and cooked the meals in accordance with the following routine: one wife prepared breakfast two days in a row, another lunch and dinner also two days in a row, and the third was relieved of domestic work for the same period. The same procedure was followed when sleeping with the husband. Each wife went to him two nights at a time by turns, except during periods of menstruation and childbirth, when the woman was considered unclean for forty days after giving birth. The wife who prepared lunch and dinner shared the husband's bed for the two nights.

In Fatou's polygamous household the cost of the food was often financed in part by each respective wife, who competed with the others in offering the husband a tasty meal of particular variety. The only ingredients the husband was obliged to contribute were the daily ration of rice and the millet, which provided the breakfast porridge. The husband either appeared with the rice and millet he calculated were needed for those people eating that day or he gave the wife in turn a 500-franc note to cover the cost of food for the entire courtyard; hardly one euro. The wives paid most of their own expenses and those their children themselves, whether it concerned matters as distinct as school fees, medicine or clothes.

The subject of the village men's contributions to the household economy made Fatou especially upset. "Totally insufficient," claimed Fatou. "The cost of food can never be met with such a small contribution." In the normal course of the day five or six kilos of rice are required to satisfy the needs of a large household such as Fatou's, including the husband, the four wives and their children as well as an unknown number of relatives who often turn up around mealtime. Fatou said there might be as many as thirty people eating together with the family at times.

Later during my stay I consulted the village headman about what he considered was a reasonable amount of money a married man should provide towards the food bill, and he proved to be loyal to those men who gave a minimum amount to their wives' and children's maintenance. He made a point of telling me he was a rich man himself, with a lot of land his sons in time would inherit. This circumstance differed from that of the other villagers whose small fields of one and a half to two hectares were usufruct property. Besides himself, the only exception was of course the marabout, the largest landowner in the village. The headman was also the village shop-owner, with large stores of millet and groundnuts he had bought up from the village farmers when the price situation was most favourable. This occurred every year as everybody was obliged to sell more or less at the same time in order to pay off their debts after the harvest. In his opinion, against this background it was natural he should defray the costs of the food and other expenses in his polygamous household. He could afford it. If not, it was equally natural that the wives who were part of the household should help out with provisions. This was as far as we got in our discussions.

Consequently not only Fatou's husband but also many other village men let their wives bear the greatest part of the burden of maintenance. In addition, the women have the main responsibility for their children. The wives search the land around every day for twigs and branches to use as fuel; they fetch water; they pound and prepare millet, buy food and cook it; they wash their children's and their own clothes, and sweep the ever-present sand out of the house. On top of this comes the growing of crops for their own needs and for those of the husband, not to forget the time and energy spent working in the marabout's fields and those of the highest Murid leader in Khelcom. How are the wives able to acquire the money for the foodstuffs which their husband does not provide them with? It has to be by finding time, apart form the usual tasks, for other remunerative activities. The women devote themselves to trading at various market places in the vicinity of the village, including the sale of vegetables they have themselves grown. They busy themselves with the breeding of animals, manufacture and sale of groundnut oil, dyeing of cloth and embroidering dresses and petticoats....all while the men sit snoozing or chatting under the *neem* trees in the afternoon heat, or else – it went through my mind – flee the village.

I asked Fatou what she thought was the biggest difference between men and women in performing their tasks. Her reply was immediate: women are better at organising than men. They learn how to organise from their mothers when they are little. Above all it concerns planning domestic work in order to have enough time over to earn their own money. Why, then, must women address themselves at an early stage to earning money of their own? How does this tally with the fact that they are taught that men are to enjoy every benefit rather than the women since they stand for the livelihood? Quite simply because the men don't earn enough money. Or what they hand over to their wives is, at any rate, too little. They save up and watch every penny in order to acquire more wives. They are lazy, and just not 'on the ball', in Fatou's words. And they're not here most of the time! They are away from the village at other places in Senegal for long periods of time, or abroad. What's more, when they are short of money they would rather borrow from friends and acquaintances or from relatives than work hard to obtain what is required. The women are expected to remain at home, looking after the house and the crops. In other words, the men have got accustomed to the women with their scanty earnings keeping the family financially afloat, and assuming responsibility for the children in every respect.

Women's associations

This was plain speaking on Fatou's part. There was a sharp tone which surprised me. All the same, what she had said was nothing new. The fact that West Africa was the promised land of female organisations I already knew. In Mbacké I had witnessed the large percentage of women's lives devoted to the associations, and to the efforts to conjure forth money needed for female club fees. Fatou had previously referred to the fact that every woman in the village was a member of the associations which existed. Nobody could remain outside and expect to be fully accepted in village life. Here Fatou enabled me to see new aspects of the club and association phenomenon. Having your sights set on earning money and relying on the associations' communal spirit from early childhood, you had access to a sort of individual female savings box and financial reserve fund which was collective in nature at the same time. Such informal organisations inspired a certain degree of security and stability in a risky world with men whose capacity to earn a livelihood you could not rely upon. The principal strategy was geared towards finding means of making money, albeit in small quantities. The money would be immediately invested in rotating savings credit clubs of various types. Some of the money was used as financial aid at other women's family celebrations in self-help organisations of the *mbotaye* type. This aid was intended to be reciprocal. It meant you could always count on this help as credit when you needed it.

The same financial arrangements applied to the monthly and yearly fees paid into the religious associations dedicated to the marabouts. Regular payments and donations to the marabouts together with work performed for their benefit served as a type of insurance guaranteeing the benefit of the leaders' magical powers to bring success in trade and business and an entry into Paradise. Fatou made use of purely business terms whenever she spoke about her investments in a certain marabout or in religious figures such as mame Diarra Bousso. She and other women with her evidently thought such more or less mystical personages were profitable figures. They were purported to possess *barke*, capable of 'repaying' many times over the money that had been given them. In actual fact all forms of association and social activity were geared towards boosting the financial situation.

The members of the village *mbotaye* were solely married women. Each member paid 500 CFA francs and donated a package of soap at each family ceremony to the woman holding the family celebration, ensuring that at least part of her expenses were met. This avoided the risk of a competitive spirit growing among members. In Fatou's view, these female associations played an important part in maintaining well-being and stability in the community. She added that the initial fee for the newly married woman fluctuated between six and ten thousand CFA francs, money which usually went to bolstering the association's store of pots and pans and other kitchen utensils. Kitchen equipment was supplied on loan to the larger feasts and festivals when an extra number of cauldrons and water vessels were required.

Apart from *mbotaye*, gifts would be exchanged on a mutual pattern among the women under such names as *ndeye dické*, *sanni jamra* and *takri kharfit*. Such bonds led to the friends or neighbours competing with each other as to who gave most money or presents at the celebrations, which Fatou considered stupid. She maintained that the entire gift business giving *ndawtal* in which one woman would outdo the others merely added to the exorbitant waste that characterised family festivals. One's own resources were drained in order to impress others while at the same time there wasn't enough to satisfy hungry mouths in the family.

There were a number of other, more modern types of association in Fatou's village. One example is the *Groupement de Promotion Féminine* (Women's Economic Development Cooperative), which followed the traditional pattern of female organisations in its operations. Fatou explained to me how the women's fees when paid in made the association a sort of savings club. Through the village Development Aid Programme women as well as men could borrow money from a rotating savings fund which lent its existence to the system of rapid repayments. In the case of the women the sum of 10,000 CFA francs was such a small loan that the members complained it was not sufficient to initiate any profitable activity. Fatou, on the other hand, thought women would hardly be able to hold on to larger sums. Many instances had been recorded of husbands laying their hands on their wives' loans. They were notorious for their inability to repay, which often led to the women being without their loan and obliged to assume responsibility for a penalty charge. Fatou insisted that you couldn't say no to your husband if he demanded having access to the loan. Much better, then, to have your money tied up in several traditional loan organisations. There, at least, the money was inaccessible for the husbands.

Religious activities

Fatou declared that the village Murid association, comprising both a male and female section, for its women's part had the same committee as in the female cooperative organisation. In this *daira* members paid 1,200 CFA francs a year to Mor Mbacké. Other tasks were performed for the marabout's benefit within the framework of the association. Fatou was keen to tell me about the work she did for Mor Mbacké and for the Murids' highest leader in Touba. She was convinced that the specific deeds she performed by the sweat of her brow on behalf of these men would benefit her in both the short and the long term. It was therefore a joy to work for the *khalifa général,* a feeling she also wished to be able to share with me. There would be no greater pleasure for her, she said, than having me work alongside her at Khelcom. That way I would be able to appreciate that I had advanced a little way towards reaching Paradise. I could at least start to entertain the hope of a happy eternal life. Her account of how she takes part in collective farming in the village on behalf of Mor Mbacké is as follows:

> When the rainy season is approaching, every member of the *daira* reports and brings two kilos of groundnuts as seed for sowing. Then we go out to the field and sow. Later, following the harvest, we sell it all and the money is handed over to the marabout at his *magal* in Touba. The most useful thing we do at the *daira* is cultivating the field, because that is how we gain merits in God's eyes, and our husbands are happy and grateful to us. I donate 1,000 CFA francs to the marabout every year, and he'll put everything right for me. All the tasks to perform are important when working for our marabouts, as they provide us with their blessing.

The most important work, in Fatou's opinion, was done on the highest Murid leader's land at Khelcom. In this, she shared her conviction with Awa, the president of the Mame Diarra *daira* in Mbacké, as described in an earlier chapter. Fatou told me that until the middle of the 1990s, the place had been a vast wooded area, declared a nature reserve by the French from colonial times and used by nomadic tribes and their cattle. The khalif had pressed the government for permission to clear-fell the land, and together with the help of his disciples he had sown millet and groundnuts over the entire area. Each year the disciples were summoned by way of the marabouts belonging to the Mbacké Mbacké family to sowing and harvesting by turns. People lived and ate at the field under primitive conditions, toiling in scorching heat for about one week. The only breaks allowed were for prayers, meals and the night's sleep.

Fatou considered working for such a holy purpose to be more than a token of favour, in spite of its heavy nature and the hardships it involved. She was one of those people who accepted the tough life as almost a gift, and she described her experiences at the spot in something approaching ecstasy. She returned from the Khelcom adventure every year so much the thinner and worn out, not to mention the number of people it made ill from lack of sleep and proper hygiene. Persons lucky enough to enjoy good contact with the organisers – i.e. the marabouts and their families – were able to work under slightly better conditions, and their meals did not consist solely of cooked rice and millet couscous, Fatou said. I was already aware of this from what Awa in Mbacké had told me earlier. Fatou told me how she bent down in the blazing heat together with long rows of men, women and children, harvesting the groundnuts by hand from the dry, warm earth. The communal spirit that prevailed made her particularly happy. She stressed once more that she would willingly have shared this experience with me so that I could understand what it was like to live and function as a Murid.

When I finally asked Fatou to suggest what she thought was the most important aspect of religion for the women, how they should live as Murids, and what they could expect at life's end, she concluded in the following way:

> Since we have sworn our oath of obedience to the marabout, the *djebelu*, clearly we expect *barke* from him. He can't give us merits (*tiyaba*); only God can do that. We believe we can obtain *barke* by working for the marabout. If he issues an order, a *ndigël*, that we shall go to Khelcom and work there, I will receive *barke* for doing what he wants, and for accepting his prayers with cupped hands when he prays for me, obtaining what I wish to have.
>
> *Tiyaba* differs from *barke* in that it comes directly from God. If you come upon a blind man and help him across the road, God will give you *tiyaba*. Every charitable action on your part affords you *tiyaba*; God makes a note of it and keeps account of it, and He provides you with merits for the good you have performed. When you show *soutoura* by being loyal to your husband in every circumstance, this will be rewarded with *tiyaba* by God. That's why I put up with the wrongs my husband does me.
>
> *Yakar* is what gives me the energy to push on in times of difficulty. For me, *yakar*, expectations, are the same as hope. Imagine, Eva, that when you come here and put a number of questions about village life, this gives us certain expectations that you might have something to contribute to our village. We hope that when you return to Europe you might get in touch with someone in a development aid programme and suggest to him a donation for our village. That's having expectations of Eva, although one can never tell the future. Likewise we have expectations of the marabouts. And we have our hope for Paradise, too.

Other villagers' remarks

On asking a group of women in the village whether they were Murids, I was met by the joyful and proud cry of: "Yes indeed! Muridism means everything to us! We thank God we are Murids!"

Fatou could well have been one of the group saying the same, just as proud of being a Murid as the others. It may appear contradictory, demonstrating the happiness and satisfaction these women radiated after having revealed the structural and institutional shortcomings in evidence in the village, and the individual woman's private problems. Nonetheless, with Paradise a far-off illusion and the marabout within sight in a neighbouring village, the women seemed undeniably content. They were without financial resources, true enough. They desired larger loans in order for their projects to be profitable – loans at a low rate of interest, and loans fully accessible and entirely at their disposal, free from interference from their husbands. Running water, too, and a petrol-driven millet mill which functioned. Briefly, they wanted concrete, time-saving measures to be taken and elements reducing their workload, enabling them to have the time and opportunity to make money of their own.

The headman was asked what he thought about the women's associations. His view was that it was a good thing the women had all these associations. The fees involved were so small, he suggested, that it was not difficult to work to get money enough to pay for them. The expense was not heavy, he added, since you didn't have to pay all of the fees every month but often only once a year. The fee for the marabout's annual feast, for example, only had to be paid once a year. He assured me there was plenty of time for the women to save up the amount required. The family feasts, moreover, did not take place every month, either. The headman emphasized the fact that the most important feature of the associations was that the women could meet and get together and live in peace. They made each other's acquaintance there, and became accustomed to working together. "It's *mbolo*," he said, "working in unison is what they should strive for."

With this, he put his finger on what I interpreted as the central theme in the men's conception of women. Alone and individually they were conceived as dangerous and quarrelsome, inclined to resort to black magic in an effort to improve their lot. The best scenario was to have the women in groups where they could exercise control over each other. This was the men's view, and it was this view which played a dominant role in the community. The associations were like assembly points for women where the collective prevailed over the individual, and where the woman's more harmful features could be neutralised. On this issue all the men in Fatou's village appeared to be in agreement.

Senegal: some facts and figures

Capital: Dakar, with approximately 2 450 000 inhabitants, including the suburbs Guediawaye and Pikine
Area: 196 723 sq.km
Population: 13 635 927 (2014)
Currency: franc CFA (1 Franc CFA = 0,00152000 EUR; 100 Francs CFA = 0,15 EUR)
Type of state government: Republic. From 1982, Democracy.
Languages: French and Wolof (together with languages of other ethnic groups).
Ethnic groups: Wolof 43%, Halpulaar (also called Peul, Toucolor, Fulbe, Fula) 24%, Serer 15%, Lebou 10%, Jola 4%, Mandinka 2%, Moors, Europeans, Lebanese, Chinese, Mauritanians and Bassari approx. 2%.
Religion: Islam 95%, Christianity and native creeds 5%.
Within Islam, the following Sufi orders are common in Senegal: Tijaniyya, Muridiyya, Quadriyya, les Layennes. The majority are Sunni Muslims. There is a smaller group of Shia Muslims.
History: The inland areas of Senegal formed part of powerful West African realms from the 4th to the 17th century. An independent Wolof kingdom existed for 300 years, up until the 17th century. In 1445 the Portuguese settled on the island of Gorée outside Dakar. They were followed by pirates from the Netherlands, and later from the French, who founded the city of Saint Louis in 1659. The British, too, showed an interest in the coastal area in the period up to 1815. Trade was mainly in rubber and slaves. Senegal was officially made a French colony in Vienna in 1815 and remained so until 1958. The French divided up the native kingdoms, and soon an élite of Muslim leaders appeared. They partly cooperated with the French in matters of economy, mainly within the range of agriculture. During this period a groundnut cash crop scheme was initiated and prospered, particularly in the years prior to the outbreak of the Second World War. Groundnuts became the chief export item, a considerable source of income for the Muslim leaders and the French alike. In 1960 Senegal gained independence under Léopold Senghor as president of a single-party state, up until 1982. Then Abdou Diouf took over and introduced a multi-party system. Abdulaye Wade was elected president of Senegal in 2000 and was succeeded by Macky Sall in 2012, leader of the political party he founded in 2008, the *Alliance for the Republic*. Senegal is a secular state, as in French colonial times, with French as the first language in schools. A majority of the Senegalese are pious Muslims, belonging to Sufi branches of Islam, as members of different *turuq* (Arab.sing *tariqa*, Sufi orders or brotherhoods) under the leadership of powerful marabouts.

Senegalese emigration: Emigration of men and women from Senegal to Europe started off in conjunction with the huge drought which plagued the Sahara regions in the 1970s and destroyed large areas of the groundnut cultivation in Senegal. Migration increased still further as a result of the economic losses which followed the economic restructuring programme in Senegal. This programme, undertaken with the assistance of the International Monetary Fund and the World Bank from 1982 to 1992, led to the 1994 devaluation of the CFA franc in West Africa.

The Senegalese have always been a trading nation, travelling world-wide. Some of them had already settled in France and in other West African countries when the devaluation of the CFA franc took place. Others had started to seriously consider such a move. The rapid rise in the price of foodstuffs led to serious problems involving the supply of commodities. Inflation caused a rising number of Senegalese to decide to emigrate. As from the 1990s, they often chose to head for the south of Europe. People from the northern parts of Senegal, from the groundnut belt around Louga, Diourbel and Mbacké, but also as far south as Casamance, made for Italy and Spain. Many of them went on to reach the United States and Canada.

It is claimed that more than half a million Senegalese have emigrated and are living abroad. Exact figures are impossible to obtain. It was reported in a Senegalese daily newspaper that 45% of all those living in Senegal wish to leave the country for good, owing to unemployment and a general poor standard of living. Even if this item of information cannot be corroborated with verifiable proof, it reflects an attitude which is alarming with a view to the country's future. At the same time, however, the emigrants are tied to their home country to such an extent – not least of all by the force of their religion – that I do not believe that the large emigration implies any threat to Senegal's development. Large sums of money are regularly sent home by those who emigrate. Their remittances, apart from meeting food and living expenses, are also to some extent used in projects designed to improve the country's infrastructure. A number of the emigrants who have chosen to move back to Senegal are franchise holders starting up companies of various types.

Spain: some facts and figures

Area: 504 782 sq km
Capital: Madrid, around 6 600 000 inhabitants (2014)
Languages: Spanish/ Castilian, Catalan, Basque, Galician.
Type of State: Constitutional Monarchy.
Currency: Euro.
Population: 47 737 941 (growth rate: 0.81%); (2014)
Unemployment rate decreased to 22.37 percent in the second quarter of 2015 from 23.78 percent in the first quarter of 2015.
Unemployment Rate in Spain averaged 16.40 percent from 1976 until 2015, reaching an all time high of 26.94 percent in the first quarter of 2013 and a record low of 4.41 percent in the third quarter of 1976. Unemployment Rate in Spain is reported by the National Statistics Institute, 2015.

Immigration into Spain: In 1981, there were 198 042 foreigners registered as living in Spain. They made up 0.52% of the population.

In 2010, this number had increased to 5 708 940 equivalent to 12.2% of the country's total population.

In 2014 Spain had 4 676 022 foreigners, equivalent to 10% of the population. In 30 years, that is, Spain has changed from being a country with relatively few immigrants to one with quite the opposite. Until recently Spain figured among the countries in Europe which admitted most foreigners. The rate of immigration has, however, diminished of late and in 2012 inflows fell to 0.8% and outflows rose to 1.2% of the domestic population.

Latin Americans have previously formed the largest immigration group owing to their historical connections with what was the mother country, following the Spanish conquests of the 16th century. Nowadays this group comprises 36% of the total number, followed by western and eastern Europeans, Moroccans and – in fifth place – Africans, chiefly from West Africa. On January 1, 2008, the number of Senegalese in Spain was reported to be 61 383, according to the National Institute of Statistics (INE).

At the end of 2009 the number of immigrants was reported to have reached 4.8 million. This figure includes foreigners duly registered in the country and in possession of a valid residence permit. They are registered with the police authorities or at a department known as *Observatorio Permanente de Inmigración.* INE: *Instituto Nacional de Estadística, 2015.*

Senegalese in Spain: some facts and figures

Most of the Senegalese arriving in Spain find their way to Madrid, Alicante, Barcelona, the Balearic Isles and the Canaries.

In the area around Alicante and Murcia the Senegalese work in the agricultural sector, engaged in the cultivation of fruits and vegetables. In the cities and at the tourist spots on the coast they devote themselves to trade, plaiting of hair, and occupation of various types connected with the tourist industry.

Most of the Senegalese in Tenerife work in the tourist trade, in both the formal and informal sectors. An unknown number of Senegalese have come to the Canary Islands illegally. A number of Europeans, who have come to Spain on a tourist visa and have not renewed their papers before they have expired also live there.

TENERIFE: SOME FACTS AND FIGURES
Area: 2 034 sq. km. A National Park covers 48% of the island's total surface.
According to INE data of 1 January 2011, Tenerife has the largest population of the seven Canary Islands and is the most populated island of Spain with 908 555 registered inhabitants, of whom about 25% (220 902) live in the capital, Santa Cruz de Tenerife, and nearly 50% (424 200) in the metropolitan area of Santa Cruz – La Laguna.
Indigenous inhabitants were called the Guanches.
Capital: Santa Cruz, with approx. 225 000 inhabitants.
Highest mountain (also in Spain): El Teide, at 3,718 m. above sea level.
Foreign tourists visiting the island: from 3.5 to 4 million each year.
Senegalese with legal status on the island, 2009-12-31: 700 men and women.

The Canary Isles are situated outside the administration of the European Union Customs authority, but politically form a part of the EU. Exemption from duty is reserved for the Canary Isles as regards foreign business. Spanish goods are therefore less expensive than in the rest of Spain. The Canary Isles are included in the Schengen Treaty.

Figures pertaining to the number of Senegalese in Tenerife are, however, difficult to consider as definite since they do not take into account transfrontier workers, or those applying for political asylum, as well as those whose documents have expired and are applying for renewal of their visas and temporary residence permits. The number of foreigners living in Spain "sin papeles", i.e. illegally, is probably quite large, and liable to vary considerably over time. It is not possible to quote reliable statistics concerning the entire extent of immigration.

(INE: *Instituto Nacional de Estadística, 2011* and *2014*)

ON TENERIFE:
ANTHROPOLOGIST, SAINT, TOURIST

Las Verónicas, Playa de las Américas

"A L KATT YANGOK! THE POLICE ARE COMING!" This warning is yelled out in *Wolof* and is rapidly transmitted from one street vendor to the next all along the broad street. Within seconds, the men have kicked away the stacks of cardboard boxes that they have been using as tables to display watches and key rings. Everything disappears into pockets and bags. The women sweep up the sheets of plastic on which have laid T-shirts and hair-plaiting items. They stuff everything they can into their bags and then throw these into the cars that are parked nearby before everyone vanishes from view until the police have passed by on foot, on scooters or in cars.

Sometimes the street vendors are too slow – the women simply grab their foldaway stools, roll up the plastic sheets and run, laden with the goods they bear on their shoulders and the fear and anger burning in their eyes. The tourists who witness this stand by, watching and laughing as the Senegalese flee. What a spectacle! The odd client can be seated with half of their hair in tight plaits, waiting for their hairdresser to dare to return. And, after a while, they do indeed return and business is resumed as normal. However, sometimes somebody is caught for selling goods or services illegally and their wares are confiscated. If they have no visa or permit, they will also be deported. Many of the Senegalese who live and work in Spain do so illegally and this is why it is imperative to get away in time when the police arrive.

Just in front of McDonald's is an area known as Las Verónicas. Here, the street narrows and the stream of pedestrians is slowed by all the women sitting in a row with their goods displayed on the ground before them. The women are black and clothed in colourful, exotic dresses. The Spaniards working nearby scowl at them – they want the street cleared of vendors. A young man arrives with paper and pen and a bag over his arm in which he is collecting money from the Senegalese, both men and women. He writes down the amount he receives from each one. A little later, another man arrives and does the same thing. They are collecting *addiyya*, gifts of money for various marabouts back in Senegal. I watch as these men disappear off to other parts of the Playa de las Américas, where the Senegalese gather around marketplaces, or outside the palatial Santander Bank or along the esplanade.

The above description of a street scene from Playa de las Américas on Tenerife was from late 1996. Things looked much the same when I returned to the area in 1998, 2000 and 2001 but on my last trip, in 2009, the situation had changed somewhat. The tourists were still there and so were the Senegalese and I recognized some of them. New ones had arrived while others had left. The collections for the Senegalese marabouts were less frequent and now took place only once a week. With their regular checks, the police had reduced the number of street vendors but the hairdressers were still there, fashioning rasta plaits for their clients. But there was now a tension that had not been in evidence before. It was clear that the 'old' Senegalese looked askance at the 'new' ones. The divide was now between the illegal boat people, who had come from the Senegalese coast across open sea in recent years, and the established immigrants, who had become locally integrated over the years. The latter retreated to their homes in the mountain villages above Playa de las Américas when they were not selling goods or plaiting hair. They were no longer so helpful or generous towards the boat refugees as they had been initially. They had been arriving in increasing numbers and their helpers' resources were running dry. The situation was becoming untenable for the established Senegalese. I discussed the situation with the spokesperson of the Senegalese association on Tenerife when I visited in January 2009. He explained that most people now kept a low profile and tried to avoid becoming involved in the provision of help. There were apparently a few established Senegalese who were willing to take care of new arrivals but for the most part, everyone was waiting for the stream of newcomers to cease. And this appeared to be happening. Efforts by the European Union and intensified surveillance of the waters meant that fewer refugees arrived from Senegal by boat in 2009 and 2010 than in the previous year.

I was visiting Playa de las Américas and the area known as Las Verónicas because these are focal points for the Senegalese and very convenient for me to explore Muridism among Senegalese Murid women on Tenerife. Having studied the religious practices of Murid people in Senegal I now wanted to broaden my horizons and follow the women who migrated to Spain to work, with or without their husbands. These women are primarily involved in selling goods and services. My intention was to study how these women's religious, social and economic lives took shape away from their homeland. I wanted to compare the lives of Murid women in Senegal with those of female Senegalese immigrants on Tenerife. My methodology consisted of participant observation and interviews. Salimata Thiam, a university student from Dakar, worked with me as assistant and interpreter on all three field trips.

My focus in this work is upon the way in which women shape their identities in the meeting between a Spanish lifestyle and Murid values and customs. I look at the strategies these women use to act independently in Spain and in Senegal. It should be remembered that Senegalese men generally discourage women from trying to earn money outside the home and this can become a source of tension between men and women on Tenerife. However, the marabouts who pay visits to the Murid diaspora gather donations from both men and women. Everyone knows that this money is earned through trade, making rasta plaits or performing other kinds of work outside the home. The marabouts are more inclined to support than complain about women engaging in this kind of work. In exchange for their donations, the Senegalese immigrants expect both material and spiritual help. They wish to benefit from the *barke* that the marabouts are believed to be able to transmit to their disciples. These religious leaders are said to be able to provide their followers with whatever they ask for, which is usually to be able to avoid deportation or confiscation of goods by the police. Also, in both Senegal and on Tenerife, followers expect their prayers to these religious leaders to be rewarded with an easier passage to Paradise.

It is particularly interesting to examine the changing relationship between women and their religious leaders in Senegal as well as in the diaspora. It is the links between the marabout and his disciples and followers that form the foundation for creating and maintaining a Murid identity. Do these links persist among migrants? Does the attitude of Senegalese women towards the Murid leaders alter in any way while they are in Spain?

If a woman's view of and sense of obedience to the marabouts change, does this also affect her relationship to her husband, father and brothers and her understanding of herself as wife, mother, daughter and provider? It would be wrong to assume that female Muslim migrant workers necessarily become less pious or active in their religion while they are in a foreign country. The opposite may apply, as it does among men. Since most Murids equate national identity with religious identity, instead of searching for signs of weakening identity it may be more appropriate to ask in what ways national and religious identity are preserved among the diaspora.

Yakar: expectations

I stepped off the bus at Las Verónicas, Playa de las Américas one January afternoon, trying to track down a woman trader whose nephew I knew in Dakar. He had made out a letter of recommendation which I had in my possession. An address was lacking, however. All he knew was that his aunt was living at a big centre somewhere on the island of Tenerife. "It has to be Playa de las Américas", a Senegalese had told me in the town of Santa Cruz. "There's at least a hundred or so Senegalese living there." All the same, I could see no-one answering the description. "Try the market place on the outskirts", a Spaniard advised me. "That's where they can usually be found at this time of the day."

The market, right on the sea front, was crowded with people. Many Senegalese men were selling wooden sculptures, belts and other leather goods at their stands. A few women had hired tables to sell textile goods, mostly T-shirts and underwear. On the other side of the tables I glimpsed several Senegalese women working together plaiting the hair of one customer at a time, with trade and business carried on all around. I started a conversation with a man and enquired about the woman I was seeking. He knew who she was as soon as I mentioned her name. After a while he promised me he would go and telephone her apartment. I asked whether he was a Murid, whereupon he swiftly assured me: "Of course I am!" In order for him to understand that I felt quite at home among the Senegalese, and that I was eager to be accepted by them, I told him about the legends and tales I had heard and collected among Murid women in Touba and Diourbel concerning mame Diarra Bousso's life. I wondered whether there existed any association in the name of Diarra Bousso on Tenerife, in which case I wished to become a member. My enquiry took the man completely by surprise. It wasn't until much later that I realised what a sensation it was that a *toubab*, a European, came along talking about Amadou Bamba and Diarra Bousso. For the man I had approached, this very subject was the essence of his creed. No outsider could have an inkling of what the prominent figures in Muridism meant – he thought – and here a European woman turns up, standing right in front of him, chatting away about them as if it were the most natural thing for her!

Within a few seconds I found myself surrounded by people, mostly men, staring at me as if I were an angel just descended from the heavens. I could hear people muttering about a miracle having happened, surely a sign from God, and the fact that the marabout who was at that moment visiting Tenerife most certainly had to meet up with me. In a flash a meeting had been arranged at the flat of one of the men the following day, together with all the Murids who wished to attend. The marabout, whose name was serigne Moudou Kara Mbacké, would speak with me and hear me give an account of my knowledge of Muridism. The marabout, better than the market people, would be able to place this unique event in its proper context and explain to them who I really was.

Later on I was to meet the Senegalese woman I had been looking for. I decided to return the following day and stay the night at her place after the evening spent with the marabout at the home of my new Senegalese friend. She might somehow be able to help me sort out a few of the issues I was tackling concerning the commotion my presence was causing.

I met the man from the market place at the bus stop at Los Cristianos the following afternoon, and we travelled up to a little village in the hills overlooking the coast. He was still very excited over our meeting. That very day, the evening before, he had phoned his marabout in Senegal and told him what had happened. The latter had contacted the *khalifa général* in Touba. The caliph had said I was welcome to visit him, the very serigne Saliu Mbacké himself, the next time I was in Senegal.

Moudou Kara Mbacké would, then, be coming to the meeting in the village together with a large number of other Murids. In the 1990s Moudou Kara had not acquired the great fame within Muridism he was to achieve later. It was common knowledge that if you wanted to earn his respect it was advisable to give him what he expected. People were wary of him; he possessed magical powers which he would use on you if you displeased him. On the other hand, he was able to use these magical powers in your favour. Moudou Kara paid frequent visits to Tenerife. He would come once a month and expected 5,000 pesetas (some 30€) to be handed over by each Murid he met and prayed for.[1]

At a later stage his name has been associated with political unrest, especially in connection with election campaigns in Senegal. He has, however become something of a hero and model figure for many young people. Boys see in him a masculine ideal, while girls are drawn to his virile charisma.

We stepped into a four-storey building in a state of bad repair, entirely occupied by Senegalese. The meeting took place in a two-room flat on the third floor. The marabout partly lay on a mattress on the floor in the largest of the rooms while ten men sat in front of him on the bare floor. The rest of us – five women – sat on the sofa and the floor behind the men, who had their backs to us. Apart from the hostess, I found out that the female 'president' of Tenerife's Diarra Bousso association was there together with a few other women. They tended to come and go in the course of the afternoon, and were difficult to start a conversation with. The meeting began with a round of questions. The men put their questions to the marabout, who answered them in a thorough manner. We women, with the exception of the female president, retired to the bedroom where we sat on the bed and chatted. Finally we returned to the room where the marabout concluded the discussion with the men by requesting a donation to the poor at the mosque in his district in Dakar, as well as for books for educational purposes at the Koran school. He received a gift

---

1. In 1996 Spain was still using pesetas as national currency.100 pesetas was worth approx. €0.6 centimes.

of money from each of us, after which he gave a short prayer for all of us and delivered a blessing ritual, a *ñaan*.

A hot meal consisting of rice, chicken and vegetables followed the prayers. The men ate apart, sitting on the floor around a bowl, while we women enjoyed the meal in the bedroom, grouped around another, smaller bowl. Subsequently, the marabout summoned me to his presence. He wondered whether I could put into words what my interest in Diarra Bousso instilled in me. What had it produced? He was not content with my nervous and rather vague wording but insisted: did mame Diarra have anything to offer me, and in such a case, what? When I finally suggested that her example in the legends as the serene and submissive wife was interesting, he lit up. That's the way every wife should be, was his opinion, but sadly enough reality was something else. The marabout promised me he would ask his disciples to translate all the texts and interviews on mame Diarra I needed help with from the *Wolof* language into French. All I had to do was get in touch with him. He handed me a visiting card and seemed to be quite pleased with our little talk.

And now it was my turn to put the questions. The first thing I wanted to know was how he defined *barke*, the central concept in Muridism. His answer confined itself to a single word: "Power!" He then expanded a little, explaining that there was political power and religious power. "But don't the two interweave in each other?" I rejoined. Yes, by all means, Moudou Kara agreed, but he seemed to be suggesting that power which has its origin in religion is justified, which is not always the case with secular power. His standpoint on *barke* was certainly revealing with regard to the Murid establishment he represented, and differed significantly from the doctrine of classical Sufism, which lays more emphasis on divine power and inspiration.

My second question concerned the matter of the father figure in Muridism. I had learnt that it was the mother's moral behaviour which determines a child's future prospects. What role did the father play in the moulding of a child's personality? The men gathered around us suddenly looked worried. Had they made a miscalculation and siphoned in a feminist? What would the marabout be thinking? Only the female president looked a little stimulated. In the course of the afternoon she had shown signs of not fully appreciating the marabout's intervention when he had not let her finish what she was saying on an earlier occasion. Moudou Kara was, however, a seasoned debater. Without any hesitation he said he was quoting the Koran by asserting that a good fertile field must be sown by a good sower. Briefly, the man's role was to beget the child, and the woman's not to deny him this task, imposed by God. My host and the remaining guests looked satisfied, and they proceeded to sing a series of *khassaïds*. The women went on with their conversation in the bedroom, and I was given a lift down to the coast and back to the tourist spots.

Later I heard from a Senegalese that the marabout had said that I possessed *barke*. I had acquired it through my studies of the Diarra Bousso legends. My new friends from the Playa market place were of the opinion that I possessed a combination of worldly and spiritual assets which turned me into a valuable contact for them. They placed certain hopes in me, and expected new opportunities to arise bringing money and success through me. This rumour gradually spread among the Senegalese around Playa de las Américas, but my later visits led to disappointment for them. As time went by I was unable to prevent the heavy-handed interventions by the police, or to work miracles of any kind. I was reminded of the event in 2009 when I last visited Tenerife. One of the men who had been there that first time at the market place told me of the wave of *yakar* – expectation – which had been ignited among the Senegalese as I wandered among the stalls of clothes, leather belts and wooden sculptures and expressed my desire to become a member of the mame Diarra Bousso association on the island.

That time I was eager to gain access to the Murid migrants' religious institutions, whereas they were pining for *barke*. The marabouts, acting as middlemen between God and the people, in the common view had the power to give the disciples what they were demanding. But you had to placate the marabouts; otherwise they might not share their *barke* with other people.

Unfortunately, some of the marabouts lacked the power to its full extent. It was never quite certain whether they were able, or were willing, to help their disciples. This uncertainty was rife, and the marabouts were able to exploit this in their ambition to gather in gifts of money. I was drawn into this world of ideas, and was awarded by the marabouts and their disciples the same tag: I possessed *barke*, and nobody knew how much. It was all very confusing, both for me and for them.

What, then, did my colleague's aunt – a successful woman trader who belonged to a different Sufi order, the *Tijaniyya* – have to say about the excitement caused by my arrival at Playa de las Américas? She felt a small but well concealed contempt for the uneducated Murids who came from an impoverished area of Senegal and for their money-conscious marabouts. At the same time, however, deep down inside, she probably felt sorry for them. Time after time the Murids on Tenerife ended up spending their money on the marabouts. They constantly lived in the hope of making a success of things and acquiring all they asked for, instead of having to work hard to gain some control over their own lives. My presence on the island, however, may have brought into action unknown forces. I believe she decided to treat me with extra care in order to play it safe, in the event that I might just be in possession of some special capacity. She also donated money to the visiting Murid marabouts at times in order to be on the safe side, protecting herself from unpredictable evil forces. All the Senegalese I met on Tenerife inhabited a similar religious universe in their quest for well-being and eternal life in Paradise.

The same evening I left the meeting in the mountain village, I accompanied this friendly tradeswoman down to the beach promenade so as to be there when she sold her wares. She usually chose working hours at times when the Spanish police would be having their meals, normally between 2 and 4.30 p.m. and 9 and 10.30 p.m. While other Senegalese would sell and plait hair until the early hours of the morning, the same woman assured me that her working hours were the surest if you wanted to be there on the street pavement relatively undisturbed by the police. She had her *permiso de residencia*, her permanent residence permit in Spain, and thus did not need to leave the country every three months in order to extend her visa. The problem she shared with almost all other Senegalese who participated in street vending was that she was unwilling to pay the expensive fee required to obtain a permit to sell in the streets, the *permiso de venta ambulante*.

This woman laid out her articles of trade on a plastic sheet on the ground, while tourists strolled past on their evening walk close to the beach. There wasn't much to choose from – a few small statues made of wood nestled behind a couple of felt hats which her daughter in the United States had sent over and asked her to sell for her. Right at the front lay a number of colourful elastic hair rings, the sort that young girls use to tie their pony-tails. In addition I counted three pairs of Moroccan-style leather slippers. Indeed, a rather modest assortment. The explanation for this well-situated tradeswoman's handsome earnings, I discovered, lay in the fact that she mostly sold wholesale. She bought and sold in bulk to customers in both Spain and Senegal. Her apartment and her balcony were crammed with cardboard boxes and bags full of merchandise. She slept together with her daughter and three other women on mattresses in the only room the floor of which was not jammed with articles. There were no basins in the bathroom, yet there, too, were plastic bags heaped one on top of another right up to the ceiling.

In striking contrast, however, was the elegant, spacious villa the woman had had built in Dakar with the money she earned from her activities both within and outside Spain. When I visited Dakar a few years later, I was shown around the house by one of her daughters. The villa contained six bedrooms each with its en suite bathroom on the upper floor, and large beautiful sitting rooms on the ground floor. Outside the house a guard, fully armed, sat and kept watch. He had been employed to ward off all the acquaintances and distant relatives who suddenly appeared like jack-in-the-boxes to claim their close relationship and squat down there for food and shelter, as soon as the house had been built and was ready to move into. The guard was also the woman's chauffeur whenever, perhaps once or twice a year, she came home to

Dakar and wished to travel around in her white Mercedes. The car stood next to the house, a tempting object to steal, and a further strong motive for the presence of the guard 24 hours a day. Part of the house, however, was rented out temporarily to a woman who sold cosmetics bought in the Canaries. The entire building looked like an emigrant's dream come true; it was all the work of this tradeswoman, a widow and mother of twelve children. She had come ten years previously from the capital of the Ivory Coast, Abidjan, with no possessions of her own, to start a new life as a woman trader in Tenerife.

Back at the pavement where the tourists were strolling by, I wandered over to a middle-aged Senegalese woman who was sitting in the dark a little way from most of the other street vendors. She had arranged her leather belts on a sheet of plastic, and I started to talk to her. She told me she had decided to sell belts for the simple reason that they were easy to cart off whenever the police made an appearance. Then she added that she had difficulty in running because of what she had in her shoes. This gave me a bit of a start as I remembered what I had been told in Santa Cruz about the drug trade in southern Tenerife. Apparently the Senegalese women were supposed to stuff narcotics in their shoes when travelling between the two continents and in this way obtain free air travel. Was this her way of making it known to me that she had drugs for sale if I was interested? Yet she was, on the other hand, a very robust person and could quite naturally find it difficult to dash off at full speed in shoes that weren't made for running. I decided to change the subject to a more spiritual issue, the annual pilgrimage to Porokhane. The woman informed me of who was in charge of applications for the trip, and stated that 42 persons, men and women, had already registered for the journey to attend mame Diarra's pilgrim site. Application fee was 5 000 pesetas (30€), to be paid in as soon as possible.

I remained silent for a few seconds and thought about what I wanted to ask her next. Then, out of the blue, came: "I love you, Eva." I thought I'd heard wrong, but suddenly came her explanation. She felt a great need of love, and it had been such a long time since she had experienced an enjoyable intimate relation; the men in Tenerife were not at all to her liking. All they did was gossip about the Senegalese women among themselves, and make every effort to disgrace the women. Instead, she had decided to pick out a woman she took a liking to, and I was now her choice.

I was of course bowled over by this situation and at first didn't know what to say. At the same time I realised it was my interest in the Porokhane pilgrimage which had aroused her feelings and given her the wrong signals. I had thought she was in charge, and she had misinterpreted my interest in her. Once more my presence had roused certain expectations without me being aware of it. My assurance that I was feeling tired and needed to go home met no protest, however. The woman remained at the beach, and one of the young Senegalese drove me home. The next morning all of us who had been at the beach trading area had breakfast together in the flat I had shared with the others. After that, I never again saw the woman who had declared her love for me. On my return to Tenerife two years later, it turned out that she had moved home to Senegal.

I consulted one of my friends in Dakar as to what really lay behind that declaration of love. My friend was of the opinion that pretty well everything was on sale in Tenerife, even love in some form or other. I recalled then that the neighbour living in the flat next door to where I had spent the night was a woman from the Ivory Coast who shared a relationship with a Spanish woman. The Spanish girl's mother financed the rather expensive lives these two women led. Could it be that the fact that I came alone, with no husband, and engaged in a special study of women and their religion, was construed along similar lines? There might be something in such an interpretation. In hindsight I realise how unprepared I had been in analysing the way my informants, as I called them in my notes, saw me. I had attributed to these people such a role, so to speak, without them being aware of it. They involved me in their lives, as it were, in what would be for them a natural manner, and had their own expectations of me. It all seems so very clear, thinking back, and I can't help giving myself an embarrassing nudge at my earnest attempts to come to terms with Muridism and those women's religious lives in Tenerife at that time, when I was right amongst them.

Then I recalled the words that Fatou, frustrated and yet hoping for a better future, uttered in her village in Senegal (chapter 8):

> *Yakar* is the driving force which eggs me on in moments of difficulty. For me, *yakar* is the same as hope or expectation. Just think, Eva, when you come here to our village and ask your questions about us, we start to have certain expectations that you will be able to contribute something to our village.

I realised that the female Senegalese immigrants in Tenerife adopted similar attitudes. Expectations that the marabouts and the Europeans would be of help in acquiring the material benefits were combined with the spirit of 'do it yourself' and 'we are each the architect of our own fortune' which met the immigrants in Spain. Support was necessary from other quarters apart from one's own efforts in order to deal with the pressure from families at home; those people who were constantly expecting financial assistance and expensive presents. The hope for fortune in this world and eternal life in Paradise was the star guiding them through all the difficulties they met in the diaspora and in the home country.

TIME IS MONEY:
SENEGALESE WOMEN AT
PLAYA DE LAS AMÉRICAS

Everyday life

URING THE 1970s MOST Senegalese wanting to emigrate made their way to France. Ten years later Italy and the United States began to be attractive migratory destinations for Murids from Senegal. Soon it was Spain's turn, including the Canary Islands, the popularity of which as a target for emigration gradually increased during the 1980s and 1990s. The number of immigrant Senegalese in Tenerife, according to police records, reached approximately 100 persons in 1996, while the number of people living there illegally was unknown. 85 persons had been deported during the period January-October 1996 for lack of residence permit and work permit. As a point of comparison, I was told in July 1998 that the number of Senegalese men legally residing at Playa de las Américas was 150. I calculated the number of women as about 20 per cent. In 2009 the chairman of the Senegalese association in Tenerife claimed that the number of Senegalese in possession of a permanent residence permit in the southern half of the island was about 600. Nobody could hazard a guess as to how many were there illegally. The normal pattern of migration has been for the men to make the journey leaving wives and children back home in Senegal. Those women who accompanied their husbands did so primarily in their capacity as housewives. As from the 1990s, however, women have begun to venture out in the world, mostly to the United States and to Spain, in order to earn their own money through trading and plaiting hair. I am referring here first of all to those women from Dakar, Saint Louis and the Groundnut Belt whose lives as immigrants I am personally acquainted with in Tenerife and Madrid. Most of them belonged to the Sufi order called *Muridiyya*. Around Alicante in south-eastern Spain and the surrounding areas where there are large fruit and vegetable plantations, other Senegalese ethnic groups can be found who do not devote themselves

At Playa de las Américas, Tenerife: nocturnal scene, Senegalese women selling detachable plaits. 2000.

primarily to street and market selling. They are agricultural labourers who to some extent come from Casamance in southern Senegal.

Those Senegalese women who emigrate either on a temporary or on a longer term basis are relatively few. In Spain they amount to about 20 per cent of the number of the men, as in the 1990s. Their preference is to establish themselves at tourist spots, and therefore they try to find their way to the Canary Islands, the Balearic Isles and the Spanish east coast, as well as to the cities of Madrid and Barcelona. The female immigrants from Senegal I got to know in Tenerife during a number of summers made up a relatively homogeneous group. Most of them belonged to the same so-called 'caste', the *griottes*, and the same ethnic group, the *Wolof*, and they came from the same, or almost the same, districts (Louga, Saint Louis and Dakar). Together with me they would talk freely about themselves as of one big family, emphasizing the fact that, just as in their villages back home, they experienced what they called *mbolo*, that is, fellowship, peace and strength in being together.

Most of the women were not used to travelling, nor were they particularly well-educated or had any knowledge of languages. More often than not they were illiterate persons who had decided to leave their city, suburban slum or village in the hope of being able to carve out a better living for themselves and for their families. Behind the official explanations for their departure from the home country – poverty and unemployment – there were sometimes other factors involving female emigration. It might concern escaping the clutches of a violent husband, a failed matrimony, a history of infidelity or a petty crime. In this respect the women differed somewhat from the male immigrants. Some of the men had been students who had failed to find a job which could bring them a reasonable income, and were consequently both able to read and write. Others only brought with them what their childhood Koran school had taught them.

When the female immigrants arrived at Tenerife they mostly knew only their own African language. The men on the other hand often spoke the French they had picked up in their home country, and quickly got to learn a little Spanish. The women appeared to be mildly interested in speaking the tourists' languages. This, together with their inability to count and read, stood in their way when dealing with tourists. It was only when the foreign tourists were sufficiently drunk that the Senegalese women seized the opportunity and gained the upper hand. They therefore did their best business in the evenings and at night. They had learnt the value of the various currency notes by their colours.

On my visit in 2001 I found that many of the women traders who had come a few years previously had learnt to count much better, and mastered quite a few Spanish words and phrases. Some of them were using calculators to

At Los Cristianos, Canary Isles: various products on sale and plaiting hair. 2000.

produce the prices they would show their customers. The apprehension they had felt in a foreign environment far from home had dissipated. It seemed as though they had grasped the fact that trading with tourists, just like at home with Senegalese, was a matter of communication and not merely making the quickest possible profit.

Among the twenty-five women traders at Playa de las Américas I interviewed, sometimes with the help of my Senegalese assistant, there were a variety of ages represented. Women between the ages of twenty and thirty dominated, while nobody was over fifty-five. A few of the women lived together with their husbands and children in the villages up in the mountains above Playa de las Américas. Others were divorced, unmarried, or had husband and children in Senegal. Geographically, distances between the Canary Islands and West Africa are relatively small and contacts with the home country quite lively. The use of cellphones between members of the family in the different countries was quite widespread, as were conversations via public telephone booths.

The business dream of most of the women was to be able to travel freely between Senegal and Tenerife and make the most of their access to both worlds. The purpose was to buy products in Senegal and sell them in Tenerife, and vice versa. Acquiring a residence permit was one step towards this end. Such a permit in Spain is obtained after living there for five consecutive years without incurring any trouble with the Spanish legal authorities.

The really big earnings were hardly feasible through trade in the street and in the market place, while the wholesale activities were a more profitable business. The largest incomes came from criminal trade in narcotica, smuggled cars and forged visas. This sort of activity was not performed by the women I got to know in Tenerife, as far as I could make out. Apart from plaiting hair, the women sold almost without exception handbags (falsely marked), T shirts, underwear, belts and socks while the men concentrated on sun-glasses, watches (falsely marked as well) and other goods. Capriciousness was a hallmark of the trade. The immigrants' situation was of course rather delicate. Sometimes they suffered from a dearth of tourists, or else the police seized their wares in an unexpected raid. Quick profits could be made, but quick losses too.

The size of the women's income on Tenerife depended more than anything else on whether they had their husbands with them or not. The women who were most efficient and earned more were those who had come without either husband or children. This enabled them to concentrate on the demanding work they were engaged in and the various trips that were involved. A number of 'marriages of convenience' took place among the women who had arrived alone. These were arranged between Senegalese men in possession of a residence permit and Senegalese women without valid documentation.

Such an arrangement evaded the problem of applying every three months for a new visa, a compulsory condition for those without a residence permit. At times there might be a dispute over what the marriage of convenience was supposed to involve. It was difficult for the women to achieve a balance between their independence and their dependence on the men. They were sometimes forced to accept having a relation with a man in order to avoid appearing as fair game for all the other fellows. Some had found a solution by surrounding themselves with their brothers and sisters, thus lessening the risk of getting married to a man who made a financial profit out of his wife. To judge from some of the women's talk, such cases were not uncommon. The stories I heard mirrored the fear often latent back home in Senegal. The wives were anxious that the men might accumulate assets behind their backs and one fine day present them with an unwanted co-wife.

The women who lived unaccompanied by their husbands in Tenerife mostly squeezed themselves into the same flat in order to save money, with five or six of them sharing a room and sleeping on mattresses on the floor. They took turns in cooking Senegalese food for everybody in the household. Whatever ingredients were unavailable on the island were brought over from the home country by fellow-countrywomen and sold to them. This applied to fashion, too, as women returning to Playa sold the clothes and materials they had acquired in Dakar. As a rule, every effort was made to follow what was going on in Senegal; the women found moments of leisure and pleasure not only in the field of entertainment but also through videos showing pilgrimages and festivals in connection with some of the solemn religious occasions.

The lives of all of the Senegalese in the Spanish diaspora were governed by the host country's requirements concerning visa, residence permit and work permit. Anybody without the proper documentation led a life in constant fear of the police authorities. As from the end of the 1990s women stopped selling wooden sculptures in the streets. Instead, lighter goods were preferred which could be smartly packed away should the police stumble upon the women traders. Trading in wooden sculptures was confined to wholesale activities, and plaiting customers' hair came to dominate business. Multi-coloured loose plaits were applied to little girls' heads, or false hair was plaited into hair styles, mostly for young people.

Many of the Senegalese women had no means of going home to Senegal once they had settled in on the island. It was quite simply too expensive to leave Spain every three months and return with a new stamp in their passport. Sometimes, too, out of pure negligence they would forget and exceed the date of expiry of their visa. If they left Spain, there was always the risk they might not be able to return without the valid documentation. In the face of such circumstances, the Senegalese women made the most of adapting their lives and their Senegalese traditions to the Spanish community as smoothly as possible. When festivals were held to celebrate a wedding or a name-giving ritual, or for the big religious ceremonies like the day for the sheep sacrifice – *Tabaski* – the women would show off their most attractive dresses. These were the occasions when the immigrant women could parade their expensive clothes and jewellery.

For those Senegalese who belonged to the *Wolof* and *Halpulaar* ethnic groups, and were *geer*, i.e. not members of a professional status group, plaiting human hair was properly speaking a taboo activity. It was considered improper to handle other people's bodies, hair and nails. In Tenerife, however, this taboo was observed less than in the home country. I have only met a handful of women who refused to plait tourists' hair for this reason. For them the problem was solved by not plaiting hair out in the street where they could be seen. In one instance a teenage girl was ashamed of her mother plaiting other people's hair. The daughter couldn't accept her mother's way of earning money and instead wanted to go home to Dakar where the proper distances between human beings were observed and maintained in a manner she was accustomed to.

Most people, nevertheless, disregarded the taboos and seized every chance to make a little money, not least through plaiting hair. They couldn't afford to foster prejudices in Tenerife. On the other hand the male Senegalese immigrants never plaited other people's hair. Admittedly, however, there did exist in Tenerife certain limits which could not be exceeded between the different social groups. The dominant female group at Las Verónicas was made up of *griottes* and persons belonging to similar low-status 'castes'. At other more fashionable places, such as near the large bank building and along the beach promenade, a socially more mixed group of Senegalese women was in evidence, but among them there were no *griottes*. Most of those selling there were *geer*, the social group who regarded themselves as free and independent.

The new circumstances that life in Tenerife offered these Senegalese women underlined the importance of time, or rather lack of time, as a factor in day-to-day life. Never before had they felt the pressure of time in such a way in their home country. In the diaspora the scarcity of time wielded a strong influence on their economic, social and religious lives more than anything else. Clearly there was a lot of money to be made, but there was precious little time to do it in. A day's twenty-four hours flew by far too fast, the women thought. They gave themselves little rest, bustling through long working hours which were only shortened by the police's crackdown on the street-vending community during certain hours of the day. Then was the moment to keep a safe distance, with time over for bulk purchase of fresh goods.

The Murids of Tenerife see the year as divided into different cycles of recurrent tasks and rituals, duly arranged in patterns of time and space. This partly concerns the annual cycle of Islamic festivals, common to all Muslims, and partly the big specifically Murid events, particularly the *magal* in Touba, and of secondary importance the pilgrimage to Porokhane. On these occasions Senegalese around the world who belong to the *Muridiyya* wish to travel back to their country and take part in the various ceremonies and rituals. In addition, there exists a special time cycle connected with the tourist season in the Canary Islands. The truly big earnings are to be had in the summer months and in December and January, particularly around Christmas and the New Year. Some years the time for good business coincides with the period when the religious festivals are held. The Muslim calendar is flexible, depending on the movements of the moon. The tourists' calendar, quite clearly, is not. Very many of the tourists plan their visits to Tenerife in accordance with the possibilities of spending sunny holidays when northern Europe is at its darkest. The immigrants, however, sometimes have to make the choice between not missing out on the big earnings at stake, and relinquishing them in favour of the religious and social values of going home to Senegal and attending the various rituals, possibly together with their families.

The Spanish inhabitants afford all the Senegalese in Tenerife the same treatment, regardless of the social status the immigrants might have among themselves. For the Spaniards the Senegalese are *negros* – blacks – from whom they distance themselves by treating them as little more than air. My assistant, Salimata, from Dakar, told me how unpleasant it was that Spaniards tended to look right through her as though she didn't exist. Many other Senegalese confirmed this feeling. I myself gained the impression that they were met with an air of contempt or in a patronising fashion, by tourists and Spaniards alike. Business alone brought Spaniards and the peoples of Africa together in Tenerife. The police view the Sufi order of Muridism in Tenerife as a kind of internal African mafia whenever they meet representatives of the movement.

Senegalese of different social groups mix more easily in Spain than in Senegal. However, those *griottes* who have made good money and return home generate a certain social mobility because of their newly acquired wealth. The offer of expensive presents from persons of low social status to people of a higher ranking in Senegalese society may lead to a casual shift in social relations, although a deeper change in the make-up of the Senegalese social organisation would not appear to be imminent. The most obvious sign of this is a closer study of how marriage partners are chosen. Endogamy – marriage within one's own social group – is still a dominant factor both within so-called 'castes' and outside, among those known as *geer*. Members of the different ethnic groups seldom intermarry, and much less in Senegal than in the diaspora.

At Los Cristianos, Canary Isles: plaiting hair and minding babies. 2000.

The physically tough pace at which the women worked and the mentally trying estrangement they felt tended to wear them down. I often wondered to myself how long they would endure this strenuous life. They claimed that the dream of a better life in Senegal kept them going, and that they as Murids did not share the sad reality of life in Spain, with its racial aspects and police harassments. They were boosted by a common vision of the holy city of Touba in the home country. In Senegal these same women were mainly experienced as temporary visitors showing much *teranga* – generosity – clearly alluding to their hotly desired gifts and donations of money. In the imagination of those at home, the immigrants were living in a gold-rush Klondike beckoning them back to Spain as soon as they had fixed a new visa. None of the visitors made any attempt to disillusion the family in Senegal. Any Senegalese who was unable to conform to the image of a rich emigrant simply did not go home, so as to avoid being exposed to his or her relatives' disappointment and irritation.

Religion

Shortage of time and the lack of access to living quarters within a reasonable distance of the work place produce an effect on religious life. Prayers are rationalised to take place in mornings and evenings only. The evening prayer session will include the five occasions prescribed for prayers during the day which have been skipped. As with all Muslim believers, the month of fasting, Ramadan, is carefully observed. The big Muslim ceremonies are celebrated, and Spanish food, which might contain pork and pig fat, is avoided. In other words, their religious practices are adapted to the Spanish surroundings without the distinctive characteristics being lost. But the hours go quickly by, and Time rears its ugly head to hustle and bustle the women in a way they all complain about. "Time leads the way for me here in Tenerife", said one woman trader to me, "while it's me who leads the way for time back in Senegal". The work they perform and the money they earn are seen by the women as a form of religious act, as long as they donate money to the marabouts and live as true Murids and believers of Islam.

On Tenerife the Murid identity is linked to a sense of community and access to assets of a kind even non-Murids find attractive. Therefore the latter, too, make their financial contribution to the Murid religious leaders. Thus many non-Murids are also incorporated into the wide network of lucrative traders. The successful woman trader I got to know at Playa de las Américas made regular contributions to the Murid fund-raising drives for this very reason, even though she belonged to the Sufi order *Tijaniyya*. She required all the customer contacts she could get through the Murids.

The Senegalese women in Tenerife went about their business in an atmosphere blending spirituality and crass financial considerations. Marabouts and money travelled in a steady flow over the sea between the two continents from and to the religious centre,[1] while all the time the disciples on the geographical edge of Muridism were endeavouring to provide for their families in the impoverished home country, paying huge sums of money to the religious leaders. Simultaneously they acquired religious and social prestige in Senegal and among other Murid diaspora groups according to the size of the sums of money they managed to accumulate. In a certain sense these disciples were not at all peripheral but rather of great importance for the marabouts, and for Muridism's continued existence and future expansion.

While the Murids were present on Tenerife their contacts with the religious leaders underwent a certain change. In Senegal the followers or disciples normally meet up with their marabout no more than once a year. On Tenerife the individual follower achieves a much closer contact with the marabouts, who pay frequent visits to the followers in order to pray for them and gain access to some of their accumulated capital in the form of gifts. Whether the visiting marabouts are accommodated at a five-star hotel, in a private apartment or in the house run by the Tenerife *daira*, the immigrants come to see them, deliver their financial contribution, and request a religious intercession. The money facilitates personal contact between follower and marabout in Tenerife, and this situation applies to men and women alike.

The Tenerife Murids live their lives on the island with Touba and Amadou Bamba "deep in their hearts", as they put it. The male Murids particularly discuss religion a lot and very often. They read booklets in *Wolotal – Wolof* written with Arabic characters – and they sing *khassaïds*, maintaining close contact with other active Murids. Their brotherhood is based on a collective creed, and they constantly refer to this creed. Such is not the case with the women. They seldom discuss religious subjects among themselves, something which the men criticise. The women are in the habit of leaving the room as soon as the visiting religious 'specialists', as they call themselves, or marabouts offer their interpretations of the texts and put questions to the male Murids. It would seem the women show no interest, but the fact is that the women on the contrary do involve themselves in religion and their involvement is most serious. When, through the medium of my assistant, I asked the female Murids a number of questions of a religious nature, I was given the same type of replies as the men gave, expressed with the same degree of intensity and active interest.

What the men had told me in the shape of criticism was in a sense true, however: the women spoke mainly of the purchase and sale of goods, of the Spanish police harassment, of the moments of stress, of the advantages and

---

1. See Evers Rosander in Eade and Coleman, 2004.

disadvantages of selling in the street or in the market place, and of applications for visas and permits. "We're not living here, we're working", was a constantly recurring phrase you heard. Yet the women did work much harder than the men, and got more deeply involved in their work and in providing for the family. They repeatedly insisted upon how heavy the burden was of keeping for the household, plus the fact that they actually supported the whole of the family back home in Senegal with their income. Moreover, they were eager to save up so as to buy a house for themselves and their children home in Senegal. They would then be able to live their lives without having the husbands' other wives and children around them.

"And what about a house in Touba?" I might ask. "That's not for me," the answer would be, "that's for the marabouts". As soon as the subject of Touba and Porokhane was broached, their tone became more intimate and they would express themselves more easily. The women professed to have an infinite love for serigne Touba, and were willing to make enormous financial sacrifices in order to travel to Touba for the annual pilgrimage. One of them told me how she had bought an exquisite perfume in Mecca and asked the person in charge of Amadou Bamba's tomb in Touba to spread the beautiful aroma there. "We live for Senegal, for Touba, and for Khadim Rassul Touba", said another woman. Just like the others, she claimed to be in Tenerife only to earn money, but lived in as Senegalese a way of life as possible in regard to food, clothes, language and religion, with her sights set on Touba and her home in Senegal.

Women and the Tenerife-Touba Association

The religious association bearing this name established its headquarters up until 2005 in Santa Cruz, the capital of Tenerife little more than an hour's bus ride from Playa. It wasn't always that easy to get free and attend the monthly meetings of the *daira*. Women living at the southern end of Tenerife considered it too far, unnecessarily expensive and time-consuming. The general view was that one had done what was expected with one's gift of money, the *addiyya*. Those women resident in Santa Cruz had to cooperate and cook the meals which were served at the meetings. Other women usually stayed where they were and sent along their subscription together with the men, who generally took part on a more regular basis.

The association, dedicated to Amadou Bamba, met in the home of the president, the venue selected for all the meetings that were arranged. In addition to the fund-raising operations, the men sang the habitual religious songs. Any women who were present would listen in silence, or would be in the kitchen cooking. In the summer, at the height of the tourist season, few would find time to attend. Nowadays the association's headquarters are situated in the village of El Fraile in the south of Tenerife where most Senegalese are living.

In August 1998 thirty or so men had turned up for the meeting, and six women. In the course of the afternoon the men came and left at irregular intervals, making it difficult to register how many had actually been on the premises. The main activity, as far as I could gather, was dealing with financial matters and collecting funds. They all, it seemed, were in a hurry to get back to their sales spots and not lose business.

The women at the meeting in Santa Cruz seemed to be quite marginalised. They sat on a balcony and chatted, while the men went through the financial matters, discussed plans for their various activities, and sang their *khassaïds*. My assistant was bored with the *daira* proceedings in Santa Cruz, she told me afterwards, something she had never experienced at her own *daira* in Dakar. It was an association for women only where the members did not feel ill at ease. In the absence of men the women were able to speak their minds and take centre stage. They enjoyed their own management: a female president and board. Such a female association was in embryo on Tenerife with a woman president, but she was often away on trade and business and unable to give regular attention to the various activities. In addition, as already indicated, she did not receive much support, and the situation was unstable as a result of the women's intensive work rate and frequent travels. Concentration on economic activity in what was formally, at any rate, a mixed male/female association led to the women occupying a secondary role.

The men were loath to hand over control where big sums of money were concerned. My assistant's comment is worth reflecting upon: when the women join the men, as in the mixed *daira* in Santa Cruz, they seem to adopt a passive role and remain powerless. The female members of the Tenerife association appear more segregated than ever from the men and from the power centres.

In 1997 the members of the association handed over some 11 million CFA francs to the highest Mourid leader in Touba, a considerable sum of money coming as it did from a single association. Comparison may be made, for example, with what a women's organisation in the Senegalese town of Mbacké had managed to accumulate in 1994: 150 00 CFA. Large material efforts on the part of the immigrants are of course essential if they are to retain the respect of people back home in Senegal. Murids living in Tenerife otherwise run the risk of appearing not only marginalised but mean and ungenerous. The fact that they are living outside the local community far from their home environment, contagiously near Europeans who are not even Muslims, is a handicap for these Senegalese in Tenerife, and needs to be compensated by generous donations, interpreted as a sign of God's benevolence.

Visiting marabouts at their hotel

The aura of 'holy space' and religious aesthetics which the marabouts' presence generates in Senegal is completely non-existent for the general population in the Canary Isles. All the religious images of Murid leaders depicted on cars, buses and walls in Senegal underline the deep popular roots of Muridism and other Sufi orders in the home country. The frequent visits paid by 'big' reputable Murid marabouts to Tenerife may be construed as a form of compensation, an important line of contact with the Muslim world and with Senegal. The visiting marabouts stay for the most part at the house run by the *daira*, where they receive their followers. As already described in earlier chapters, the leaders offer advice on matters of religion, relate a series of religious legends, impart blessings, promising to pray for their disciples and followers in the diaspora, and finally obtain donations of money.

The position these marabouts occupy in the Murid hierarchy is a determining factor for the kind of treatment they are given and the respect they are shown by the Senegalese in Tenerife. The closer the visiting marabout is related to the Mbacké Mbacké family in Touba, the greater the honour felt and the more blessings are bestowed. Marabouts of low or middle status, who visit too frequently, may be regarded as parasites or spongers. They are afforded a polite and generous reception, as religion and tradition demand, but little more. Their popularity and the status they are perceived to enjoy can be measured by the size of the sum of money they receive during their visit. When the last living son of Amadou Bamba, shaykh Mouhamadou Mourtada Mbacké, also called 'The Marabout of the Diaspora', came to Tenerife in 1998, he was invited to stay at a five-star hotel. People felt genuinely honoured by his presence. Each member of the association donated an amount equivalent to 30€. The general opinion was that a person who was the son of Amadou Bamba must be in possession of an exceptionally large portion of *barke*.[2] Shaykh Mourtada died in 2004.

Very often the women take time off from their street peddling to go and see the visiting marabout, and are introduced to him when offering their donation. Sitting on the floor in front of him, their heads lowered, they listen to what he has to say after they have submitted a list of some of their problems through an intermediary belonging to his retinue. The marabout's replies are given them via the same confidant. The women regard this close contact with the 'religious experts', as the marabouts like to see themselves, as of great significance. Meeting a marabout is something they have never experienced in their home country, providing them with strength and the hope of concrete results. Both women and men are convinced that, in order to make a success

---

2. See Evers Rosander, 2003.

of their trading operations and outfox the Spanish police, they must partake of the marabout's intercession. There is a need to feel that they stand under the marabout's protection. This attitude repeatedly surfaces in conversations with Senegalese women at Playa de las Américas.

Male dilemmas

The women's personal integrity and their degree of independence and financial success appeared to be a somewhat complicated matter for the Senegalese men in Tenerife. They claimed they were worried about the women's moral conduct in Spain, complaining about this issue at every opportunity. As noted before, the men were constantly critical of the women's way of life in Tenerife as it reached beyond their control. They criticised their country-women for a supposed obsession with money and material objects, and were horrified at what they called the women's indifference towards religion. The very fact that the women were out in the street bargaining with tourists, male and female alike, particularly upset a number of male traders. It seemed as if they had a guilty conscience over their being unable to manage the conduct of these women in a way they deemed proper. This feeling of powerlessness and guilt causing problems for the men made the women suffer for no fault of their own. Releasing their hold on the women was almost a heresy, it seemed, as if they were acting "against their religion", as the men themselves expressed it. They knew perfectly well that the women would have been much more restricted by family and community home in Senegal. They also knew that most of the female migrants' families had not the slightest idea of the fact that their mothers, daughters or wives sat out on the pavement in full view of passers-by, shouting at the top of their lungs to attract the attention of the prospective tourist customers. It would have been considered a matter of pure shame and truly embarrassing for all the members of the family if it had become common knowledge back in Senegal.

The women, for their part, adapted their ways of living in order to exploit their opportunities to earn money to the maximum. This was their greatest ambition. As a consequence, they spent very little time at one and the same spot. My impression was that they they travelled a lot, and often, to other places on the island of Tenerife as well as to Gran Canaria and to the Mediterranean islands of Mallorca and Ibiza. They could also travel to the Spanish mainland, and drift off as far afield as Italy, the Netherlands and Belgium. Their trips were determined by rumours which seemed to promise where the best trade was to be found. They would choose the places where they had sisters or other relatives they could stay with while they tried their luck as female traders. Those of them who were able to travel home to Senegal and return without any visa worries did so on a regular basis. Others who sold on both a wholesale and retail scale made trips to countries where goods were inexpensive to purchase and stockpile. They often purchased clothes wholesale from the United States and had them sent in containers to be sold in Spain and Senegal. Another important reason for the many trips – perhaps the main one – was the feeling of insecurity which invaded the women traders concerning their surroundings. They were scared of being smitten by the evil forces of magic, the result of envy, in the event that their business plaiting hair and selling goods turned out to be a success. If their trade became a financial failure, they saw this as a consequence of other people's evil intentions, and both of these motives drove them to make a move.

While the female immigrants were constantly exposed to their countrymen's criticism, they themselves, on the other hand, generally made an effort to not get involved in their husbands' lives. As far as religion went, they appeared to be less indoctrinated than the men – more 'free-thinking', so to speak. In the diaspora the men sought an identity in religion which could provide them with the strength to keep them going. The women could do without any public manifestation of their religiosity – they found enough comfort in their own selves as Murids. The men suffered from the women not showing as much discretion and tact in their dealings with their husbands in Spain as they would have done home in Senegal. In short, the women's attitude towards their husbands was less humble and patient. This was interpreted by the men as one of indifference, something which hurt their self-esteem, which had already been tarnished as a result of the Spaniards' offensive racial attitudes.

The women, in turn, said they were not insensitive to the demands their husbands placed on them with respect to their behaviour. The fact that many of them had married Senegalese men in the diaspora was surely a sign that they were keen to earn a reputation as decent and modest women, while they were living on Tenerife too. They were, however, busy with their main objective: earning money for their family, for the marabout, and for themselves.

It is of some interest to note that polygamy was not at all as widespread among the Senegalese on Tenerife as in Senegal. Admittedly almost all the men had one or more wives home in Senegal, but in Spain they were content with one. Polygamy was first and foremost a manner of demonstrating their wealth and power. The type of status and prestige the acquisition of more than one wife brought could not be enjoyed in the diaspora but only in Senegal among the house-bound husbands. On Tenerife, on the other hand, if a Spaniard discovered a household where several wives were living together, the man would be met as often as not by ridicule and contempt.

The idea of seeking a divorce, or rather the threat, was latent in the minds of women who lived alone in Spain, without their husbands. It was difficult for them to keep track of their legal rights should the husband who had stayed behind in Senegal request a divorce in her absence. Sometimes the wife only learned much later that her husband had divorced her. This might be the case, for example, where the wife was on Tenerife illegally, without the proper documentation, and would be unable to leave Spain without forsaking the opportunity to return. Such divorces could give rise to minor tragedies, where the women, having allowed the husband's family to take care of the children while they were away working in Spain, ended up losing the right to bring up their own children after the ex-husband had remarried.

Nonetheless, the female immigrants were happy to be able to be in Tenerife and enjoy the opportunity to work their way towards earning an amount of money they could never have dreamed of making back in Senegal. They felt privileged. It was a sentiment which made up for the hardships they had gone through in the foreign land. There was a countless number of wives who had seen their husbands emigrate and waited in vain for an airline ticket enabling them to follow after them. The Senegalese men were not, however, all that willing to take their wives with them to Spain. It was an expensive trip, the wives might be subject to the negative (in their eyes) influences of the Western ideals of gender equality, and all sorts of problems and conflicts might arise with the wives the husbands had already acquired in Tenerife...

I recall an angry conversation in a telephone booth between a male Senegalese immigrant at Playa de las Américas and his wife in Dakar. He was yelling so loudly he brought some of us pedestrians on the pavement to a halt. I was given the gist of what was being said by some Senegalese women street-vendors, whose interest was aroused by the conversation. They knew something about his case, it appeared. The wife was accusing him of being a liar, and he was defending himself by raising his voice bit by bit. It turned out that he had promised to buy her an airline ticket so that she could come to Spain and seek medical aid; she was childless, and had put her last hopes in getting help abroad. The husband had let her down, claiming he was penniless, and anyway had a new wife who was now pregnant, and he intended divorcing the wife in Dakar.

The women on the pavement gave me a knowing look and shook their heads, while one of them said to me in Spanish: 'Hombres senegaleses'... 'that's Senegalese men for you...'

THREE WOMEN:
KHADY, COUMBA
AND AMINATA

THE DIFFERENT FORTUNES OF THREE Senegalese women which I have been following up during my visits to Tenerife have deeply affected me, and their
personalities have left a particularly strong impression on me. The first
woman concerned appeared to be able to maintain a balance with regard to
the unwritten cultural laws which were advantageous to her and fully acceptable to her environment. I've called her Khady. The second woman's name
is Coumba. She suffered from a certain social maladjustment on Tenerife,
and in addition was trapped between the expectations she placed on herself
and those that her mother had for her. Coumba failed to be as successful a
woman trader as Khady. Both of them, mutual friends, spent a comparatively
large sum of their money on marabouts and funds for religious purposes.
The women were firmly convinced that this was the best investment they
could make in order to achieve success and obtain protection from others'
outbreaks of envy and evil intentions. The third woman of my choice I have
called Aminata. She is the one I know best among all the Senegalese women
I met on Tenerife.

I chose Khady as an example of a woman who was financially successful as
an immigrant and a woman trader. There are of course other less successful
women who from a number of points of view would be quite as interesting
to focus attention upon. Nonetheless, the reason why Khady fits so well here
for a closer presentation is that her life story provides a contrast with Coumba's in several characteristic ways. At the same time they both share many
common features and a similar background from the same neighbourhood in
Saint Louis, the big city in northwestern Senegal. A study of the careers of
these two women shows how the lives of female Senegalese immigrants can
vary, while at the same time both women move within a relatively uniform
system of norms.

This system obviously includes the third woman, Aminata, even though
she represents another category of woman trader. Her profile is a more profes-

sional one, more accustomed as she is to the world outside Senegal. Talking to Aminata is a thrilling experience; she is a true entrepreneur, a woman who busies herself with helping and sharing her practical know-how with newly arrived Senegalese at Playa de las Américas. My conversations with her have broadened my perspectives concerning female immigration to Tenerife, and have provided interesting individual variations along the women's paths of life.

Khady

Khady is a *griotte*. She arrived on Tenerife at the start of the 1990s together with a group of young African dancers. They all obtained a residence and work permit in Spain. The ballet dancers toured not only around Spain but also in France, Latin America and the United States. It was a hard-working but enjoyable time, Khady thought, and she loved the freedom of travelling and dancing. She was in her thirties and divorced when I met her. She had abandoned the dance routines and devoted her energies to the wholesale and retail trade, and to plaiting tourists' hair in the street at Las Verónicas at Playa de las Américas. She also rented stalls at market places around Tenerife, selling textile goods. Khady told me she would usually spend three days a week at markets in different spots not far from Playa de las Américas. Once in a while she would go to New York and buy up a large stock of T-shirts and other clothes which she then sold to buyers in the Canary Isles. The continent of Asia was a tempting source of business with the price of gold relatively cheap and with its fashionable jewellery. Khady had therefore made a number of trips to Dubai and Saudi Arabia. She would then sell the jewellery in Senegal and on Tenerife, mainly to Senegalese women. As a trader she earned much more than she had done as a dancer, and enjoyed a varied and independent life.

The first years she was abroad her family remained in Senegal. Khady sent remittances home every month and travelled there a couple of times a year. She and her sisters had been brought up in the grandmother's house, which she had later repaired and given a modern touch, at the same time purchasing a building site outside Saint Louis. A relative helped her build an elegant house with a swimming pool. In the manner of many other emigrants, she rented the newly built house to a well-situated European.

One January day in 1999 I visited the family in their older house in Saint Louis. I was surprised to find that the two sisters were home in the middle of the day together with the grandmother. There was no sign of Khady's mother, who had remarried and lived with the new husband together with their children in another house in the same city. Khady's father had died a long time ago. Unemployment combined with the monthly instalments sent by big sister Khady from Spain appeared to have left her siblings in a state of unconcern as they passively sat around and whiled away the time listening to pop music and watching television. In the evening I saw her brothers hanging around at a street corner. My impression was confirmed when I brought the matter up with Khady. She had made up her mind that later that year she would bring all of the family save the grandmother over to Tenerife, to live and work alongside her at Playa de las Américas. It was extremely important for her to have her family around her being a single woman. It was clearly more sensible that they should be able to provide for themselves through trading and plaiting hair on Tenerife rather than go idle at home.

Khady's grandmother was keen to chat and had a lot to say about the phenomenon of migration. Her own and her family's lives had been strongly influenced by Khady's success as a trader. In her opinion young girls who leave Senegal are not to be criticised for going to Tenerife as unmarried women. Being young, they are able to get by without feeling the pressure of marrying for the sake of honour and decency. However, those women who are thirty to forty years old and still at a fertile age, find it difficult to remain on Tenerife and not get married. Men in Senegal mostly have one wife at least, but on Tenerife they need a housewife-cum-mistress. As pointed out in an earlier chapter, they are reluctant to take their wives with them to Spain since, as they see it, providing for the women is expensive and the travel costs are high. In their way of thinking the wives cost almost nothing in Senegal compared to Spain. It's better to live with the women who are already there on Tenerife and who are working and making their own living. "What's more, they don't want their wives to go to the West and have their heads filled with odd ideas from Spain," Khady's grandmother said laughing. "Look at our Khady, she looks after herself and a lot of men can't understand how she does it." Western style 'secular' life, involving the notion of human rights and gender equality, is evidently a source of worry for the men, was my immediate reflection. It was not the first time I had met this attitude among the male immigrants.

"But," said the grandmother, "it's better for migrating women not to be married. Because if they are, then the husband keeps all the money he has earned and gets a new wife for the money. Or they behave like Khady's husband: run through all her money and not do a bit of work."

The grandmother told me how she had ruined her eyes plaiting hair earlier in her life, and her body was worn out from all the singing and dancing. She was a *griotte* of the old school, earning her way by dancing and singing the praises of the fêted guest or the hero of the occasion at family ceremonies. Salimata, my assistant, passed her a 1,000 CFA franc note on our departure, and gave me an explanation later on. The fact that the grandmother was a *griotte* and had been talking to us for a very long time at our request was equivalent to a work session. "That's the way it is with the *griottes*," Salimata said, and she knew best. "They're used to being paid for everything they do, while the *geers* might see it as an insult."

In the summer of 2000, Khady is living together with her mother and her two brothers and two sisters in a flat in the centre of Playa de las Américas, not far from Las Verónicas. Her feeling is that it will be cheaper in the long run and more practical to live in town rather than renting a place up in the hills as most Senegalese do. Others, though, believe that you can save money by living up there in one of the villages above the Playa. Khady tells me that up there they pay something like 180€ a month for a room in an apartment shared with many others. Not my cup of tea, says Khady, who finds such an arrangement uncomfortable and prone to conflicts.

In the centre where she now lives she does not have to think about expensive transport arrangements for herself and the members of her family, at all hours of the day; each and everyone can go home as they please and enjoy home cooking. The others feed themselves on hamburgers at McDonald's. The fact that *halal* meat, from animals killed in accordance with Islamic ritual, is not available at such an establishment means that many of them end up eating French fries and drinking Coca-cola at high costs. This isn't Khady's style of living: when she drives off to the market places far from home with the pick-up loaded with merchandise, she always has home-made food with her.

The members of her family "respect the visa", as they are wont to say. By this they mean that they remain in Spain the stipulated three months that their tourist visa allows. They then leave the country and apply for a new visa which is granted on condition they do not exceed the time limit. As soon as they get the visa stamped in their passport they are back again for a new three-month period. Unless you have a residence permit, this is the only way to remain legally in the country.

Khady is clearly the head of the family, paying all the daily household expenses. Whatever each of them earns trading and plaiting hair, they keep for themselves. As head of the household Khady has great authority since she is the one with most experience abroad and who has the most money. She is also the only one in the family to have a car, which her brother borrows on occasion. The others' chief target is saving up enough to buy a return flight to Dakar every third month.

The members of the family are not particularly happy living abroad, and remain in close contact with the relatives in Saint Louis, making long telephone calls to them on a daily basis. Khady goes home to Senegal too, but only once a year. She cannot afford to go more often, she says, because all the family and the many relatives in Senegal live in expectation of a number of presents and donations of money from her. This is not taking into account all those who have fallen ill and who ask for help in meeting medical and hospital costs, even though she hardly knows them personally . People's needs for help are endless, Khady says, adding what women in similar situations have already told me: "I was forced to leave Senegal as my money was at an end. All I had left was my return ticket to Tenerife."

Salimata on her own visited Khady's grandmother in her home on one occasion and met Khady, who had come to stay a month at Saint Louis in 2002. Salimata's description of her visit was recorded in these notes to me:

> A lot of people were gathered on the pavement outside the house. When I went in I saw Khady sitting in the middle of the floor in an armchair, sort of on a pedestal, surrounded by people crowded around her, a bit like disciples usually sit in front of their marabouts. She was dressed in a beautiful, expensive *boubou*, wearing a lot of jewellery. There were other *griottes* present, praising her and her family continuously. Everybody wanted to talk to her, stretching their hands out to reach her. She didn't look at all as happy as she usually does, but seemed rather embarrassed. As soon as she saw me she brightened up. As she got up, she suggested we go out into the garden. She told me she was keen to get back to Playa because it was a less noisy place than here in Senegal. While we were standing there a woman completely unknown to her approached us and whispered something in Khady's ear. Khady told me the woman was begging for money for her son who was sick and was about to go into hospital. After listening to her she gave the woman a little sum of money. Then we went into the house again and she handed over some money to the griottes who were still singing in praise of her. I found it rather tiring with all the noise and din, so I left after a while and went home to a relative.

In contrast to almost all other Senegalese, Khady will admit that she enjoys living in Playa de las Américas, and appreciates having the chance to travel to other countries. "I'm an *aventurera*", she repeatedly says, assuring me in Spanish that she is a bit of an adventuress. She will soon be off again, this time to the United States.

I asked Khady which Sufi order she belonged to, and she said she was a Murid. Before she arrived in Tenerife she was not at all active in any religious association. She gave no donations to the marabouts visiting from Senegal, nor to the Murid leader in Touba. When she first settled down in Playa she didn't even say her daily prayers. One day, however, she was engaged in conversation with a marabout on a flight from Dakar to Las Palmas in the Canary Isles. He did not approve of what seemed to him her indifference towards religion, and suggested she should approach shaykh Amadou Bamba and ask him to take care of her. One day, the marabout declared, she would find herself in need of his protection. A few days later the house she was living in burnt to the ground in an enormous fire, but not being there at the time she suffered no harm. She saw what happened, however, as a sure sign, and not long afterwards met Amadou Bamba in a dream. In the dream Amadou called upon her to follow him, and since that moment she has been a Murid and goes on a pilgrimage to Touba once a year.

During our conversation about Muridism one day, Khady brought up her great love for not only Amadou Bamba but also mame Diarra Bousso. She uttered the same solemn words as I have heard from many other Murids: "If the son is so wonderful, imagine what the mother who gave birth to him must have been like!" There is a close connection here with the current notion whereby the character the child acquires is dependent on the mother's moral conduct.[1] Mame Diarra is to be seen as the perfect wife and mother in Khady's opinion, and she bemoaned the fact that most women – herself included – found it difficult to live up to such a perfect female ideal. She was, however, trying to be a good Muslim, she said, by praying, fasting, giving to charity and making donations for religious purposes, by going on pilgrimages and behaving in a decent and respectable fashion.

Generous donations, of course, are conditional upon financial capital of some considerable size. Khady earned enough money to provide both her family and the marabouts with plenty of presents and donations. She was the owner of a new house in Saint Louis and a building site in Touba. She also sent money to the mosque in Touba and to the Murid hospital being constructed there. Although she said she had bought this property, it was difficult to know what she actually owned and didn't own. Almost all the capital goods, such as the house and the cars, had been purchased on instalment, and the situation was similar regarding furniture, clothes and jewellery. In other words, Khady was continually obliged to see that she was acquiring enough money to be able to pay off her running debts. This was why from morning to night she was constantly busy plaiting tourists' hair and selling T-shirts, leather belts and imitation branded goods at different market places around Tenerife in addition to importing similar merchandise in containers from the United States. Selling the goods and buying fresh stock, she would find her customers among the island tourists, among Senegalese compatriots in various spots throughout Spain as well as in her home country.

Nevertheless, even though Khady used the hire-purchase system, she refused point-blank to sell on credit. She would only accept what the Senegalese trading community called 'red money'- cash payment, in other words. She had tired of being cheated out of payment for the goods she delivered. Her own and her customers' geographical mobility was a further factor in

---

1. See Sylla 1994.

her preference for selling for cash. The hire-purchase system requires a permanent address, or at least a situation in which one has a fixed abode for a longer period of time so that the money can be sent there and a customer can be reached. Such was not the case in respect of Khady and those clients she mostly sold to.

As I interpret Khady's situation, she has undertaken to set herself an enormous amount of work in order to keep herself and her family afloat living in the style she had chosen. All the instalments she must pay on a regular basis bind her to the necessity of having access to a considerable and regular income. There are large expenses involved, and the safety margins are small. I have no idea how much money she has saved in the bank, but my guess is that it is a quite modest amount of money. Her view is that money shouldn't stay idle in a bank, and this way of looking at things is shared by her Senegalese business colleagues. Money is to be used in such a way that it performs efficiently for its owner. The day she is unable to carry on owing to illness, old age or a general financial decline, she risks sudden ruin.

Furthermore, Khady suffers from the expensive but irrepressible habit of buying luxury presents for her relatives in the home country. She knows that she must spend money – a lot of money – in order to be 'someone' in the eyes of her environment, gaining status, prestige and respect in Senegal. The respect she meets through the prosperous life style she can show and pass on to others provides her with moral protection against criticism and legitimises her trips and living abroad. A respectable, single but *poor* woman would never enjoy the esteem such as Khady can count on as a successful, generous and pious Murid woman trader in Tenerife. It might be suggested that Khady has landed, a prisoner, in the moral treadmill, with financial and moral obligations expected of her. This would go to explain her quite recently adopted religious involvement and her nigh on fanatical obsession with making money.

Most people wherever they live try to have a reserve of economic resources to avoid the risk of finding themselves in a tight financial corner. The Senegalese tactic of achieving such reserves has always been to spread their eggs and put them in many baskets. By this I mean the existence of rotating savings and credit associations, both on Tenerife and in Senegal. The money saved up in these institutions can be used to initiate a business venture or rescue a financial project under threat. In 1998 Khady informs me that she puts a certain amount euros into her Spanish bank account every day. This money will later be transferred to her Senegalese bank for use when she is back home in Senegal. The remainder of what she earns, after deducting daily expenses, is placed in a rotating savings association, called a *nat* in *Wolof.* These are the traditional financial societies, already mentioned, which still constitute the very foundation of women's economic savings. The regulations for their participation have, however, been influenced by the special financial and formal circumstances under which the women live in Spain.

Whoever is without a permit to be in Spain is, by definition, an illegal immigrant. Such people risk being arrested by the police and deported, with their goods confiscated. Persons living under such conditions are naturally not suitable as members of a rotating savings club. The system requires a regular contribution of one's savings to a common fund over a period of time. This is to ensure that every member has access to the same sum of money. There are, for instance, women such as Khady who travel a lot and might find themselves in the most unexpected places at times when the association meets and contributions are handed over to the presiding official in Tenerife. In such cases it is imperative that family members can act on Khady's behalf, for instance, and deposit the money due. In many cases, however, the *nat* savings system can be a risky business for members. When the turn comes to those who are the most recent savers in the system, there might be many participants who have already left the island and are no longer making a contribution. In order to avoid such a situation only persons with valid residence permits are allowed to belong to the rotating savings associations which span longer periods of time and require large deposits of money. Illegal immigrants in Spain have to be content with savings clubs operating on a daily basis or weekly at the most. An example of such a club is the one in which Khady's sister is a member. She is without a residence permit and a valid visa, and gives the following description of the savings methods she uses:

> There are three types of *nat* for people like me who don't have the proper documents. You can choose to deposit the equivalent of 12€, 30€ or 60€ a day for a maximum of five days. There are ten of us in such a club. I'm unable to earn more than 30€ a day with my work so I deposit that sum of money together with nine other women. When it's my turn, I have access to five times 300€. With this sum I can buy more goods and hopefully increase my sales.

Khady is a member of several rotating savings and credit associations. She mentions one *nat* in particular at Playa de las Américas which meets once a month. A sum of money – the equivalent of 180€ – is decided upon and deposited by each of the ten members. Each time one of the ten women is allotted the total sum, which should amount to 1800€ if all have made their contributions as agreed. This is a suitable quantity of money for the purchase of stock and the cost of the transport of goods, on a rather larger scale than Khady's sister's. Sometimes, at the meetings, the women are in such a hurry to get back to their place of work that they just hand in the money and have no time for a chat, while on other occasions they send a person in their confidence with the money instead. Others are in the best of moods; they storm in, do a little dance turn lifting their *boubou* skirts, and make provocative movements with their bodies, which raise a laugh. Many of them stay on for a cup of tea or a glass of water, just as they do in Senegal. On Tenerife, however, the first things spoken about are goods and prices. A recurring subject of conversation is the question of where there are bigger sales opportunities, higher prices to be asked, and more customers to have their hair plaited: on Ibiza, at Palma de Mallorca, at Sitges on the Spanish mainland. Places which are all the rage for the moment vary from year to year, while the word quickly gets around as to where the best deals may be made.

Another subject of conversation at the savings club meetings, always high on the list, is the current price of gold. Khady tells me of another type of get-together at which they devote themselves to saving up gold in the shape of gold jewellery. She belongs to such an association. The way it works is by members handing over a piece of gold jewellery worth a certain sum of money at the end of every month. Each woman in turn becomes the owner of all the jewellery deposited that month. Many of these pieces of jewellery have originally been purchased in Mecca or Dubai, are 24-carat gold and have a reddish tone. The style is generally classical Arabic.

A third, very popular type of savings club concerns saving up to purchase beautiful and expensive *boubous*. Senegalese women like to acquire elegant dresses of splendid material as a reward for their hard work on Tenerife. According to Khady, they will even go as far as buying dresses which can cost up to 300€ each (this in 1998). These *nat* are formed with the purpose of putting together a certain sum of money to purchase such luxury items, in the same way as with other rotating savings associations. However, as distinct from the others, this time it is the president of the association who selects a particular dress for the woman in turn. At each get-together a brand-new beautiful dress, sewn in the latest fashion in Senegal or Mali of the highest quality, is lying there waiting for the lucky new owner. Khady has told me that she herself buys her own *boubous* during her trips to Mali and Senegal. Those women, however, who cannot leave Tenerife for lack of a valid visa are happy to have this type of *nat* to satisfy their needs. It helps them to keep up to date with the current vogue in the world outside, as far as attractive clothes and jewellery are concerned.

I make a special note of Khady's friendly manner on my visits to Las Verónicas where the *griottes* generally meet in the evenings, whether selling, plaiting hair or just having a chat together. She is careful to spend time listening to the women and sharing experiences. Sometimes I will find her sitting among the other *griottes* at Las Verónicas plaiting tourists' hair. The Senegalese appreciate the fact that she does not behave in a self-important way adopting a pompous attitude, even though she is a more successful trader than most of them. She appears to be not at all bothered by any possible symptoms of envy which might have a damaging effect on her. She claims to have full confidence in Amadou Bamba, and that her marabout will be praying for her and providing her with protection. Muridism is her sure guarantee of security.

How is it possible, one might ask, to earn so much money merely by plaiting tourists' hair and selling T-shirts and leather belts? It must be borne in mind that she is also involved in the lucrative wholesale business as well as import/export operations in gold jewellery between Arab countries and Senegal and Spain. The chief explanation, however, lies in Khady's enormous capacity for work. Her job extends over both day and night, and she is a tireless person in the art of doing business. Khady has only a few hours' sleep every night from three or four in the morning to seven o'clock, when she loads up her car with goods and drives off to different market places, returning home late in the afternoon with whatever she has not been able to sell. Her next work schedule begins in the evening at Las Verónicas where until after midnight she plaits the hair of tourists many of whom are often in a more or less inebriated state. At the same locality the Senegalese men are selling imitation brand wristwatches. Khady is often plaiting hair as early as six in the evening, taking a rest around ten o'clock for a meal. Either she has her own food with her in the car parked nearby, or she drives home for a quick meal.

Around midnight the atmosphere changes at Las Verónicas and the immediate neighbourhood. "Crime hour" has arrived, as the Senegalese are wont to say. The district is crowded with tipsy young people, both boys and girls, who have come on cheap charter trips to the island. They are easy bait for the smart African sellers and the Senegalese women traders' insistent offers to plait the tourists' hair. As they hustle the English girls along the street the tone they use is more aggressive than in the daytime. Prices have suddenly jumped sky-high – the later into the night the more expensive the job! During daylight hours the normal price for attaching a colourful plait into the hair is about 5€, while it can cost double as much or more at night. Plaiting a person's hair or applying detachable plaits daytime costs between 50 and 100 euros, but at night there is no fixed limit. Customers often stumble in their inebriated state over rates of exchange, and are persuaded to accept prices which the following day seem to be glaringly unjustified. Furthermore, the plaits may be of a lower quality and the work carried out sloppy since the customers are not in a fit state to take much notice. They are quite simply not sober enough to understand they have been cheated. This exploitation of the foreign tourist applies not only to the Senegalese in the street but also to Spanish barmen and disk jockeys.

Some of the tourists, resenting the Senegalese methods of hard bargaining, make a complaint the following day with the police but without any tangible results. Whoever feels cheated can seldom point out the woman who has plaited her hair. As soon as the tourist accompanied by the police approaches the street-plaiting community, the women down their tools and vanish. The customers remain, their hair partially in plaits, and have to wait until all is calm and quiet again and the hairdressers return. During the darker hours of the night it is difficult to make out who is who, and the following day you can't recognize the 'culprit'.

Khady has tired of being a part of the really late work shifts. At about one o'clock she begins to pack up her things and make for home, to relax, watch a video or two or listen to Senegalese music. She will also probably pray one of the five prayers she has not had the time for earlier in the day. She does not have to work all through the night any longer for the sake of her economy, she explains to me, and she has never really approved of the tough language and night scuffles in the streets. The members of her family, however, mostly work at night, when they consider it safer to avoid the police as there are fewer of them around at those hours.

The money Khady earns goes straight into her pocket. She has few other expenses connected with her work other than hiring the stall at the market places and paying for the fuel she needs for her car. Her starting price when selling to customers is generally five times what she pays for the whole-sale purchase of T-shirts. Though free of income tax, she nonetheless pays a monthly amount for her Spanish health insurance plus a work permit charge.

The key to Khady's financial success is undoubtedly her huge work capacity. With no children to care for and no husband to demand her presence at home, she can come and go as she pleases. She chooses her own working hours and the places she prefers to confine her activities to in order to do the best business with the greatest possible access to customers. It was not without good reason that Khady made up her mind not to remarry after the divorce from her former husband. She learned from married women on Tenerife she had spoken to that she earned much more than they did. The movements of the married women were limited, and the time they had at their disposal outside the home to sell and plait hair could in no way compare with Khady's. It was merely the fact that there were only twenty-four hours in a day which stopped her.

From experience Khady knew, moreover, that some men kept a close check on their wives' doings. Their pangs of jealousy could put a spoke in the wheel for many a plan and project. She also had little trust in men's intentions for marriage. In line with most other well-situated women, she feared that a possible husband would take advantage of her and line his pocket at her expense. Khady repeated what every other woman had already said: there was always the risk that the husband would some day appear out of the blue with a younger, fresh new wife for the common household.

Khady had no intention of letting this happen. She made every effort to keep on good terms with the visiting Murid marabouts by donating money to their cause. When the Murids' annual festival in honour of Amadou Bamba took place in Touba, she paid for the trip for the entire family. The following year she intended going with her mother and sisters to Porokhane to attend the mame Diarra Bousso *magal* or pilgrim festival. The generosity she showed her relatives and neighbours in Senegal when she was home attracted a good deal of attention far outside the part of town where the family's house was situated. Her investments in the shape of exemplary conduct, open-handedness and proven piety gave dividends in the form of a large moral capital.

Khady was proof for many Murid men and women in Tenerife that religion provides the believer with access to a large number of resources of many types. Taking part in the pilgrimages to Touba or Porokhane and there praying for a better life brings visible results according to the Murids. Consequently it would be true to say that Khady not only in an indirect way contributed to the spread of Muridism via her donations of money just as the male Murids do. She was, as it was commonly reported, a living example of the outstanding success of Muridism throughout the world. The very fact that she was a successful woman trader strengthened her own and others' faith in God and His protection of her.

The religious doctrine, on the other hand, emphasizes the subservient and obedient role of woman in relation to man. How does this tally with Khady's actions as an independent trading partner in business of every shade? The answer is to be found partly in what we have just said. Through the moral capital and good reputation Khady had acquired she was able to function perfectly well outside the home. As a divorcee neither did she need to hide or disguise her financial independence, as was the case with the married women in similar positions. They had to be careful not to degrade their husbands and their authority by openly demonstrating their independence in matters where decisions had to be made. At the same time it should not be forgotten that much of Khady's success was bound up with her personality. She had a keen nose for easily adapting to a new situation, and her manner towards her fellow-beings was, as referred to earlier, exceptionally friendly.

Nevertheless, even in her capacity as a visibly rich and God-fearing woman, her gender was a disadvantage for her and played on her moral vulnerability. With Khady as a point of departure, however, we can establish the fact, I think, that economic change undoubtedly exerts an influence on the life careers of immigrant women. Women see that positive alternatives exist to being married and staying at home. On the other hand the social structure appears to be firmly established in prevailing gender relations. The dominant religious ideology maintaining men's superior position over women here on earth undergoes a very slow change through the new work opportunities on offer. Khady's example plainly reveals the fact that we have to move with great care within the system of norms in order to be able to achieve independence and be one's own boss, fully retaining respect for one's own person.

Khady's mother Codou

Khady had suggested her mother Codou coming to Tenerife to earn money of her own. Her mother had got the ticket for the flight from her daughter, who had also arranged a visa for her – and now she was there. Unfortunately Codou was not all that happy over the arrangements but instead worried all the time about the children from her last marriage who she had left in her husband's household. Codou sent the husband each month a sum of money equivalent to some 250€, covering expenses for food and whatever else, which she did not specify for me in our conversations. Every three months Codou returned to Senegal in order to renew her visa, and saw then how hard life had become for her children. She told me there was an unpleasant atmosphere around the house. The two wives who belonged to the polygamous matrimony were envious of Khady and her mother, who were capable of travelling abroad and earning a good bit of money. Codou lost a lot of sleep in her anxiety that the feelings of envy might find expression in acts of evil hurting the children. She spent a lot of money seeking out marabouts who, she hoped, would be able to ward off the malicious intentions.

None of the people back home in Saint Louis knew anything about the toil and trouble Khady's mother went through out in the streets in the darkness of the night at Playa de las Américas, plaiting the hair of inebriated tourists. She told them nothing of all this as she was unwilling to reveal that part of her life in Tenerife. It would have made her co-wives spiteful and her own children depressed. It was much better coming home and living up to the picture of the successful immigrant, enjoying everything that money can buy in a modern and wealthy community like the Spanish one. Months went by, however, and there was no change in sight. Every third month Khady's mother and the sisters would travel home only to renew their visa and return to Playa. On my own return a year later, in 2001, she had ultimately wearied of plaiting hair night after night, with the constant concern for her children at home in Senegal.

In order to keep the people living in the husband's large household in a good mood and avoid the curse of the 'evil eye' – envy of a type that could cause damage, explained Codou – she always brought with her a number of presents for the co-wives and their children. It might be cosmetics, perfume and toys. Her hard-earned money quickly vanished buying these gifts, but they enabled her to give the children something by way of compensation for the constant absence of their mother. The older ones would ask for cellphones and digital cameras while the younger ones wanted different brands of trainers and gym outfits. Loving mother that she was, she always tried to meet their desires. On the first trips home she also took along large quantities of products from Tenerife with the purpose of selling them in Dakar and Saint Louis. She stopped doing this as soon as she realised that she would never get paid. Nobody at home in Senegal professed to be able to afford paying cash, and the instalment plan didn't work.

I wonder, in fact, whether Codou might not just as well have stayed at home in Senegal in view of the amount of money this elderly woman spent on travel, presents, monthly maintenance of the household in Saint Louis, and fees paid to the marabouts for their prayers, talismans and anti-witchcraft rituals. She could not possibly save up enough capital the way she was spending her money during the periods of time I was able to follow her life at a distance. Plans she had of opening a small shop in Saint Louis went no further than plans during the years I got to know her. Age took its toll, and as a fifty-year-old she was unable to cope with the late-night and long-hour shifts at Playa de las Américas. All the same, and in spite of everything, Khady's mother preferred to live on Tenerife and work there in three-monthly periods. Her goal was, as for all the other itinerant Senegalese, to crown the five long years of following the visa rules and regulations by acquiring a residence permit in Spain. She would then be able to travel at will between the countries.

Coumba

If Khady can be considered the typical woman trader, manoeuvring herself forwards without husband or children but with a notion of herself as something of an 'aventurera', then Coumba is the opposite. She is the family girl who has no experience of working outside the home, and who has been cast out, as it were, into the immigrant way of life on Tenerife for which she is not particularly well equipped. Most important of all for her is her marriage and living as a good mother and obedient daughter, ideals which are not so easy to achieve in the diaspora. I find the task of portraying Coumba also more difficult to perform. I should like to present Coumba's life story in as favourable a light as Khady's, but this would be twisting the truth, I fear. Notwithstanding, it would be wrong to conceal the problems which present themselves among the Senegalese in Spain as well as in Senegal. They are partly rooted in the social and economic structure which quite often embroils people in conventional ways of life and impedes their freedom of action, and partly in the personality of each and every one.

Khady and Coumba had lived as neighbours in Saint Louis and were close friends since childhood. Their mothers knew each other, too, having grown up in the same district. When Khady's mother remarried and moved to her new husband's house, Khady started to spend more time at Coumba's home than previously. Coumba was not, like Khady, of the *Wolof* ethnic majority group, but belonged to the next largest group, the *Halpulaar*. She was fluent in *Wolof* but her native tongue was *Pulaar*, which she always used at home with her family. The *Halpulaar* had their roots among the nomadic tribes in the north of the country and retained their traditions raising cattle. Marriage was almost without exception within one's own ethnic group. Many of the young boys who wished to live with a woman from an ethnic group other than the *Halpulaar* attempted to make their way to Europe or the United States, where they would often be able to freely choose a life partner without the family meddling. Thus social flexibility was helped along by migration, which made it easier for people from different groups to meet each other and start a family eschewing ethnic and status barriers. Crossing these limits, however, is not a problem-free business, as we shall see an example of in the following.

Coumba was a *geer*, which as implied earlier meant that she belonged to the large part of the population which was not divided into any professional status group. Khady, on the other hand, was a *ñeeño* and of lower social status than Coumba. Most of the Senegalese immigrants in Tenerife were *ñeeños* and were affiliated to Muridism.

When Khady got the opportunity to travel to the Canaries and perform African dance, Coumba's mother wanted her daughter to go along too and keep Khady company. Coumba could not afford the trip, however, so she was compelled to bide her time and wait until Khady could lend her money for the ticket. Six months after Khady had gone, Coumba made the journey to Tenerife via Gran Canaria. Coumba's mother found out that Khady was earning good money in Spain and she naturally hoped her daughter would be able to do likewise. Coumba admitted to me her apprehension about the journey, but her mother persistently urged her to go. The mother was always short of cash and often complained of the miserable life she was leading. With her demands that the daughter send money home to her as frequently as possible she came to sabotage Coumba's every effort to build up seed capital for her trade in Tenerife. Coumba always gave way and did as her mother wished. The next nail in the coffin for Coumba's finances was her husband, or rather her husband's customs and habits.

Coumba was 21 when she arrived on Tenerife, and had little experience of standing on her own two feet. With Khady's help she acquired living quarters and the essential information for newly arrived immigrants on the island. In time one of the more experienced women traders took care of her. Coumba was given good advice concerning the kind of goods she should buy for her stock, where to buy them, and the prevailing prices on the market. The wholesaler gave her a loan for her first purchases in order for her to get started. We are dealing here with a period twenty-five years back in time, at the start of the 1990s, when very few Senegalese women were in Tenerife. Most of the women there were the wives of Senegalese immigrants. Women who were living there without a husband's watchful eye found themselves constantly hounded by Senegalese men, and Coumba was no exception: she felt their interest for her all too closely. She was also worried over her situation as an immigrant with no more than tourist status, without a residence permit and always running the risk of being deported for lack of a valid visa. How would she ever be able to compile enough money to pay for a return ticket Tenerife-Dakar before the visa expired?

It was at this point in time that Coumba's husband-to-be, Ousmane, made his appearance. He offered her protection from the Senegalese men's constant harassment if she agreed to marry him. By accepting she gained the right to live in Spain for as long as she was married to him, and without a visa since Ousmane was a naturalised Spanish citizen. Ousmane, ten years older than Coumba, belonged to the *Wolof* ethnic group, and was a *ñeeño*, a *griot*. He came to Tenerife for the first time as early as in 1983 and after a year or two decided to stay on. Ousmane was among those people who had obtained a residence permit and later Spanish citizenship at a time when it was relatively easy. Immigrants were required as a labour force within the construction industry. There were not many Senegalese, and they were as a whole fairly well looked upon.

Home in Diourbel remained Ousmane's first wife and four children. His intention had always been to send money home to his family every month. As time went by, however, the amounts he sent became smaller and smaller, or nothing at all. It turned out that Ousmane, otherwise a charming, open personality and a helpful and generous man, lived beyond his means, something which had caused him a good deal of problems over the years. Soon Coumba was to feel the consequences of her husband's style of living. Ousmane had lost several well-paid jobs as a construction worker, and four times within a couple of years had been arrested by the police for selling in the street without a valid permit. This happened at great cost to him since each time his stock of imitation brand wrist-watches and sun-glasses was confiscated. His friends and colleagues had on each occasion lent him money to replenish his stock.

Eventually the other Senegalese began to tire of helping Ousmane out of his financial straits, urging him to be more observant. He had to be quicker in mind and body to escape the police when they appeared. Generally speaking, Coumba's husband was one of those people who found it difficult to make their way in a society like the Canary one. A lot of work was needed and a good deal of self-discipline in order to get on. The men were often sorely tempted by the many bars and other pleasure spots on the island.

Putting on a charm offensive Ousmane had also tried to interest tourists in some sort of business idea. He suggested he could be useful in a kind of project they might finance mutually, but no tourist had yet shown any interest in his proposals. All of this I was told by the women traders before I got to know Coumba's husband more closely.

When I met Ousmane one day out at the market place he offered Salimata and me a refreshment and told us of his problematic life situation. He said he felt ashamed every time he had something nice to eat in Playa as it made him think of his poor family back in Senegal who might be without sufficient food for the day. He could only afford to travel home and see them once a year, and sometimes he was not able to do even that. His present troubles concerned his five-year-old daughter with his second wife, Coumba. She was old enough to be sent home and go to a Koran school and learn Senegalese manners and customs. Ousmane was not keen to have his daughter follow in the footsteps of Spanish children who he found were too badly brought up, while the Spaniards themselves had become too secularised and lacked respect for traditions. But who would take care of her in Senegal? His own mother didn't like Coumba for various reasons. Ousmane's mother considered her son should have married a woman from the same ethnic group and the same 'caste' as himself, and she wasn't interested in looking after the child. What's more, there were already enough children in the house – the first wife and the four children Ousmane had had with her lived with his mother. However, if she were paid for the extra costs involved, she would certainly agree to take charge of the girl, who liked her grandmother very much. The problem lay on the financial side. Street-vending was not making much headway and Coumba wasn't very good at plaiting hair. She didn't like the job, and the result was, said Ousmane, that their finances had left them in desperate straits. His own work, or lack of it, he didn't say a word about.

A few days later I met Coumba among the other women at Las Verónicas. She had become, just like her husband, a very committed Murid. Ousmane would ask for the marabouts' help whenever he could afford to donate money. Coumba told me the Murid marabouts' visits were becoming less frequent. Their followers on Tenerife were no longer in a position financially to pay the spiritual leaders' hotel bills, and instead invited the marabouts to stay with them, the immigrants, in their own flats and apartments. This was not at all as inviting as staying at the splendid five-star hotels they had been used to. Nevertheless, they still received donations of money for the prayers they were expected to say on the immigrants' behalf, and for the miracles it was hoped they would perform. Coumba said to me literally about the donations: "It's a duty we have towards the marabouts. They have every right to receive the *addiyya* we give them. This money isn't even for themselves. They say it's for serigne Touba."

Coumba chose to take her own husband as an example in order to convince me of the marabouts' supernatural powers. Ousmane had been seriously ill during the winter and the doctors were unable to help him. One of the most important and well-known Murid marabouts, serigne Mourtada by name, and a brother of serigne Touba, had however cured Ousmane by praying for him and sending him holy water from the spring in Touba. Because now he was healthy again! She made a point of paying the marabouts and praying five times a day. She usually said her prayers and read a few extra verses from the Koran in the morning before leaving for work. She would generally save a few prayer occasions for the evening because out in the streets where she sold goods or plaited people's hair there was no suitable spot for the necessary ablutions prior to saying prayers.

I asked whether she had gone on the annual pilgrimage to Touba like many of the immigrants. No, she hadn't, but she had donated money to the event. She had *intended* to go, she told me; the money had to go in her stead... Making a financial contribution counted too, didn't it? Why, of course, I mumbled, a little ashamed at having put such a tactless question. All the Murids who could afford it and whose papers were in order travelled every year to the *magal* in Touba. It was part of the reward for having slaved away at their work all the year in Tenerife. I should, of course, have realised that such a trip was far too costly for Ousmane and Coumba. Moreover, I was fully aware that it was just not on to go back home without lovely presents and a load of money for all those who were expecting a gift. No – it was far better to sit tight and avoid the feelings of shame induced by not being able to live up to the expectations placed on immigrants. Those who were successful went home and basked in the admiration of their environment. The less fortunate stayed on Tenerife.

We entered McDonald's and had a cup of coffee together. Coumba looked relieved at being able to withdraw a while from the hustle and bustle of the street, with its honking cars, screaming pedlars, and the tense atmosphere in the air outside – you never knew when the police might turn up. I wanted to broach the subject of the different marabouts who usually came to Playa de las Américas, but Coumba was full of her problems with her mother-in-law.

As I listened I tried to give her some comfort. Her situation, though, was a textbook example of what happens when you contravene social rules. The mother-in-law blamed her son's bad luck in business on Coumba. It was her fault their economy was so bad; it was all her fault, because she quite simply did not make enough money. The way the mother-in-law saw it, Coumba was not accustomed to putting her back into the job and working hard, being a spoiled *Halpulaar* woman and socially occupying a higher position than her husband.

Coumba said that, if the truth were known, she did not enjoy plaiting other people's hair. She was not used to touching other people's hair; at the most, she could plait the hair of the closest members in the family. Moreover, she felt uneasy about sitting out there in the street on a dirty pavement, in full view of foreign European people streaming past. Neither could she pluck up enough courage to call out to tourists and attract their attention, as the other Senegalese women did. I knew that under these circumstances she would often look unhappy, while in point of fact she was frightened and unsure of herself. Such facial expressions were not conducive to good trade.

In the course of time, however, Coumba gradually got used to her life selling in the street. Her daily income was generally less than the other women's since she sold too little and plaited hair too slowly, and that rather reluctantly. Compared with what she would be earning home in Senegal, she was nonetheless quite happy. The difficulties lay rather in the fact that her work schedule was reduced owing to her domestic duties as a housewife and as a mother whenever her daughter was not with grandmother in Saint Louis. The other women without their husbands on Tenerife lived communally, taking it in turns to do the cooking. They generally had no particular hours to pay attention to other than the police force's work schedule, which they kept a special eye on in order not to be caught in the street. They were mainly out in the evenings, sometimes far into the night selling and plaiting hair. Coumba partly lived a different sort of life as she had to be home to cook the food at definite times of the day, and her husband was unwilling to have her out late in the dark.

This was the usual dilemma facing female immigrants on Tenerife. Living alone without a husband easily gave a woman a bad reputation, yet on the other hand it gave her the freedom and opportunity to make a lot of money. The married woman, with her responsibility for the family household on Tenerife, enjoyed a good reputation and a higher moral status but was less likely to bring in a large income. In Coumba's case, the fact that a lot of demands were placed on her within the family served to increase her anxiety for the future and the financial situation. She realised that trading in the street, tending to the needs of the household, and looking after her child were becoming too much of a burden for her. On top of this was the duty of being a good wife, at the beck and call of her husband. Still, she also knew that she shouldn't complain about her husband in front of others. In Tenerife, too, it was important to observe the three words of honour for the conduct of married women: *muñ...* patience and endurance; *kersa...* shame; and *soutoura...* tact and discretion. This was why she never said a bad word to any Senegalese about Ousmane's inability to provide for his family. Neither did she let on to me, although she did give me to understand that she was worried for the family's future and their financial situation.

Since Coumba's reputation remained virtuous and her loyalty towards her husband, at least superficially, never faltered, Ousmane felt a greater trust in her than many other married men in Tenerife. He needed in any case more money to cover living costs, and consequently allowed his wife to trade out in the street. She felt quite free and independent if she were to compare what her situation would have been like living with her husband in Senegal. Supervision and control in social matters were much harder there. She would have had to put up a bigger fight to find suitable ways of coming out and earning money, partly behind her husband's back. There was always a potent risk back in Senegal of rousing the husband's anger and being punished with a beating. This conclusion was shared with other Senegalese women in Spain. In Tenerife everybody was plainly aware that they were there to make money, and nothing else. Everybody knew, too, that you were unable to do that by staying home all day.

Coumba's mother-in-law did not appreciate her daughter-in-law's many merits as a loyal wife to her son. Coumba, in turn, was troubled by the mother-in-law's dissatisfied attitude towards her. She blamed her poor income on witchcraft, probably in some way connected to the mother-in-law. It was not unusual for a woman to associate her mother-in-law with negative elements in Senegal, explicable in terms of black magic and vice versa. Coumba was convinced she could be assailed by evil powers, set in motion by her mother-in-law. By getting in touch with people specialising in long-distance black magic, the mother-in-law would clearly be able to wreak damage on Coumba's life even when she was living in Tenerife. Coumba telephoned marabouts in Senegal to seek help, hoping they would be able to render the powers harmless.

A further source of discontent was the attitude of her own mother, who would refuse either to trade or plait hair when she came visiting, and who was in general a rather demanding lady. She sat for the most part at home in Senegal waiting for her daughter to send her money.

The bulk of what Coumba earned as a woman trader she used in order to cover rent and food. She was only able to save a little for her own personal use since her husband appeared to take it for granted that she was the one who stood for the expenses they had in common. Her working hours increased somewhat whenever her mother came over to Tenerife to take care of the child. She persuaded her mother to take a flight from Senegal using money they had managed to get on loan. Coumba held out hope that her mother could earn enough with petty trade or plaiting in her idle moments so they could repay the loan. The plan fell through and their financial situation gradually worsened. The next idea that occurred to Coumba was moving from Playa to Sitges south of Barcelona. She thought things would be much better there as she had heard from a number of Senegalese that high prices were in demand at the seaside resorts around Barcelona and sales were brisk. The venture fizzled out because they were unable to find anywhere cheap and comfortable to live.

Both Coumba and Ousmane were highly respected among the Senegalese community, where they were regarded as friendly and pleasant persons. They had had a bit of bad luck, that's all, people said. Nobody criticised Ousmane openly for living beyond his means. In spite of the friendly reception they were always given, however, Coumba felt isolated from the rest of the women traders. The family ceremonies in Senegal in conjunction with marriages and name-giving were replaced in Tenerife with parties celebrated there, and they required support in the shape of presents and donations. Coumba could not always afford to make a contribution. The system relied on mutual give and take. When you knew you couldn't give or give back, then you knew it was time to withdraw, and the same unwritten rule applied in Senegal as well as on Tenerife. On account of her faulty financial position, Coumba could not count on the women's full confidence to participate in the activities of the rotating savings associations. She had to be content with the minor clubs which operated on a short-term basis and involved smaller investments. This left a bitter taste in the mouth for Coumba, who had needed so well a large sum of money to put into her business.

In spite of the disappointments of her marriage Coumba was not keen to seek a divorce. She intended to stay in Spain, and she was aware of the privileged position her matrimony with Ousmane had given her. She could not be thrown out unceremoniously like so many other of her sister traders! Her hope remained to make enough money to be able to fulfil the three demands required of her: providing for her mother and daughter in Saint Louis, assuming responsibility for the Tenerife household, and being capable of saving up money for her personal use. The dream of obtaining in time a house of her own back in Senegal and opening a little shop there remained remote, but it was at the back of her mind all the time. It gave her the inspiration to carry on working at Playa de las Américas as much as she had the time for and was able to cope.

In 2005 I looked up Coumba in Saint Louis where she was staying at home with her mother for a couple of months together with her daughter, while her husband was visiting his own mother, his first wife and the four children in Diourbel. By that time Coumba was quite probably rather tired of her husband, who let her bear the brunt of the responsibility for the family economy. He seemed to have adopted an attitude common among a variety of married men whose wives feel they must leave the home and make some money. These husbands appear to have completely given up as regards the domestic economy. Criticised, they claim that the wives desire this responsibility, in spite of the fact that the women in the majority of cases are obliged to earn money for the essentials in the house since the men's contributions are so small and practically amount to nothing.

Coumba's mother openly expressed her discontent with her daughter's marriage to Ousmane, a *griot*, and a *Wolof*, to boot. It was a failed venture, she thought, even though he lived in Spain and through his Spanish citizenship allowed her daughter to live there and travel to and from Spain whenever she wished. The son-in-law had in any case not turned out to be the golden calf Coumba's mother had set her hopes on.

Aminata

Aminata, just as Coumba, was married, but I never met her husband on the island of Tenerife. He remained in Dakar, and as far as I could make out, seldom went anywhere else. It was easy for me to get along with Aminata. She was evidently used to being with Europeans and was influenced by her many years spent in Western settings. One could even suspect that she had changed in the direction of a more secular world view. This was by no means the case, however. Animata's religiosity was profound, even though she was not the least afraid to express herself concerning both religious leaders and men in general. She appeared less dependent on social pressures among the Senegalese on Tenerife, and behaved in a more independent manner than the other women traders, particularly concerning questions of economy. Perhaps the fact that she was one of the most well-off of all the trading women in the Canaries was a contributory factor.

At the same time, however, Aminata stood out as a woman well-entrenched in Senegalese culture, with deep roots in her home country. She was constantly returning there following her long and many business trips. The fact that she occasionally felt frustrated both there and in Spain had more to do with her fear of magical powers of evil. She considered, on a par with Coumba, that such powers were called forth by other people's feelings of envy. They constituted a constant threat to her, wherever she might be. This phantom occupied Aminata's world both translocally and internationally, and consequently she found it almost impossible to be rid of.

Aminata was of the *Wolof* ethnic group and was a *geer*. Her husband was too, but he belonged to the *Tijaniyya* order while Aminata was a Murid, a rather unusual state of affairs since the wife normally would pertain to the same Sufi order as her husband. He was employed as a government official and earned much less than she did. In fact, his monthly take-home pay was no more than what she would earn for a day's work on Tenerife.

Aminata told me that when she was a poor young girl and not yet married, her present parents-in-law had nasty things to say about her. They spread the word that she was a prostitute, not wishing their son to have anything to do with her. At this time she was working as a maid in the home of a French family. Aminata assured me that she can never forget the humiliation she was subjected to on that occasion. Now that she is a rich woman they are of course silent on this matter. Her matrimony is monogamous, and Aminata would accept nothing else. If her husband chose to take a further wife she would first threaten him with divorce. If he persisted he would run the risk of having no more than his meagre salary as soon as she carried her threat into effect and disappeared out of his life.

All of Aminata's family have been in trade and commerce for a number of generations. They used to travel around several West African countries selling their merchandise in the Ivory Coast for long periods of time. There exists a tradition and a know-how in the art of buying and selling in the family which most of the *griottes* in Playa de las Américas are lacking. Aminata, her mother and her sisters, are all married, or have been married, to men living in places other than they themselves, either in Senegal or in Europe. The women believe that, for the sake of their own reputation and their children's, they need the social status a marriage provides. They work better, however, without their husbands breathing down their necks, so to speak, since the latter would only take to meddling in their affairs. Of Aminata's two sons and two daughters, the eldest two commute between Spain, Italy and Senegal. They have already started their international career trading clothes and items of fashion. The youngest children live at home in Dakar with the husband's family and are cared for by his mother and sister.

The finest dwelling in the family's possession is situated in a fashionable suburb of Dakar. It doesn't belong to Aminata but has been built with her sister's and mother's money. The villa Aminata is having built in the district called Sacrecoeur in Dakar is European in style, and the furniture has been purchased in Spain. This is where she plans to stay during her visits to Senegal and when she is older. She has bought her husband a BMV and another car for her father-in-law.

It was Aminata's sister who first came to Tenerife in the mid-1980s. Her sister has travelled widely in Spain selling wooden sculptures produced in Senegal. In her opinion the best trade was to be found in Valencia, Madrid and the Canary Isles. She told me about how inexpensive gold was in Mecca where the enormous department stores bought up the gold jewellery, and about the infinite range of models there were.

I had for a long time been wanting to obtain a little more information about what goods Aminata and her friends and family sold and which made them so prosperous. I suspected that it could not be the usual assortment of T-shirts, leather belts and other sundry items the *griottes* displayed on their stalls. One late evening in July I was at Aminata's home in Playa de las Américas interviewing her about her activities as a woman trader. She was staying at the same apartment hotel as I was with people from all over the world, cramped in small flats and paying a small monthly rent. It was two in the morning, and Aminata had made herself comfortable on a sofa after finishing a long work shift. Spanish public television's Channel One was on, the sound turned down. A detective film flashed by on the screen, while a CD bought in Dakar blasted out loud Senegalese music through the open windows.

Aminata showed no signs of wanting to talk, and the volume of music made verbal communication impossible. I myself felt tiredness creeping up on me and the thought was just going through my mind: "Pity. So few occasions I get to talk to her in peace and quiet", when all of a sudden a neighbour, a woman from the Ivory Coast, stormed into the room, accompanied by another neighbour dressed in a colourful *boubou* and a head scarf of the same material. The latter woman was balancing on her head a large bowl of *tjebb-o-djenn*, the Senegalese national dish of rice, fish and vegetables. She put it down on the floor and invited us all to sit down around the bowl. After Aminata had been eating for a while she began to cheer up and asked the woman from the Ivory Coast what the following day's activities were to be. "Have you hired a car? You know I refuse to give you driving lessons in my own car!" she laughed. Aminata told us about the risks involved in driving with the woman in question, who was a learner. She would whizz along the road like a rally driver, but the main problem was that the traffic signs meant nothing to her, and neither the traffic rules. Aminata said she sat on tenterhooks while the car flew along the road. The woman, it transpired, intended to buy a car of her own to transport her merchandise to various market places on the island, and would therefore need to learn to drive. "Then you'd be better off trading in gold," the other neighbour retorted, referring to gold jewellery, and added "you don't need a car to move those goods around, just a solid bag and patience, loads of patience, going home to the customers and sitting down with them and showing them what you've got with you."

We were soon all involved in a discussion around the subject of gold: the price of gold per gram, the latest jewellery models, the best places to purchase... This was now the moment to ask Aminata straight out how she had entered the gold branch. She replied that the inspiration came from her sister, and that she had just kept going as it seemed to be a profitable business. She would buy the jewellery in Dubai and Mecca and sell it to Senegalese in Spain and Senegal. Previously she had often done some purchasing in Bahrein and Hong Kong. She enjoyed the collaboration of her husband in that he stored the jewellery at home in Dakar while Aminata was away on her business trips. She explained to me that this was a strategy of hers with the purpose of preventing the husband from acquiring another wife. By allowing him to watch over the gold she demonstrated her trust in him.

In 2001 Aminata chiefly traded in bags which bore the imitation brands of Klein, Calvin or Nike. I wondered whether there was any other merchandise Aminata and her neighbours sold in Tenerife. The women nodded, saying they certainly did not confine their activity to gold jewellery, imitation goods and the sale of T-shirts and stockings, wholesale and retail. They had realised that there must be an interesting, growing market among the Senegalese women who had got caught in Tenerife when their papers were not in order. The lively trade with cosmetics and sexy underwear seen flourish in Dakar and Abidjan had its equivalent in the Canary Isles, and Aminata had been among the first to exploit that clientele. Senegalese women living permanently on the islands but illegally were extremely interested in getting hold of a man to provide for them. Aminata assured me that, apart from trading and plaiting hair, among the *griottes* there existed a hardly concealed prostitution. The idea was to pin down Spaniards and Senegalese who had residence permits, get married to them and thus ensure for themselves the possibility to leave Tenerife and return at their leisure. It had turned into a popular means of solving the problem, Aminata pointed out, and the others agreed with her. It meant the endless trips from Spain every three months to renew the visa were a thing of the past. "As long as you don't do a foolhardy thing like me", chirped in the one from the Ivory Coast. The others gave her a sympathetic look and assured her she did the right thing by divorcing her lazybones of a husband who had been living at her expense. I gathered that Aminata on principle in no way approved of the *griottes* who consistently used and abused the Spanish men for their purposes. They gave all the Senegalese women a bad name in Spain, regardless of the others' conduct. For her own part she had no particular desire to suffer for the questionable behaviour of some of the *griottes*.

Nevertheless, Aminata as a saleswoman made some good money using the women's charm offensives. Some of the women competed with each other for

A female dancer *(griotte)* and a male dancer *(griot)* at a meeting of the Senegalese women's association in Madrid, 2009.

the favours of the Spanish and Senegalese men using every means at their command. Aminata told me about some of the seductive arts employed, including the small, delicate transparent strips of cloth which the women wear next to their bodies and between their thighs and which, in good Senegalese fashion, egg the men on with the tempting pattern of the embroidery. These popular strips of cloth are called *petits pagnes* in French and *bethio* in *Wolof*. Other items which are particularly in demand are the strings of pearls intended to excite men by rattling and clattering around the woman's hips as she moves prior to and during intercourse. Such a string of pearls goes under the name of *perles de reins* in French and *bin-bin* in *Wolof*. Incense is another attractive aphrodisiac. "What I sell most, though, are various types of Senegalese cosmetics, such as *khezal* (a cream for bleaching the brown skin. It is chiefly used on the face but also other parts of the body), and creams and herbs which have a drying effect and which smell nice down there." "Oh yes," I said, "Senegalese men want their women to have really tight vaginas, don't they?" "That's right," said the woman from the Ivory Coast, "and at the same time they want children by the dozen. How on earth are we going to manage that, producing the children the men want while the little babies have to come out the same way and not leave us big and sloppy down there? That's why there's a need for different creams and suchlike that can only be bought in Africa."

Aminata added a critical observation to the effect that since the majority of the men were potentially polygamous types, a woman who was eager to capture a husband and keep him for herself had to make a supreme effort to give him what he wanted. "Because, who wants to share a man in your home?" was Aminata's almost rhetorical comment. She was definitely not the sort of woman who could imagine having one or more co-wives. The other women, however, were not totally in agreement with her. "Sometimes it can be better to remain second or third wife rather than have no man at all, as long as you can live in a house of your own and provide for yourself," was the conclusion the other two neighbours came to. Neither of them would envisage sharing a household with another woman or women. Rather let the husband come and spend a couple of nights a week with them.

The hour was late, close to four in the morning. The neighbours left for a few hours' sleep before tackling their work the following day. I expressed my gratitude for the evening spent with them, and decided to save the rest of my queries for a more fortuitous occasion.

Aminata often criticised the *griottes* at Playa de las Américas for their trading methods. Her assessment of the situation was that it was unwise of them to sit all together in a row at Las Verónicas. She said it was much better to spread out and avoid the constant harassment of the police by attracting less attention. Moreover, there would be more customers for each of them. What Aminata didn't bear in mind in saying this was the fact that these women had not previously worked as saleswomen on a large scale as she and her family had.

Another aspect of Aminata's greater experience as a trader compared with other Senegalese women was her command of languages. Her knowledge included Spanish and French and a little English as well as the native *Wolof*, and she had no difficulty in conversing with her customers. The other women showed little interest in acquiring languages. Khady was the *griotte* who was most open towards the tourists, but there was nobody like Aminata for attracting customers by chatting with people. Another sign of her professional attitude was the diplomatic way in which she treated her customers. She eschewed the aggressive tones common among the other trading women, preferring a calm and friendly but firm approach, which more often than not gave profitable results on both a large and small scale.

Equipped as she was with both a residence and a work permit, Aminata therefore preferred not to sit on the edge of the pavement exposed to the exhaust fumes of the passing traffic, but instead she rented a stall and sold her goods fully legally at the different market places around Tenerife. She drove her own pick-up, loading in her wares early in the morning before she left. In 2001 she was mostly selling Chanel brand imitation handbags, T-shirts and belts at the market places, or else she sold wholesale to the retail trade.

From time to time she would plait tourists' hair together with her daughter down at the beach promenade, and occasionally had customers visit her in her home to have their hair plaited. Evenings she would spend watching DVD and video films from Senegal or enjoying Senegalese music, phoning friends and putting her business affairs in order.

"Corruption is rife in Tenerife," Aminata once said to me when we were talking together. "You can't avoid being affected by it as a saleswoman." I wondered how it manifested itself, and I was told you had to bribe your way into renting a table at the market places. You could always try handing over a T-shirt with a banknote wrapped inside. Some people, however, never managed to obtain a permit to sell from a market stall, and were forced into illegal street peddling of cheaper goods often of poor quality. According to Aminata her stall only sold good quality articles. When plaiting hair alone or together with her daughter, she took good care to apply thin, fine threads, not too thick, so as to make them last longer. Aminata did not have much time for people who were sloppy with their plaiting – they gave a bad name to the traders for whom plaiting hair was a serious occupation. Furthermore, she was eager for customers to be happy with her work and the products she sold. It paid in the long run, she knew, to be meticulous and honest.

The natural consequence of Aminata's personality and ambitions to perform a perfect job and offer a faultless product was that the family always enjoyed a host of customers and made good money. This, however, gave rise to pangs of envy in other Senegalese women, which Aminata was most afraid of. Such feelings could easily be channelled into curses and maledictions and harmful actions directed at Aminata and her family on the part of those who considered themselves to have suffered as a result of Aminata's sales success. Aminata claimed to have heard that some Senegalese women accused her of using black magic to steal customers from them. Such imputations frightened her. She regularly requested of her marabout that he protect her against every form of black magic. She also went to great expense in making long-distance calls consulting specialists in magic, home in Dakar. Shortly after I had left Tenerife in 2001 she moved, together with the part of the family that was living with her, to the Balearic Isles in the Mediterranean out of fear for magic powers which might assail her if she stayed on Tenerife. In 2006 she telephoned me from Mallorca to let me know all was well with her family, but that she had moved around a couple of times to two or three places since last. This led me to conclude that she continued to be a successful trader but still felt the object of envy and therefore insecure.

While we were both still on Tenerife I asked Aminata how her marriage could function at a distance with her husband in Senegal and she herself in Spain. She then explained she was in daily contact with him on the phone.

She kept him informed about where she was and what she was doing. In addition, she did go home as often as money and circumstances permitted. Her husband not only saw to it that the gold jewellery was stored in a safe place in the home, but also helped by investing wisely; in gold bars, for instance.

Nonetheless, Aminata's mother was still not happy with her son-in-law. For such a well-to-do daughter this son-in-law was a rather miserable match, she thought. She wanted her daughter to get a divorce and remarry a man with higher social status and a better education, leading to a better-paid job. The mother feared the son-in-law was taking too much advantage of Aminata financially. On the other hand, Aminata, now a forty-year-old with four children, knew she could hardly find a man who did not already have a wife or two; she was, of course, not interested in landing up as a second, third or fourth wife. On top of that, she depended on her husband and his family to take care of the two children who were still at school. Living as a married woman alone, far from home, had of course its price to pay, and Aminata had to be willing to spend a certain amount of her financial resources on her husband. All in all, however, she preferred to pay the price rather than run the risk of ending unhappily in a new home with a stepfather for the children.

The sociologist Fatou Sarr has argued that the tendency for Senegalese women to submit to their husbands' wishes in accordance with social norms has undergone no change. She maintains that it appears as though successful female entrepreneurs have not been able to alter the ideals the traditional wife represents. A patient attitude and the capacity to take suffering in their stride are still seen as outstanding merits in a matrimony.[2] All the same, her research shows that an unexpectedly high percentage of wealthy female entrepreneurs have managed to keep their marriages monogamous. The women Sarr has studied have provided their husbands and their families with a number of possessions in a similar way to Aminata. Their parents-in-law have enjoyed the generosity of the daughters-in-law by receiving gifts the women traders have donated at family ceremonies, and this has improved the family's status. Under such circumstances it follows that the husband's parents would wish to exert influence on their son so that he would retain his wealthy wife and not provoke her by taking a second.

The option of maintaining a monogamous matrimony is not always so obvious to the man. For one thing he is unable to show off his several wives to his male friends and family members; he remains the father of fewer children, and he misses out on the various aspects of extra service that competing wives in a polygamous household can offer the man they share.

The competitive spirit shown by the co-wives can sometimes lead to real highlights in the art of cooking as well as in the art of seduction in polygamous

---

2. Sarr 1998:163.

households. It can, according to Aminata, go to exaggerated lengths when the women endeavour to excel at any price. She tells me that the women often compete in preparing the most delicious food, which might, for instance, be enjoyed by the husband on a sofa while the wife whose turn it is to serve his every need massages his feet. Women traders in particular, Aminata points out, have every reason to be on their guard concerning the husband's chances of saving up enough money to acquire a further wife. Not all the women are as successful as she has been, and the majority are unable to offer their husbands extra money and handsome presents. Animata thinks that almost all marriages in Dakar are polygamous. "And the men always have the law on their side..." Aminata sighs. Nearly all the women she knows are disappointed in their men. But what's to be done? You need a father for your children, and what would life be like without children? Aminata is convinced the only way to enjoy a more or less acceptable life for a Senegalese married woman is to have money, so that one can in any case be a little more independent by living in a house of one's own with the children. Money and a house of one's own are top priorities.

Aminata further told me that she never raised her voice in public against her husband or called into question any of his decisions. She avoided making it obvious for others that she owned any form of authority in matters which concerned both her and her husband. In actual fact I do not believe she was playing a double role when she allowed her husband to get the credit for decisions she had made and deeds she had performed. Growing up in a Senegalese family had taught her what sort of conduct was expected and what norms existed in gender relations. Such norms did not vanish by the wave of a magic wand, even though migration and new economic opportunities for women had given rise to a modest process of change. The relatively large portion of independence Aminata actually enjoyed would have been a threatening element for both her husband and her environment if her daily phone calls to her husband and her willingness to make the financial decisions he proposed did not demonstrate the opposite. Neither her customers nor her trading partners would have respected her in the long run unless her husband had been there as her male source of protection and the person with the ultimate right of decision in the business operations. It was quite simply not enough to be a woman trader; without having established a sound reputation as a wife and as a mother her authority sooner or later would have eroded.

Aminata shows much less esteem, however, for the Senegalese men in Tenerife, intolerant as they are towards their countrywomen's style of life in the diaspora. When we once broached the subject of the male immigrants she was not slow in expressing her negative opinion with respect to their attitudes towards women in Tenerife. In her view the men were showing more and more signs of envy of the women's financial successes. Their way of reacting was to criticise the women for too intense an interest in money, while the men entrenched themselves in a narrow form of Islam. Aminata believed this was not the true form of religion as expressed in the Koran. "Look at all these young men strolling around the streets holding their prayer-books and constantly praying, thinking they're good Muslims," she commented, "instead of working as hard as we women to make some money for our families." By observing the work routine and religious practice of the Senegalese men and women in their daily life in Tenerife, Aminata was expressing an opinion of men and religion scarcely possible for public consumption in Senegal. There negative remarks concerning men or religion are strictly taboo. Above all, you are unable to criticise men's religious practices in whatever form without disgracing yourself as a woman and as a Muslim.

Aminata's views on Senegalese men and their reading of prayers at all times of the day should not be interpreted as implying that women are indifferent towards religion or the native spiritual leaders. As noted earlier, Aminata is herself profoundly dependent on contact with her marabout and the set of values he stands for. She feels that without him her fear of the evil powers would be unbearable. She has a great trust in his capacity to protect her. She never misses an opportunity to visit her marabout in Senegal when he holds the annual feast with his followers.

Animata's mother, who has been working all her life in trade and commerce but without selling at the market places or having a residence permit in Spain, made the following remark to me one day: "The marabouts are needed here when you are away from home. You never feel really 'free' here (from the police, it is implied, and from the threat of confiscation of your goods). It's not the big pilgrimages to Touba that are most important. It's going to see my own marabout at his *magal* in Senegal, and seeing to it that he prays for me so that I can count on his help." The mother proceeds with her street trading while the police are having their lunch. When the police have left work for the day she does a few more hours' selling. She is engaged in a constant struggle to elude the police and avoid being deported after her visa has expired. In 2001 she would say that the marabouts sometimes helped her with the visa. "We have got shaykh Amadou Bamba to thank for being here," says another woman who sells her goods at the different market places. "He is helping us because he wants us to get out into the world, and that's why we are here. And why the marabouts support us." This is an allusion to the two deportations to Gabon and Mauretania suffered by serigne Touba, alias Amadou Bamba, at the hands of the French when his movement began to rouse considerable interest among the Senegalese masses. The Murid migrants have converted these reluctant journeys made by Amadou Bamba into a type of mission they now perform themselves after the founder in the name of modern Muridism.

THE SUBORDINATION
OF WOMEN

Limited freedom

I N THE COURSE OF THE PREVIOUS chapters we have become acquainted with Senegalese women from town and country, in Spain and in Senegal. All of them belonged to the Sufi order Mouridiyya and were in close or distant contact with their spiritual leaders. Some of them were female marabouts themselves while some were followers.

What is so striking about the women's life situation? My first impression concerns their limited freedom – both in terms of physical space but also ideologically. There are enormous differences between the options open to me and those open to Senegalese women when it comes to everyday questions concerning family, work, accommodation and travel. The notion of the strong independent West African woman who provides for her family and enjoys a certain freedom from her husband is true in one sense but misleading in another. These women are often compelled to take charge of their own and their children's maintenance against their will. Like the men, they have learnt that a man's right to decide is related to his role as provider while a woman's duty is to obey. But when a husband fails to bring home either money or food, his wife must take over. So then who decides over the family? Men are given considerable leeway in practice even when they are no longer the chief provider and may therefore seem undeserving. Since they possess all the power, whatever the circumstances, no negative consequences ensue when they fail to comply with their ideals.

Although men know from experience that women are well able to take over responsibility for the livelihood of the household, they do not readily yield any of their power. Since they hold the highest positions in the spheres of both religion and family law, men continue to dominate in society at large as well as in the household. In the eyes of the law, women are ranked as minor citizens who must obey the male head of the household. Women are supposed to tolerate men's inadequacies and they tend to remain silent rather than complain for fear of being considered bad wives or mothers.

The absolute authority enjoyed by men persists to a large extent even in the diaspora. Women must make the most of niches that are out of sight. This reinforces men's views of them as dangerous and needing to be reined so that they will not create chaos and disorder in the family and society.

Money of one's own

It is against this background that the frantic pursuit by Senegalese women of a way to *earn their own money* is so significant. They themselves maintain that they cannot rely on their men. Their economic security is threatened not only by men's unemployment or sickness but also by polygamy. A husband may, sometimes without warning, suddenly bring home a new wife. This has an immediately negative impact on the household's economy and the "old" wife (or wives) often has to draw upon her own resources to secure the situation for herself and her children.

Although polygamy does not represent the most common form of matrimony in Senegal – approximately 45 percent of the women living in marriages of long duration have co-wives – most of the women I got to know sensed the ever-present risk of ending up in a polygamous marriage sooner or later. In the large, powerful marabout families, polygamy is a well-established way of building broad, influential networks. But even poor farmers' wives in the groundnut belt of Senegal and migrant women in Tenerife worry about their husbands' long-term marriage plans. Women often try to build up their own financial reserves in case their husbands find a new wife. The ideal solution for many wives would then be to buy a house of their own. They also like to hamster some money for buying themselves nice clothes, make-up and jewellery so that they can remain attractive to their men. A woman must try to earn the respect of the women in her husband's family, of neighbours and others and she may do this with the help of her possessions. What is more, if she can, a woman will be expected to help provide for her mother and other relatives. These expenses are among the most burdensome for women and they can seldom ask their husband for help since he will have his own unemployed or ageing relatives to care for.

In Senegal men and women often keep their economies separate and this has both advantages and disadvantages. I am more used to the idea of the household being an economic unit than are most of the Senegalese women I have met. Shared ownership can of course be problematic, both in Sweden and elsewhere, particularly in cases of divorce or inheritance. For Senegalese women, polygamy can make matters extremely complicated if the husband dies leaving several widows making claims upon his property. Even while he is still alive, the problems for a wife multiply as soon as he takes a new wife. His income remains the same and it may take some time before a new wife decides to go out and try to earn some money. Until then, she must live off whatever her husband gives her and the "old" wife (wives) will have to make do with a reduced portion.

It is easy to understand women's drive to earn their own money in light of this. Another characteristic of marriages is the secrecy surrounding the size of one's private means. The tug of war that often takes place between husband and wife about one another's property, when neither knows how much the other one actually owns, is often intense. Both parties, as a rule, try to contribute as little as possible to the common expenses, not to mention the costs for the education of the children. Men are sometimes ashamed to tell their wives that they have no work and need money. Both of them suspect each other of keeping money for themselves – jealousy and conspiracies are commonplace and they often destabilise marriages to the point of divorce. This is one of the fundamental problems faced by Senegalese families and it follows migrants from Senegal out into the diaspora[16].

The women always hope to extract more from their husbands within the framework of their marriage than reality offers. They nourish this expectation even if their whole lives they have been told by other women that men are not to be trusted. With such an attitude towards a husband and bearing in mind the women's great need for money, it is easy to understand the intoxicating effect that migration produces in people who manage to emerge from their country and enter places like Tenerife. The relative ease with which money can be earned in Spain is seductive for these women. While they would have lived with constant anxiety about how to earn money for themselves and their children in Senegal, they are pleased to work non-stop in the diaspora. The realisation that they can earn decent money in a relatively short period of time by plaiting people's hair or selling goods is almost unbelievable for them. So what does life offer for an immigrant? For the hard-working, successful women in the Canaries there are great opportunities.

"There's nothing at home," say most of the Senegalese women I have met in Spain. They feel satisfied that they are now able to create better conditions for their children, above all by paying for education and coveted goods.

Women can also save money to establish a decent life in Senegal for their old age, first and foremost in the form of a house. Being able to acquire a plot of land and having a house built for them and the family is a huge relief for

---

1. See Dial 2008, Gemmeke 2008, Lecarme-Frassy 2000.

those who can afford it. If they are able to rent it out, they can also enjoy some welcome income.

Most of those who migrate are young. They see few prospects in Senegal and the embellished stories told by returning migrants amplify the myth of the Spanish El Dorado.

The evil power of envy

Sudden changes in a person's material circumstances provide occasion for envy, fear of witchcraft and evil forces among Senegalese at home and in Tenerife. The examples described from Tenerife show how frightened successful women are of the envy of the less successful and how the unsuccessful blame their failure upon the evil of others. The problem for many is therefore how to manage success. For others the chief concern is that their economic failure risks being seen as a sign of personal incompetence and lack of *barke*, due to weakness or an immoral life. Growing economic differences both in Tenerife and in Senegal give rise to anxiety among migrants, among families and between various groups in Senegalese society.

A better understanding of the background to this unrest can be obtained by considering what the Senegalese sociologist Hassan Sylla calls the "*Wolof moral philosophy*"[2]. This notion helps clarify why failure to make money is so shameful that people strive to find an explanation outside of themselves. Sylla notes that religion and morality are the ideological ingredients that perpetuate the belief in the evil power of envy. By religion, he means the *Wolof* people's abiding belief that there is a God whose existence can never be questioned under any circumstances. Linked to this unshakable belief in God is the conviction that morality lies at the root of all life and exerts an influence on a person's eventual passage into either Hell or Paradise. Anyone who behaves immorally is considered to disgrace not only themselves but their whole family. This is believed to be so potent that it overpowers the protective amulets made by marabouts, *gris-gris*. One family member's immoral behaviour can damage a whole family's welfare in the home and in society. This feature has been stressed in previous chapters in connection with the important concepts of tact (*soutoura*), patience (*muñ*) and decency (*kersa*). This is not the case for the husband, whose bad behaviour is in any case concealed by his good, tactful wife. However, if men and women together behave immorally it may have a negative effect on a place, which may become ill-reputed as somewhere where rash and thoughtless conduct and disrespect for traditions prevail. Therefore, all of the popular entertainments such as drumming, sing-

---

2. See Sylla 1994.

ing and dancing are prohibited before the harvest. This is a way of ensuring that the rains will come when they should and the harvest is protected from the evil eye and other negative forces.

The hierarchical, male-dominated gender system in Senegal fuels envy and suspicion in the women, whose ideal lies in a peaceful and communal existence, known as *mbolo*. The ambivalence they feel towards one another accompanies the women on their emigration to other countries. They keep a sharp eye on each other in Tenerife too. Everyone is supposed to be equal. No one should be cleverer or earn more than the others or they will represent danger.

We have already touched upon the magical antidotes to these problems. They involve consulting a marabout or fortune-teller to receive a diagnosis of the situation and suggestions for cure. Fortune-tellers use cowrie shells or sand for their predictions and clarifications. They also interpret dreams, which disclose moral deficiencies. Khady gave us one example when her house had burnt down and she dreamed that Amadou Bamba was calling her. She was told that she had neglected him and the fire was her punishment.

The marabouts also determine their clients' need of amulets for protection or fulfillment of wishes. For a fee, they produce amulets that they make with pieces of paper with words from the Koran on them that they roll up into small leather packages together with pieces of an animal, such as bits of cat skin. The amulet is then worn on the body. In Senegal the religious leaders also give instructions about what sacrifices should be made at particular holy sites in order to subdue the evil powers. For the same reasons, the fortune teller or the marabout will give instructions about giving gifts to unknown people – usually many metres of white cloth and a certain number of candles. When gifts are made to anonymous recipients, no expectation of reciprocity should be made. The gift should be free and unconditional if it is to have any effect.

The same applies to sacrificial animals. The animal is slaughtered and prepared for a meal at the mosque where all the visitors eat together. The marabout pledges to pray for those affected, usually in exchange for a gift of money. In all of these dealings, a close connection with holy men and sacred space is notable for helping those who feel the threat of malicious others. The force of religion is essential for assuaging destructive energies.

The spirits known as *rab* that were traditionally believed to cause people's trials and tribulations are still blamed, though less so than before. They are not linked in any way with Islam but with people, inside whom the spirits lodge themselves and interfere at will. Sometimes they invade a whole village, which then suffers from catastrophes such as fires, drought, floods or crop failure until they have either been driven out by force of rituals, known as *ndab*, or the village population has had to leave the village locality and move to another place. It is impossible – and pointless – to try and work out whether a man or woman has been attacked by a spirit or by the bad will of a certain person, since boundaries are fluid in the realm of magic and witch-craft. If a woman believes that she has been afflicted by uncontrollable pow-ers manipulated by someone in her environment, she will not imagine this in the form of a spirit but if she cannot identify the person responsible she will blame the spirit realm[3]. It is extremely rare for a marabout or fortune teller to identify a man as the culprit. Nor do the women themselves – as far as I can make out – believe that a man could envy someone so much that he could mobilise enough negative energy to seriously harm that person.

The subordination of women

In my encounters with the Senegalese I was struck by my own incompetence at comprehending their gender ideology, with its influences from both re-ligion and West African tradition mixed with elements of western ideas of human rights and equality. Men's and women's relationships and women's social role simply puzzled me. The discussions I was fortunate enough to have in Senegal were a great help, particularly those with Dr. Penda Mbow, who champions women's rights and civil society and who was able to clarify many of the difficult issues concerning gender equality. Overall, I feel that the position of Senegalese women is beneath them. The fact that it is shared by far too many fellow sisters in Africa and in other continents does not make it any better. Women's subordination is carefully monitored by men and, as noted earlier, is reflected in family law, religion, and in family and society at large. It permeates all social and economic activity. In addition, criticism of the gender system is more or less silenced, as is criticism of other systems of oppression in Senegal, such as the professional status system/caste system and ideas about magic. Here we witness examples of factors that have very negative consequences for the least powerful in society, of whom women are the main representatives.

This reality is concealed for the foreign consultants of the many interna-tional development aid organizations by the population's use of local languag-es and the secrecy surrounding features of caste and ethnicity. Women are silenced by ignorance, illiteracy and religiously inspired ideals about humility. They are also dependent upon men for social status, protection from violence and entry into Paradise. Suspicion is cast over women who try to protest against male dominance in officialdom and they are ignored until they join

---

3. See Gamble 1967, Sadji 1974, Zempleni 1966.

the ranks of the silent women. Unmarried women with or without children have difficulty achieving any status in society.

It is difficult to grasp the problem of domestic violence through the eyes of women. Married women have often told me that many men beat their wives at the same time as protecting them from advances by other men. These men apparently see the violence they use as a way of 'fostering' or chastening a woman in the name of God and women who protest against a husband's violence risk becoming an object of derision. Many men justify their actions through reference to the Koran verse 4:34:

> And those you fear may be rebellious admonish; banish them to their couches, and beat them. If they then obey you, look not for any way against them; God is All-high, All-great.[4]

In this patriarchal society women often compete with one another for the attentions and praise of men. The husband is the authority in polygamous households and the lack of solidarity among co-wives often works to the advantage of the man, who can blame all the household's problems on the women instead of taking responsibility for his own role in them.

Women tend to blame other women for their difficulties. By individualizing the problems instead of seeing them as part of structural inequalities, they reproduce irregularities while constructive solutions are never openly discussed. In combination with men's negative view of women, this means that more egalitarian attitudes and a positive understanding of women as active citizens in state and community are slow to emerge[5].

"*Le pouvoir de la mère est fictif*", the power of mothers is fictitious, said my assistant Salimata Thiam in 1998 in Playa de las Américas. From my western point of view, nothing could be more accurate. Allow me now to pass the issue of women's subordination to men over to two female members of the educated Senegalese elite.

Fatou Sow holds a PhD in Sociology and Codou Bop has worked as a journalist and consultant. Both of them have mixed for a considerable time in international development and social science research circles focusing on gender and human rights. Sow and Bop, together with eighteen female African specialists in various aspects of women's health, have published a report the title of which is:"*Notre corps, notre santé: la santé et la sexualité des femmes en Afrique subsaharienne*"("*Our Bodies, Our Health: Women's Health and Sexuality in Subsaharan Africa[6]*"). The authors make clear that they consider women's position to be poor and to be absolutely subordinated to that of men.

---

4. Arberry, A. 1997 The Koran Interpreted. A Translation. New York.

5. Personal communication with Dr. Penda Mbow, Dakar, January 2007.

6. See Sow and Bop 2004.

According to Sow and Bop, the oppression of women can be traced back to slavery and the caste system as they existed well before the spread of Islam among the ethnic groups *Wolof* and *Halpulaar* in West Africa. Sow and Bop note that in local warfare it was mainly women who were captured as slaves and they were seen as the victors' war bounty. This began long before the European slave trade started. Women were taken to other tribes, regions and clans. Even within each professional status group women were those who suffered most and they still are. Nowadays as well as before women of the lowest caste – *les griottes* – are expected to serve everyone else at all kinds of meetings. One example of this was described above in connection with the mame Diarra Bousso association in Mbacké, where the chairperson always used a *griotte* to run around, delivering messages on foot to the members. Sow and Bob note the contrasts in Senegal between the status of women according to international conventions that the Senegalese state has signed and the status they have in family law and everyday life. *The Convention on the Elimination of All Forms of Discrimination against Women* was ratified in New York on 18 December 1979 and Senegal signed it. The contrasts between the contents of this convention and Senegalese reality are stark – women remain second-class citizens.

Ever since independence from France in 1960 and particularly during the UN-declared decade for women 1975-1984, the Senegalese government has officially shown willingness to improve women's situation. A Ministry of Women's Affairs (*Ministère de la Promotion de la Femme*, now renamed *Ministère de la Famille*) was established alongside social and economic programmes for women. Sow and Bop argue that these efforts have not led to any significant changes. They claim that the ideas that a man should control his wife and that she should remain at home were strengthened with the arrival of French colonialism in the 1800s. It was not only Muslim leaders but also Christian missionaries who promoted these ideals. Working outside the home – particularly in trade – was seen as inappropriate for women and many husbands forbade their wives from leaving the house or farm. Women went to great lengths to try and find ways to engage in trade and make some money without losing their status as respectable wives. Sons often had to act on behalf of their mothers outside the home and this persists to an extent even today. The adage, "Paradise is in the hands of the husband" is as apt today as before.

Uneducated women generally speak with resignation about polygamy or men's rights compared to women's and say that everything is God's will. But when the same women chat with one another they often judge men harshly for their irresponsible behaviour with money, towards their family and in relation to other women. I will not use the word adultery because this would sound ridiculous to the women themselves. "Faithful? A man? Ha!", they would say. However, this kind of criticism is kept out of public view and remains within the secret world of women.

Family law in Senegal

Senegal is predominantly a Muslim country and its form of government is that of a democratic republic. After the departure of the French colonizers in 1960, efforts were made to establish family law using remnants of the French legal code together with elements of Islamic law from the *shari'a*. The objective was to lay traditional views of marriage as an agreement between families to rest and develop a legal focus on the two partners as individuals: wife and husband. The results were drawn up in 1972 and ratified in 1974 and 1979. The law met with public outcry when it first came out. Some men considered it too secular or anti-Islamic and they derided it as *La loi des femmes* – women's law. Others, particularly intellectual women with a western-oriented education, felt it was too conservative. The problem has since been to see that this controversial family law is respected and put into practice. To mention one example, it limits the privilege enjoyed by men according to customary law and also religious law to repudiate a wife without bringing the case into court. This 'modern' family law, which is now nearly 40 years old, still applies for the most part and it regulates marriage, divorce, child custody and inheritance. Islamists, however, have since argued that *shari'a* should play a greater role. For non-Muslims in Senegal there are certain variations to the law but for the most part it applies for all citizens, whether they are Muslims, Christians or people of other religions.

The most recent legal reform was ratified in 1989 but it contained nothing revolutionary for the improvement of women's situation. The debate about family law is still lively and Islamists and feminists have widely divergent opinions. One of the most controversial articles in the law from 1974 was no. 154. This article determined that a woman may only work outside the home if her husband gives his approval. In 1989, the wording was softened but there are continual disagreements between spouses about the applicability of the law in this instance. The women I have written about in the preceding chapters have mentioned the problem of husbands refusing to allow them to work outside the home and women traders have faced particularly strong opposition. Many of them therefore prefer to live without a husband, at least for a time. The more dependent a married woman is upon being able to provide for herself and her children, the more a husband is likely to oppose it, at least publicly, to save his reputation as a man who controls his women and the economy of the household. According to the law, a woman is entitled to own land. In practice, however, women are seldom landowners or inheritors of land. The reason given is that when a woman marries, she will normally move away from her father's property to her husband's home. Traditionally, a woman was seen as an unstable social element who should not be bound to land in a particular place or own land from a distance. The exceptions are the female marabouts who have inherited land as daughters or granddaughters of former kings, whose kingdoms were broken up and taken over by religious leaders. They can also receive land or even a whole village from a close male relative, as we saw with the female marabout Maimouna.

Marriage and divorce

Senegalese family law still treats women as instruments for creating alliances between groups. As long as men see no benefit from introducing new laws, marriages will continue to be silent contracts between families whose members faithfully adhere to local customs. This is so regardless of who contributes the most to the household. The minimum age for girls to marry is 16 years but this is frequently broken, particularly in rural areas. Despite the prohibition in law, arranged marriages for very young girls occur, as does levirate marriage. Levirate means that a widow marries a brother of her deceased husband so that she, her children and her property remain in the husband's family.

According to the wording of the law, a man is the head of his family. This is of major importance for decisions regarding children, particularly in relation to the education of daughters. A mother can only indirectly influence the father. He decides where the family will live and his wife requires his permission if she wishes to travel anywhere. Women migrants in Tenerife who travelled there without their husbands' permission accept that divorce will probably be the outcome of their disobedience. It is the duty of a wife and children to obey their male overlord by demonstrating subservience in the home. Since this has religious overtones it is particularly difficult to change.

In practice it is the man who decides whether his marriage will be monogamous or polygamous. According to the family law, upon drawing up a marriage contract, a man may choose one of three alternatives: monogamy, or to have two, or more than two (three or four wives) – the maximum allowed in Islam is four. If he chooses none of these alternatives, it is the last of them that is automatically applied. It is true that a bride will be asked whether she accepts her bridegroom's decision and she will often be too shy to oppose it. Women I have asked have explained that if a woman says she wants a monogamous marriage, this reflects badly upon her as someone who has been influenced by non-Islamic, secular ideas and who is too mistrusting of her husband-to-be. She also risks that her fiancé will no longer be willing to marry her. If a man selects monogamy on the contract and then takes a second wife later in life he may face a prison sentence. However, several of my male informants in Tenerife explained that "you can always divorce and then remarry but this time with the new woman as your wife".

There are at least three ways to marry. If one chooses a civil marriage, then the officiant will be a government official. The few people who elect to marry in this way are usually educated in the West and have secular ideals and they usually opt for monogamy. One may also marry according to traditional custom but the marriage should then be registered in a civil process afterwards. Finally, religious wedding ceremonies are common and these take place in the mosque and involve a ritual in which the bride may not actually be present.

If a marriage is not registered within six months after the wedding it is impossible for the woman to prove that she has been married. This may have negative consequences for her if a divorce should take place or if an inheritance issue arises. When marabouts marry the young daughters of their *talibés* the girls may be left alone for years after the wedding. Some religious leaders have so many wives that they simply do not have time to visit them all. Girls who want a divorce in situations like this often have difficulty proving that they are married as no registration forms exist.

These married girls may remain without children in their parental home waiting for their husband, who may never actually visit. Their only chance of escape from the situation is if their marabout husband takes pity on them and says the magic words: "I release you". In this case, a separation will be approved by everyone and the girl can hope for a new marriage. Similar situations arise with male migrants who marry when they are back visiting their village in Senegal without completing any paperwork and then disappear to another country. They leave their wives in a precarious situation and these women often want to divorce and remarry. Otherwise they risk ending up as unpaid childless maids in the homes of their in-laws with an absent husband who may never turn up if he doesn't have enough money or has visa problems.

It is popular for male migrants in Spain to find one or more wives back in Senegal. It boosts their status in the eyes of other men and for girls who long to go to Europe to earn money, marrying a migrant may seem like a dream come true.

However, if their dreams are broken, the disappointment can be great. Women I met in Tenerife told many tales of young girls marrying men who had returned to Senegal for a visit. In one case, the marriage was arranged over the phone while the man was in Madrid and the girl, back in Senegal.

The bridegroom sent a sum corresponding to the bridewealth via Western Union to the girl's father. As far as I know this husband never returned to his wife in the home country as he was living illegally in Spain without any 'papers'.

Men usually do not want their wives to accompany them to Europe and pick up what they consider to be the deplorable habits of the women there. This is also so among Senegalese migrant men in the USA, where women have been known to ring the police if their husbands beat them and the men have then been convicted of abuse and ended up serving prison sentences that they feel they do not deserve.

Many men therefore feel it is better to keep their wives at home in Senegal, where they know their place and where the children will receive a proper education in Koran school. Some men have also told me that they do not want to have to pay for expensive trips for the family to come to Europe.

It is not simply religious traditions that prevent people from wanting civil marriages. If the bride lacks identification documents or school diplomas it may be difficult to produce the necessary paperwork. The bride's family may not be literate and the forms are complicated and difficult to fill in. Photographs are required, but where should these be taken? And how should they be paid for? Questions like these mean that many prefer to get married in the village according to custom. The men go to the mosque, where the imam performs the marriage ceremony and the woman stays at home to await the party and wedding night.

The family law of 1974 made divorce more difficult than it had been previously. In theory, it would offer women greater protection from abandonment by their husbands without legitimate reasons. Divorces were now to be handled by civil courts and would only be permitted in specific instances, such as adultery or obvious breakdown of the relationship. Women would also have the option to file for divorce in these courts and men would have to pay maintenance to their former wife and the children. However, these rules are rarely applied, particularly in rural areas. Most people are indeed unaware of what the law says and they simply follow whatever their religious leaders dictate.

The legal stipulations for divorce reflect a male-dominated notion of justice. In practice, the law leaves a divorced woman and her children in a worse position than the ex-husband. It is far easier for a man to get a divorce than it is for a woman and, unlike her, he rarely needs to give a reason. The most common reason given by the wife is that the husband has been gone for more than six months and that he has failed to comply with his marital duties. Even if a woman does succeed in gaining a divorce, it is a tough life she faces as a divorcee. Many women describe how common it is for men to seek revenge upon their ex-wives and try to make life as difficult as possible for them, even

Going to a name-giving party: mother and her daughter dressed up. Mbacké 1995.

if she is the mother of their children. An angry ex-husband may, for instance, try to sabotage his former wife's economy. Her vulnerability is exacerbated by the fact that society views single women as less than full citizens and as unable to act as guardians of their children. She will not receive the *pension alimentaire* (employer's contribution to child support) that would be her right elsewhere, like in Spain. It is the divorced man who receives the support instead, whether he has custody of the children or not. When the man initiates a divorce, the process goes quickly and sometimes his wife knows nothing about it until it is presented to her as a fact. Regardless of what the law may say, several of the migrant women I have met have experienced this after leaving husbands behind in Senegal.

Inheritance

According to the Islamic law, women should only inherit half of what men inherit. The Senegalese law in article 609 states: "A widow inherits one quarter of the estate if there are no lineal heirs. If there are several wives, this quarter should be divided between them."

Article 610 declares that: "A widow is entitled to one eighth of the estate if there are lineal heirs. If there are other wives, then this eighth should be divided between them." This means that if the man has four wives who survive him, then they each get a quarter of a quarter, or a quarter of an eighth of his property. In practice, it is very difficult for a widow to stake her claim at all. The relatives of a deceased man are usually quick to take their pickings of his property though the goods that a woman has acquired for herself in a polygamous marriage remain hers. If she shares them with her husband, he has no right to give them to any of the other wives.

The conflicts over ownership that arise in polygamous households both while the husband is alive and after his death are innumerable[7].

Naturally, the Senegalese Constitution promotes equality between the sexes and between ethnic groups as well as between professional status groups. But it is extremely difficult for women to demand their rights when most of them lack education and there is constant discrimination against women. In rural areas in particular, women remain marginalised because they are barred from gaining education. As noted earlier, unlike in European societies, the individual in African society is more dependent on a social group, such as the extended family or clan, than upon the state. This is the case in Senegal, where efforts by public institutions to limit practices such as polygamy have

---

7. The data in this section are derived from the article "Mariage et divorce: version Code de la Famille", anonymous, in *Femmes au Sénégal, Les Cahiers de L'Alternance*, no. 10, Dec. 2006.

failed or had the opposite effect. They have not been taken seriously by political leaders, nearly all of whom are men. Men still wish to be able to practice this form of marriage and women are not sufficiently united to be able to counter it. In a society in which unmarried, divorced or widowed women are often targets for sexual and other forms of harassment, accepting a position as second, third or fourth wife may be preferable to living without a husband.

Many Senegalese have grown up in families in which the father has had several wives and men are aware of its advantages – today, there is little incentive for them to work against it. If you were to ask any Senegalese man in Senegal or in Spain what he would invest his money in if he had any, most would give the same answer: first a new wife, then a gift of money to the marabout, after that, perhaps a car, land or a house and then the family...

SMALL CHANGES,
GREAT EXPECTATIONS

Small changes

HOW DO SENEGALESE WOMEN manage to fulfil their dreams in Senegal and in Spain despite the hindrances they face? How do they manage to shoulder the responsibilities that men often leave them with for caring for the home, children and household finances? How do they have the strength?

Part of the answer lies in their ability to organise themselves, which they learn from an early age in the home and in youth associations. They also seem to be blessed with extraordinary stamina for both physical and mental labour. They know that they will ultimately have to rely upon themselves for their income and survival and they put everything into fulfilling their dreams. Anyone who catches a glimpse of their lives will be impressed by the amount of energy they spend on their homes, families, associations, ceremonies and pilgrimages.

Involvement in women's associations encourages both independence and cooperation – in the broadest sense of the term – *mbolo*. Here, women learn the crucial importance of reciprocity – giving and taking – which forms the backbone of women's social life. Various economic cooperatives also enable women who are in difficulties to borrow money to start small businesses. Other associations enable them to participate in female-dominated social spheres in which parties for weddings, name-giving and funerals play a major role. Women collaborate in organising these festivities but they also compete with one another. These events offer an opportunity to make public displays of generosity in the form of money or gifts that will enhance one's own family's reputation in the eyes of everyone present. The donor at one ceremony will become the recipient at the next and give back at least as much as they have received and ideally much more. Often, this means giving back twice as much as one received on the last occasion. Family ceremonies are expensive but also important affairs for women's social lives and they are one of the many reasons that women are constantly in hot pursuit of money.

The number of tradeswomen in Senegal and abroad is steadily growing and this makes women increasingly visible in society. Nowadays, many of them are earning enough money to live more or less independently of their husbands and if they can afford to buy themselves a house of their own, they gain considerable freedom from male control. External influence from the mass media, relatives and tourists visiting from other countries also give women an awareness of other models of marriage and family life than the traditional Senegalese one.

Migration is one way of escaping outmoded values that lock people into social groupings with little chance of making changes. These values may concern not only gender relations but also prejudices towards ethnic groups or status groups such as 'castes'. There are many taboos and unspoken agreements in the name of religion and tradition that prevent initiatives for change or development. Despite the difficulties faced by migrants to Europe, these factors make the option of leaving the country highly attractive for those who feel victimised and especially for young people. Some leave in order to escape a problematic situation at home and to find quick money and a better future for themselves and for their family back in Senegal.

It is not uncommon for women traders to live and work in Senegal or abroad but have a strong enough economy to send their daughters to school in the USA. These girls will most likely in turn influence their own daughters towards a less patriarchal way of life. Even the daughters of marginalised women such as divorcees or widows may be the embryos of change as has proven to be the case in Algeria and Morocco. Single women both highlight and challenge the prevailing norms and gender hierarchy[1].

Globalisation brings not only greater awareness of national and ethnic identity but also consciousness of different ways of life that many women and youngsters may be inspired to imitate. Those who wish to protect their privileged position over others – largely men – are often anxious to stop women from migrating and getting ideas about equality into their heads. By anchoring the discourse *against* equality in religion, men are able to claim that their patriarchal ideas are ethically correct according to Islam and this makes it more difficult for women to demand change.

I should note that none of the women I describe have been promoters of women's rights like those I mentioned in connection with the reform of family law, such as Fatou Sow and Codou Bop. On the contrary, the women I have portrayed are committed Murids who do not question the patriarchal ideas embedded in their faith. What they want above all is money and they

---

1. Jansen 1987: 244–249.

want their husbands to give them liberty to work outside the home. They do not speak of problems with social norms or with men as a group. When I suggested changes to the law, the women looked dubious. They know that they have nothing to say about such matters. Their illiteracy, their heavy workload and their habit of remaining silent in situations in which men speak means they do not participate in debates about society. Their religion is their nourishment and their respect for those who represent God and perform miracles is great. The quest for money for themselves and their children is what drives them. According to most Senegalese women, religion and money are what life is all about.

Great expectations

Of course, religion and money are important to both men and women but in this summary I focus on women. Morally correct behaviour is an important part of women's religiosity[2] everywhere and this is highly evident in Senegal. The didactic stories about mame Diarra illustrate female morality according to Muridism and it is notable how closely linked morality and devotion are for the women. Today's Senegalese values are apparent in these legends and they follow migrants out into the world beyond Senegal. In Tenerife I saw how fundamental they were for identity, both for men and women[3]. It is for this reason that I shall now briefly reiterate the central features of the mame Diarra cult.

The role of the mother is presented as one of great responsibility and social significance, particularly among the *Wolof* and *Halpulaar*. Mame Diarra's absolute obedience and submissiveness in marriage and in the extended family are rewarded by her having a son who becomes a prophet and leader. She becomes the hope and ideal of the Murid women[4].

No matter how she has been treated by her husband, a woman's duty is to show discretion, *soutoura*, and loyalty in order that she may enter Paradise. Consequently, the man holds his wife's fate in his hands and this moral notion essentially chains a woman to her husband. It also makes marriage obligatory if a woman wants to live up to the expectations that religion and society foster. Women look up to mame Diarra and her virtues because she appears to have succeeded in meeting the demands made of her as the ideal wife. Her behaviour resulted not only in a remarkable son but, what is more, also in material prosperity for her followers who ask for her assistance. "She gives me

2. See Sered 1992.
3. See Evers Rosander 2003.
4. See Thiam 1998.

everything I ask for," is the most common characterisation of mame Diarra. More poetically, women say that she is the 'ocean' that gives to everyone, who embraces all without limits in time or space – she is a mother who each individual may see as his or her own. This is how she is perceived today.

Aram is a Murid woman in Touba and she is an avid follower of mame Diarra Bousso. Every year, she goes to Porokhane for the *magal* and asks mame Diarra for various material items that she says she receives a short while after the pilgrimage. This is how Aram describes mame Diarra's generosity:

> People say that mame Diarra used to hang her washing on the trees by her hut in Porokhane. And they say that if you want a good wardrobe, you should rip a piece of cloth off your dress and then tie it to one of the branches. I took a whole skirt to Porokhane and then I ripped it into shreds and hung them all on the trees. I did it for myself and for my friends. The people I was with said I was crazy but I told them to leave me alone. I've never regretted doing it because I have more than a hundred skirts now … Everything you ask of mame Diarra in God's name you receive. People are no longer hungry or thirsty or cold like they used to be – they have more clothes, more of everything. And it's all thanks to mame Diarra.

The Murid women say that mame Diarra's son Amadou Bamba does not give as much or as quickly. It is his mother who is associated with this unconditional and almost absurd generosity while the father image is far less charged. The women claim that men are of a different nature and that they always put their own interests first except when it comes to their marabout, whom they worship above all else. A male Murid will do anything for the marabout who has accepted his pledge of obedience.

For Murid women, Porokhane, where mame Diarra is said to be buried and the annual pilgrimage takes place, is a cherished site for the mother. By contrast, Touba, where the son is buried and the great mosque lies, is a powerful symbol of Amadou Bamba and is more popular for Murids in general. The identification of Touba with Amadou Bamba is so strong that people use the names interchangeably; he is called serigne Touba as well. Murid women tend to see mame Diarra and her son as one and the same person – she gave birth to this extraordinary man and saint because of her untainted moral behaviour – while some eminent Murid men tend to see mame Diarra simply as the biological progenitor of a great religious leader.

Aram writes eloquently of her love of mame Diarra:

> Porokhane is the holy city. We say that Touba is life, it is everything. But Porokhane gave rise to Touba, and so in fact Porokhane is life, and everything. People say of Touba that 'As soon as you arrive there, you are saved (from all misfortune). If you grow up there, you'll be well-behaved. If you die there,

you'll reach Paradise.' That is true of Touba. But what can you say about Po-rokhane, which is Touba's mother and is so much more than Touba? All I can say is that *serigne* Touba is the house but mame Diarra is the door to the house and if the door is closed then you can't get in. Thanks be to mame Diarra.

The Murid men say that Porokhane is of much less significance than Touba. The *Great Magal* in Touba is the largest Murid event with millions of visitors, they assert. But over the years Porokhane too has become an important pil-grimage site. The mass media and improved communications have contribut-ed to this development. Migration has also benefitted Muridism and pilgrim-ages since the majority of Senegalese immigrants in America, Italy, Spain and other countries are Murids. This has given Muridism a boost: the mosque in Touba has been extended and there has been a building boom in Porokhane to house high-ranking visitors. Also, the Mame Diarra associations in Senegal and the migrant women have contributed with their own money and they have therefore become of increasing interest to the Murid establishment

Both men and women are expected to live up to the ideal of humility that Muridism promotes and that mame Diarra Bousso represents. But I do not think that men experience the double burden that women do. Women are subordinate to men in marriage as well as to the marabouts in religion. While a man chooses to obey his marabout in order to derive material and spiritual benefits, a woman's subordination to men is hardly voluntary. Putting up with a husband's beatings, taking responsibility for the children and all or part of the household income is often a woman's lot in life. Mame Diarra seems to give inspiration and help not only for obedience but for inner strength and self-respect. Mame Diarra reiterates and gives dignity to the wife-mother role for many Murid women in their daily lives. They go to Porokhane and are treated almost as equals to men. Aram, whom we met earlier, has never felt as happy as she does when she goes on a pilgrimage to Porokhane:

> When we go to Porokhane with our mame Diarra association it's the women who get to sit comfortably at the front of the bus while the men have to sit at the back. In Porokhane, we eat together with the men and we drink before they do. We are shown all this respect because of mame Diarra. It's mame Di-arra who elevates us to this standing. The men don't even make their ablutions before we do (before prayer). They're always after us. That's how it is in our association. So, thank you mame Diarra Bousso and thank you to the president of our association!

Given the above, I suggest that it is difficult to draw hard and fast conclusions regarding the position of women in Senegalese society and in Muridism. It is also hard to make sharp distinctions between the sacred and the profane. Women's religiosity is present in every aspect of their lives. Female subordination exists alongside women's influence over men and children in the private sphere of the home and in the family economy. Elements of Murid rituals that strike me as discriminatory, such as the fact that few marabouts permit women to join in the singing of Amadou Bamba's songs and that some do not even allow women to sit in the same room as the men during the *daira* meetings, are accepted as completely natural by the women themselves. Both men and women have their sights set on Paradise and the prospect of a life after this one and they live in fear of instead ending up in Hell. This fear transcends gender and forms the basis of religiosity in general.

It is against this background that mame Diarra Bousso takes on meaning. I can understand the Murid women's need for an ally and representative before God; an ally who has mystical powers and great empathy. I am also conscious of these women's uneasiness about me, the ethnographer from another country, and about what will become of me after death. Firstly, I am *toubab*, white and Christian, or non-Muslim from a secular western society. For them, I am a lost soul who will never enter Paradise unless I convert to Islam or, better still, follow Amadou Bamba and ask his mother for support. It is to help me onto the right track that the women take me along to Porokhane and patiently deal with all my questions. Although I came to them to try and understand their religiosity from an analytical viewpoint, they want to awaken my own religiosity and enable my salvation. They want me to not only passively observe what they do but to actively and fervently participate and to transform my life into that of a Murid. But the women also expect me to help them, above all in a material sense. I realise again and again that we have entered into a relationship of reciprocity with each giving what they can.

The women are convinced that all the work they do and the money they give to God and for the marabouts are worth it. They believe that showing submissiveness, patience and high moral standards in the family will also pay off. Expectations about Paradise are combined with hope of prosperity here on Earth. So it is all about *yakar*, expectations made of God, the marabouts and other people.

What does Paradise actually mean according to these women? What does it stand for? What do they expect to find there? Those I have asked cannot give a clear answer but one thing is certain – in Paradise they will be able to rest. There will be gurgling brooks, green meadows and trees that are laden with fruit, they are told. They will no longer be burdened with worries and, most important of all, the women will be safe from the threat of the torments of Hell.

POSTSCRIPT

ORIGINALLY THIS BOOK was written in Swedish with a view to reaching a wide audience both within academic circles and beyond. The Nordic Africa Institute (NAI) encouraged this and the book, *Nyckeln till Paradiset* (The Key to Paradise), was published by NAI in collaboration with Carlsson Publishers, Stockholm in 2011, with financial support from the Längmanska Culture Foundation, Stockholm.

This broad approach gave me the opportunity to include some of my own feelings and thoughts concerning my field of research in a more personal way than is normally the case in social anthropological studies. It also afforded me a chance to speculate over how my informants might have perceived our encounters – the purpose and meaning of my presence among them in Senegal and Spain from their own perspective, and the way I interpreted their reactions.

Later, when NAI expressed interest in publishing the book in English, we applied for and received much appreciated financial support for the translation from the Vilhelm Ekman University Foundation, Uppsala, and the Åke Wiberg Foundation, Stockholm.

Chapters 1–2 and 12–13 have been translated by Associate Professor Alexandra Kent, the Nordic Institute of Asian Studies, Copenhagen, and chapters 3–11 by Senior Reader Graham Long, Nebrija University, Madrid, Spain. I would like to express my great appreciation for their sensitive work.

Fieldwork

I conducted fieldwork for shorter and longer periods in Senegal 1992–1998, and among Senegalese migrant in Tenerife 1996–2001 and in Madrid 2003–2005. In 2009 I was back in Tenerife for a week in order to conduct interviews with members of the Senegalese Association there.

My fieldwork was financed by the Swedish Research Council, the Swedish International Development Cooperation Agency and within the framework of the following positions, including time for analysis and writing up: Senior Researcher at the Nordic Africa Institute, Uppsala; Senior Researcher at the former Center for Development Research, Copenhagen (today, the Danish Institute for International Studies) and Senior Researcher of the "Women and Religion" Research Programme, financed by the Swedish Research Council, at the Department of Theology, the Section of Sociology of Religion, Uppsala University. My last visit to Tenerife in 2009 was financed by the Spanish Ministry of Foreign Affairs, the Section for Research and Development, Madrid, in collaboration with the University of Miguel Hernández, Elche, Spain.

Anonymity and composed cases

Khady, Coumba and Aminata are fictitious names of people I got to know in Tenerife almost twenty years ago. I have changed details in their lives so that they will remain anonymous. This means that they constitute what we can call "composed cases", presented to the readers with characteristics of significance for many Senegalese women in Tenerife who live in similar circumstances.

The same applies to Awa and Fatou in Senegal. They are described using pseudonyms and have been ascribed some biographical facts taken from the lives of other women that resemble their own.

The marabout Serigne Cheikhouna in Touba Belel and his first wife Mai Habou appear under their real names. Their contribution to my study was decisive and I would once again wish to express my gratitude to them.

Collaborators

In Senegal I collaborated with Múskeba Fófona 1993–95. She was a student at the Department of Sociology, Gaston Berger University, S:t Louis, Senegal. I also worked with the sociologist Fatimata Sall, Dakar, and the social welfare worker Fatou Sy Samb, Mbacké. In Senegal and in Tenerife I collaborated with Dr. Salimata Thiam, Dakar. These women were excellent assistants and treasured friends during my fieldwork. With the exception of S. Thiam, their real names do not appear in the book as I have not been able to reach them to ask for permission. I would like to extend special thanks to my husband Göran Rosander, Förslöv, and my dear friends Irene Svensson, Stockholm, and Prof. Em. Gunilla Bjerén, for their comments and advice when I was writing the book in Swedish. Thanks are also due to my kindred soul Amparo Pozo Calvo, Valladolid, Spain for all the critical comments and inspiring talks in Spain and Senegal.

Many thanks also to the Nordic Africa Institute, Uppsala: Elnaz Alizadeh, Head of the Communication Unit, Karl-Eric Eriksson, former Head of the Publication Unit, and Birgitta Hellmark-Lindgren, former Head of the Communication Unit and current Head of the Communication Unit, Stockholm University Library, Stockholm.

Finally, I wish to thank Mercedes Jabardo Velasco, Professor, Miguel Hernández University, Elche, Spain, Penda Mbow, Professor, University Cheikh Anta Diop, Dakar, and the Presidential Representative of Senegal for *l'Organisation Internationale de la Francophonie* (OIF), Allan Roberts, Professor, UCLA, USA and Karen Tranberg Hansen, Professor Emerita, Copenhagen University and Northwestern University, USA.

GLOSSARY
WOLOF-ENGLISH

addiyya: financial offering to a religious leader or marabout

Ajaana,arjana: Paradise.

awo or aawa: first wife in a polygamous (polygynous) marriage.

Bai Fall/Baye Fall: a sub-group of Muridism, founded by Amadou Bamba's closest and most famous disciple, Cheikh Ibra Fall.

barke: blessing, divine power (Arabic baraka).

Cheikh/Shaykh: title ascribed to an eminent religious leader or marabout.

daara: collective work group serving the shaykh, often combined with a Koran school for the young boys who live in rural daaras, carrying out agricultural work and pursuing Islamic studies.

daira: a Murid association of disciples in the name of a religious leader or marabout.

djebelu, jebbelu: act of submission by a disciple, surrendering to the authority of his/her marabout.

geer: freeborn, of the nobility, 'those who possess honour'.

gewel: bard, praise singer, member of a low-status professional group.

Hisbu Tarqiyya: ('Party for a Spiritual Uplift') an association in expansion with its main residence in Touba, dominated by young fervent male Murids. They are open to modern technology and a globalised world though maintaining a conservative idea of women's status in religion and society.

kersa: deference, restraint, shame.

khabru: a tomb or mausoleum.

Khadim Rassul: another name for Amadou Bamba, founder of Muridism.

khalwa: meditation, spiritual retreat (of Arabic origin)

khassaïd: religious song, penned by Amadou Bamba, inspired by the Koran.

Korité: in West Africa (Senegal and Mali) the feast marking the end of the month Ramadan (in Arabic, 'Id al Fitr).

ligeey: work. According to Amadou Bamba, work for a holy purpose is equivalent to prayer.

maas: age group, age association.

magal: pilgrimage for the celebration of a Murid marabout or a feast of remembrance of a marabout. (The annual Great Magal in Touba is a festival on the 18th of Safari, the second month in the Islamic calendar, commemorating Amadou Bamba's return from his 12 years of exile in Gabon and Mauritania, which was ordered by the French colonial power).

Mame: title of honour for a deceased person of high esteem, often within the religious field, used for both man and woman.

mbolo: peace, cooperation, unity.

Mbotaye: traditional neighbourhood self-help (aide-entre-aide) group for married women. (Ndaye dické, sanni jamra and takri kharfit are the names of similar groups or associations).

Murid: member of the Sufi order El Mouridiyya, Muridism.

muñ: patience, capacity to endure pain and discomfort.

ñaan: blessing by a marabout

nat: rotating savings and credit association.

ndawtal: gift of money given by women relatives at family ceremonies, recorded by the receivers so that later, on a similar occasion, the same sum or more is given away

ndigël: command, exhortation to submission and willingness to follow the Murid ethics.

ñeeño: member of artisan/professional status group, musician.

pentch: courtyard, in this book referred to as a meeting-place on the marabout estates in Touba.

Safara: hell.

Seriñ, serigne: title ascribed to eminent religious leaders and marabouts.

Shaykh/Cheikh: title ascribed to an eminent religious leader or marabout.

Sokhna: title for a female shaykh or an eminent woman.

soutura: discretion, tact.

Tabaski: In West Africa (Senegal and Mali) 'the big feast' (in Arabic: Aid Al-Adha). For Tabaski, every Muslim family who can afford it should ritually slaughter a sheep in remembrance of Abraham's willingness to sacrifice his own son as a sign of his submission and total surrender to God.

talibé: disciple.

teranga: generosity, hospitality, honour.

tiyaba: (from Arabic) merit received from God.

toubab: white person, European.

yakar: expectation, hope.

ziyara (from Arabic): pious visit, visit to holy places at a pilgrim site.

BIBLIOGRAPHY

(# Indicates that the book or the article is referred to in the text.)

Augis, Erin. 2005. "Dakar's Sunnite women: The politics of person." In *L'islam politique au sud du Sahara: Identités, discours et enjeux*. In Muriel Gomez Perez (ed.), Paris: Karthala, pp.309–26

Ibid. 2012. "Religion, religiousness, and narrative: Decoding women's practices in Senegalese Islamic reform." *Journal for the Scientific Study of Religion 51, no. 3 (2012)*, pp. 429–41.

Ibid. 2013. "Dakar's Sunnite Women: The dialectic of submission and defiance in a globalizing city." In Diouf, Mamadou (ed.) *Tolerance, Democracy, and Sufis in Senegal*. New York: Columbia University Press, pp.73–98.

#Ba, Awa. 2008. "Les femmes mourides à New York. Une renégociation de l'identité musulmane en migration." In Diop, Moumar-Coumb (ed.). *Le Sénégal des migrations: Mobilités, identités et sociétés*. Paris et Dakar: Karthala-Crepos-ONU Habitat.

Behrman, Lucy C.1970. *Muslim Brotherhoods and Politics in Senegal*. Cambridge, Mass.: Harvard University Press.

Bop, Codou. 2005. "Roles and the position of women in Sufi brotherhoods in Senegal." *Journal of the American Academy of Religion 73*, no. 4, pp. 1099–1119.

#Brenner, Louis. 1993. *Muslim Identity and Social Change in Sub-Saharan Africa*. Bloomington: Indiana University Press.

#Buggenhagen, Beth A. 2009. "Beyond Brotherhood: Gender, Religious Authority, and the Global Circuits of Senegalese Muridiyya." In Diouf, Mamadou and Mara Leichtman (eds.) *New Perspectives on Islam in Senegal. Conversion, Migration, Wealth, Power, and Femininity*. New York: Palgrave Macmillan.

Ibid. 2012. *Muslim Families in Global Senegal: Money Takes Care of Shame*. Bloomington: Indiana University Press.

Callaway, Barbara, and Lucy Creevey.1994. *The Heritage of Islam: Women, Religion, and Politics in West Africa*. Boulder, Colo.: Lynne Rienner.

#Carter, D.M 1997. *States of Grace*. Minneapolis: University of Minneapolis Press.

#Copans J.1988. *Les Marabouts de l'Arachide*. Paris: L'Harmattan.

Coulon, Christian. 1981. *Le marabout et le prince: Islam et pouvoir au Sénégal*. Paris: Éditions Pedone.

#Ibid. 1988. "Women, Islam and Baraka". In Cruise O'Brien, D. and C. Coulon (eds.). *Charisma and Brotherhood in African Islam*, Oxford: Clarendon Press.

#Ibid och Reveyrand, O. 1990. *L'Islam au féminin: Sokhna Magat Diop, Cheikha de la confrérie mouride*. Bordeaux: CHEAm.

#Dial, Fatou Binetou. 2008. *Mariage et divorce à Dakar: Itinéraires féminins*. Paris and Dakar: Karthala-Crepos.

Diouf, Mamadou and Steven, Rendell. 2000. "The Senegalese Murid trade diaspora and the making of a vernacular cosmopolitanism." *Public Culture*, no 12–3; pp. 679– 702.

#Ebin, E. 1990. "Commerçants et missionaires: Une confrérie musulmane sénégalaise à New York. "In *Hommes et Migrations*, no. 1132 (May).

#Ibid. 1996. "Making room versus creating space. The construction of spatial categories by itinerant Mourid traders". In Metcalf, M.D. (ed.). *Making Muslim Space in North America and Europe*, Berkeley and Los Angeles: University of California Press.

Eickelman, D. och J. Piscatori (eds). 1990. *Muslim Travellers: Pilgrimages, Migration, and the Religious Imagination*, Berkeley: University of California Press.

Evers Rosander, Eva. 1997. "Introduction" and "Le Dahira de Mame Diarra Bousso de Mbacké, Sénégal." In Evers Rosander, Eva (ed.) *Transforming Female Identities: Women's Organizational Forms in West Africa*. Uppsala: Nordic Africa Institute.

#Ibid. 1998. "Women and Muridism in Senegal: The Case of the Mame Diarra Bousso Daira in Mbacké". In Ask, Karin and Marit Tjomsland (eds.). *Women and Islamization. Contemporary Dimensions of Discourse on Gender Relations*. Oxford: Berg.

#Ibid. 2004. "Going to Porokhane and Not Going to Porokhane. Mourid Women in Senegal and Spain." In Eade, John and Simon Coleman (eds.). *Reframing Pilgrimage. Cultures in Motion*. London: Routledge.

Ibid. 2005 "Cosmopolites et locales: Femmes sénégalaises en voyage". *Afrique et Histoire Révue internationale*. Número 4. Paris: Verdier.

#Ibid. 2006a. "Sacralizing Hotels in Spain: Mourid Marabouts in Motion". *El Awraq*, vol. XXIII, Madrid: Dirección general de relaciones culturales y científicas.

Ibid. 2006b. "Cosmopolitas y locales: mujeres senegalesas en movimiento" In Jabardo Velasco, Mercedes. *Senegaleses en España. Conexiones entre origen y destino*. Madrid. Ministerio de Trabajo y Asuntos Sociales.

#Ibid. 2010. "Gender relations and female autonomy among Senegalese migrants in Spain: three cases from Tenerife." De Regt, Marina, König, Reinhild and E. Evers Rosander (eds.). *African and Black Diaspora*. Vol.3. Number 1. New York: Routledge.

Ibid. 2011 "With Mame Diarra Bousso in Spain: Murid Women Migrants in Tenerife". In Fog Olwig, Karen and Mikkel Rytter (eds): *Mobile Bodies, Mobile Souls: Migration, Family and Religious Practice*. Århus: Århus University Press.

#Gamble, David P. 1957. *The Wolof of Senegambia. Together with Notes on the Lebu and the Serer*. London: London International African Institute.

#Gemmeke, Amber B. 2008. *Marabout Women in Dakar. Creating Trust in a Rural Urban Space*. New Brunswick and London: LIT.

#Guye, Cheikh. 2007. *Touba. La capitale des mourides*. Paris: Karthala.

Hill, Joseph. 2010. "All Women Are Guides': Sufi Leadership and Womanhood among Taalibe Baay in Senegal." *Journal of Religion in Africa* 40, no. 4, pp. 375–412.

Janson, Marloes. 2014. *Islam, Youth and Modernity in the Gambia: The Tablighi Jama'at.* London: Cambridge University Press.

#Jansen, Willy. 1987. *Women without Men.* Leiden: Brill.

#Jean, Christine.1997. *Les sokhnas Mbacké-Mbacké: des femmes marabouts,* Doctorat d'Ethnologie et de Sociologie Comparative, Université de Paris X, Nanterre.

#Khalifa, Rashida. 1998. *Koranen. Det sista testamentet. (The Koran. The Last Testament.)* Islamic Prodic.

Koktvedgaard Zeiten, Miriam. 2008. *Polygamy: A Cross-Cultural Analysis.* Oxford: Berg

Leymarie, Isabelle. 1999. *Les griots wolof du Sénégal.* Paris: Servedir – Maisonnoeuve & Larose.

#Lecarme-Frassy, Mireille. 2000. *Marchandes dakaroises entre maison et marché. Approche anthropologique.* Paris: L'Harmattan.

#Leichtman, Mara A. 2009. "The Authentication of a Discoursive Islam: Shi'a Alternatives to Sufi Orders." In Diouf, Mamadou and Mara Leichtman (eds.). *New Perspectives on Islam in Senegal: Conversion, Migration, Wealth, Power and Femininity.* New York: Palgrave Macmillan.

Masso Guijarro, Ester. 2013."La dahira de Mame Diarra en la diáspora: un desafio al patriarcado murid?" *Revista de Dialéctica y Tradiciones Populares,* no. LXVIII-I., pp. 125–144.

M'Bow, Penda. 2001."L'Islam et la femme sénégalaise. Ethiopiques." *Revue négro-africaine de literature.* N°s 66–67. 1:e et 2:e sémestres.

Ibid (ed.). 2006. *"Hommes et femmes entre sphères publique et privée".* The CODESRIA series on Gender, nr. 5, Dakar: CODESRIA.

#O'Brian, D. Cruise.1972. *The Mourides of Senegal: the Political and Economic Organization of an Islamic Brotherhood.* Oxford: Clarendon Press.

#Pajares, M. 1998. *La immigración en Espana: Retos y propuestas.* Barcelona: Icaria Antrazyt.

Parry, M. och M. Bloch, M. 1989. "Introduction: money and the morality of exchange". In Parry, J. and M. Bloch (eds.). *Money and the Morality of Exchange,* Cambridge: Cambridge University Press.

Pezeril, Charlotte. 2008. "Réflexivité et dualité sexuelle: Déconstruction d'une enquête anthropologique sur l'islam au Sénégal." *Journal des Anthropologues nos.* 108–9 (June 1, 2008), pp. 353–80.

Piga, Adriana. 2000. *Dakar et les ordres Soufis. Processus socioculturels et développement urbain au Sénégal contemporain.* Paris: L'Harmattan.

#Riccio, B. 2001 "Following Senegalese Migratory Path Through Media Representation". In King I. and N. Wood (eds.). *Media and Migration.* London: Routledge.

Roberts, Allen. 2003. "Sheikh Ibra Fall and the Baye Fall movement" in Roberts, Allen (ed.). 2003. *A Saint in the City: Sufi Arts of Urban Senegal.* Los Angeles: UCLA, pp.109–121.

Ibid. 2010."Estado láico y sufismo en Senegal". *Nova Africa,* nr 26, pp 7–21.

#Sadji, M.1974. "Le mythe de la sorcellerie". *Notes Africaines, no. 34,* janv., pp. 16–20.

#Sarr, F.1998. *L'Entrepreneuriat feminin au Sénégal: La transformation des rapports de pouvoir.* Paris: L'Harmattan.

#Schimmel, Anne-Marie. 1975. *Mystical Dimensions of Islam*. North Carolina: University of North Carolina Press.

Schultz, Dorothea. 2008. "Turning to Proper Muslim Practice: Islamic Moral Renewal and Women's Conflicting Assertions of Sunni Identity in Urban Mali." *Africa Today* 54, no. 4 (Summer 2008), pp. 20–43.

Seck, Abdourahmane. 2010. La *question musulmane au Sénégal. Essai d'anthropologie d'une nouvelle modernité*. Paris: Karthala.

#Smith, Margaret. (1974) 2010. *Rabi'a the Mystic and her Fellow Saints in Islam*. Cambridge: Cambridge Library Collection. Paperback.

#Sered, S. Starr. 1992. *Women as Ritual Experts: The Religious Lives of Elderly Jewish Women in Jerusalem*, New York and Oxford: Oxford University Press.

Soares, Benjamin F. 2004."Muslim Saints in the Age of Neoliberalism." In Weiss, Brad (ed.). *Producing African Futures: Ritual and Reproduction in a Neoliberal Age*, Leiden: Brill, pp. 79–104.

#Sow, Fatou och Codou Bop (eds). 2004. *Notre corps, notre santé: la santé et la sexualité des femmes en Afrique subsaharienne*. Paris: L'Harmattan.

Sow, Papa. 2004. "Prácticas comerciales y espacios de acción de los senegaleses en España". In Escrivá, Angels and N. Ribas (eds.): *Migración y desarrollo. Estudios sobre remesas y otras prácticas transnacionales*. Córdoba, CSIC.

#Stepan. Aldred. 2011. "Rituals of Respect: Sufis and Secularists in Senegal". In Thomas Banchoff and Robert Wurthnow (eds). *Religion and the Global Politics of Human Rights*. Oxford and New York: Oxford University Press.

Suárez Navaz, Liliana. 2002. "Brotherhood, solidarity, education and migration: the role of the Dahiras among the Murid Muslim community in New York". *African Affairs*, no 101, pp. 151–170.

#Sylla. Assan. 1994. *La philosophie morale des Wolof*. Dakar: Université de Dakar Cheikh Anta Diop.

#Thiam, S. 1998. *Mame Diarra Bousso: Un idéal de vie*. Mémoire de maîtrise, Dakar: UCAD (Université Cheikh Anta Diop).

#Zempléni Andras. 1966. "La dimension thérapeutique du culte de rab, ndop, tuutu et samp; rites de possession chez les Lebou et les Wolof". *Psychopathologie africaine* II,3, pp.295–439.

www.ingramcontent.com/pod-product-compliance
Lightning Source LLC
Chambersburg PA
CBHW080404270326
41927CB00015B/3339